THE ACQUISITION OF COMPLE

This book presents the first comprehensive study of how children acquire complex sentences. Drawing on observational data from English-speaking children aged 2;0 to 5;0, Holger Diessel investigates the acquisition of infinitival and participial complement clauses, finite complement clauses, finite and non-finite relative clauses, adverbial clauses, and co-ordinate clauses. His investigation shows that the development of complex sentences originates from simple, non-embedded sentences and that two different developmental pathways can be distinguished: complex sentences including complement and relative clauses evolve from simple sentences that are gradually *expanded* to multiple-clause constructions, and complex sentences including adverbial and co-ordinate clauses develop from simple sentences that are *integrated* into a specific biclausal unit. He argues that the acquisition process is determined by a variety of factors: the frequency of the various complex sentences in the ambient language, the semantic and syntactic complexity of the emerging constructions, the communicative functions of complex sentences, and the social-cognitive development of the child.

HOLGER DIESSEL is Professor of English Linguistics at the Friedrich-Schiller-Universität Jena. He has previously published *Demonstratives: Form, function and grammaticalization* (1999), and has written for a variety of journals including *Language* and the *Journal of Linguistics*.

CLINLING

In this series

67   P. H. MATTHEWS: *Grammatical theory in the United States from Bloomfield to Chomsky*

68   LJILJANA PROGOVAC: *Negative and positive polarity: a binding approach*

69   R. M. W. DLXON: *Ergativity*

70   YAN HUANG: *The syntax and pragmatics of anaphora*

71   KNUD LAMBRECHT: *Information structure and sentence form: topic, focus, and the mental representation of discourse referents*

72   LUIGI BURZIO: *Principles of English stress*

73   JOHN A. HAWKINS: *A performance theory of order and constituency*

74   ALICE C. HARRIS and LYLE CAMPBELL: *Historical syntax in cross-linguistic perspective*

75   LILIANE HAEGEMAN: *The syntax of negation*

76   PAUL GORREL: *Syntax and parsing*

77   GUGLIELMO CINQUE: *Italian syntax and universal grammar*

78   HENRY SMITH: *Restrictiveness in case theory*

79   D. ROBERT LADD: *Intonational morphology*

80   ANDREA MORO: *The raising of predicates: predicative noun phrases and the theory of clause structure*

81   ROGER LASS: *Historical linguistics and language change*

82   JOHN M. ANDERSON: *A notional theory of syntactic categories*

83   BERND HEINE: *Possession: cognitive sources, forces and grammaticalization*

84   NOMI ERTESCHIKDSHIR: *The dynamics of focus structure*

85   JOHN COLEMAN: *Phonological representations: their names, forms and powers*

86   CHRISTINA Y. BETHIN: *Slavic prosody: language change and phonological theory*

87   BARBARA DANCYGIER: *Conditionals and prediction: time, knowledge and causation in conditional constructions*

88   CLAIRE LEFEBVRE: *Creole genesis and the acquisition of grammar: the case of Haitian Creole*

89   HEINZ GIEGERICH: *Lexical strata in English: morphological causes, phonological effects*

90   KEREN RICE: *Morpheme order and semantic scope: word formation and the Athapaskan verb*

91   A.M.S McMAHON: *Lexical phonology and the history of English*

92   MATTHEW Y. CHEN: *Tone sandhi: patterns across Chinese dialects*

93   GREGORY T. STUMP: *Inflectional morphology: a theory of paradigm structure*

94   JOAN BYBEE: *Phonology and language use*

95   LAURIE BAUER: *Morphological productivity*

96   THOMAS ERNST: *The syntax of adjuncts*

97   ELIZABETH CLOSS TRAUGOTT and RICHARD B. DASHER: *Regularity in semantic change*

98   MAYA HICKMANN: *Children's discourse: person, space and time across languages*

99   DIANE BLAKEMORE: *Relevance and linguistic meaning: the semantics and pragmatics of discourse markers*

100   IAN ROBERTS and ANNA ROUSSOU: *Syntactic change: a minimalist approach to grammaticalization*

101   DONKA MINKOVA: *Alliteration and sound change in early English*

102   MARK C. BAKER: *Lexical categories: verbs, nouns and adjectives*

103   CARLOTA S. SMITH: *Modes of discourse: the local structure of texts*

104   ROCHELLE LIEBER: *Morphology and lexical semantics*

105   HOLGER DIESSEL: *The acquisition of complex sentences*

Earlier issues not listed are also available.

CAMBRIDGE STUDIES IN LINGUISTICS

General editors: P. AUSTIN, J. BRESNAN, B. COMRIE,
W. DRESSLER, C. J. EWEN, R. LASS, D. LIGHTFOOT,
I. ROBERTS, S. ROMAINE, N. V. SMITH

The Acquisition of Complex Sentences

THE ACQUISITION OF
COMPLEX SENTENCES

HOLGER DIESSEL

Friedrich-Schiller-Universität Jena

CAMBRIDGE
UNIVERSITY PRESS

CAMBRIDGE UNIVERSITY PRESS
Cambridge, New York, Melbourne, Madrid, Cape Town, Singapore, São Paulo, Delhi

Cambridge University Press
The Edinburgh Building, Cambridge CB2 8RU, UK

Published in the United States of America by Cambridge University Press, New York

www.cambridge.org
Information on this title: www.cambridge.org/9780521107488

First published 2004
Third printing 2006
This digitally printed version 2009

A catalogue record for this publication is available from the British Library

ISBN 978-0-521-83193-2 hardback
ISBN 978-0-521-10748-8 paperback

Contents

List of figures	*page*	ix
List of tables		xi
Acknowledgements		xiv
List of abbreviations		xv
1	**Introduction**	**1**
1.1	The scope and goal of this study	1
1.2	Hypotheses	3
1.3	Data	7
2	**A dynamic network model of grammatical constructions**	**13**
2.1	Construction grammar	14
2.2	The usage-based model	23
2.3	Language acquisition	34
3	**Towards a definition of complex sentences and subordinate clauses**	**41**
3.1	Towards a definition of complex sentences	41
3.2	Towards a definition of subordinate clauses	42
4	**Infinitival and participial complement constructions**	**49**
4.1	Literature	50
4.2	Infinitival and participial complement clauses in adult grammar	55
4.3	Data	59
4.4	Analysis	62
4.5	Discussion	72
5	**Complement clauses**	**77**
5.1	Literature	78
5.2	Finite complement clauses in adult grammar	80
5.3	Data	89

viii   *Contents*

5.4	Analysis	90
5.5	Discussion	111

6   **Relative clauses**   **116**
6.1	Literature	116
6.2	Relative clauses in adult grammar	127
6.3	Data	129
6.4	Analysis	131
6.5	Discussion	141

7   **Adverbial and co-ordinate clauses**   **149**
7.1	Literature	149
7.2	Adverbial and co-ordinate clauses in adult grammar	152
7.3	Data	156
7.4	Analysis	158
7.5	Discussion	169

8   **Conclusion**   **174**
8.1	From simple sentences to multiple-clause constructions	175
8.2	From lexically specific constructions to constructional schemas	180
8.3	Conclusion	184

Appendix	186
References	200
Author index	220
Subject index	224

Figures

1.1	Mean proportions of complex sentences in the transcripts of the five children	*page* 10
2.1	Left, right- and mixed-branching phrase structures	25
2.2	Localist network	27
2.3	Distributed network	27
2.4	Network of argument structure constructions	29
4.1	Phrase structure of a complex sentence including a passive matrix clause and a nonfinite complement clause	53
4.2	Phrase structure of a complex sentence including an active matrix clause and a nonfinite adverbial clause	54
4.3	Mean proportions of bare infinitives, *to*-infinitives, *wh*-infinitives, and participial complements	62
4.4	The development of *want*-constructions	72
6.1	The NVN-schema	122
6.2	The conjoined clause analysis	125
6.3	External syntactic structures of restrictive and nonrestrictive relative clauses	128
6.4	Mean proportions of PN-, N-, OBJ-, OBL-, and SUBJ-relatives	132
6.5	Mean proportions of the first 10 PN-, N-, OBJ-, OBL-, and SUBJ-relatives	133
6.6	The development of PN-, N-, OBJ-, OBL-, and SUBJ-relatives	136
6.7	Mean proportions of subj-, obj-, obl-, io-, and gen-relatives	137
6.8	The development of subj-, obj-, and obl-relatives	138
6.9	Mean proportions of the syntactic heads of participial relatives	140
7.1	The proportions of children's *because*-clauses that occur in response to a causal question	162

7.2	The development of bound and unbound early conjoined clauses (i.e. *and-*, *but-*, *because-*, and *so*-clauses)	165
7.3	Mean proportions of the children's early and late conjoined clauses that are intonationally bound/unbound to the semantically associated clause	167
7.4	The development of initial and final *when*-clauses	170
7.5	The development of conjoined clauses	171
8.1	The development of finite and nonfinite multiple-clause structures	179
8.2	Network of finite complement clause constructions	182

Tables

1.1	General overview of the data	*page* 9
1.2	MLUs at 2;3 and 3;2	9
1.3	Total number of the children's multiple-clause utterances	10
1.4	Total number of the children's finite and nonfinite multiple-clause utterances	11
1.5	Total number of the children's nonfinite complement clauses, nonfinite relative clauses, and nonfinite adverbial clauses	11
1.6	Total number of the children's finite complement clauses, finite relative clauses, and finite conjoined clauses	12
4.1	Infinitival and participial complements	57
4.2	Nonfinite complement clauses	60
4.3	Complement-taking verbs of the children's nonfinite complement clauses	61
4.4	Mean proportions of the children's NP-V-VP constructions and NP-V-NP-VP constructions	62
4.5	The most frequent complement-taking verbs of the children's NP-V-VP constructions and the mean age of their appearance	63
4.6	The most frequent complement-taking verbs of the children's NP-V-NP-VP constructions and the mean age of their appearance	66
4.7	Frequency of the children's *want*-constructions and the mean age of their appearance	68
4.8	Mean proportions of the mothers' NP-V-VP constructions and the mean age of their appearance in the children's data	74

4.9   Mean proportions of the mothers' NP-V-NP-VP
       constructions and the mean age of their appearance in the
       children's data   75
5.1   Finite complement clauses   90
5.2   Complement-taking verbs of the children's finite complement
       clauses   91
5.3   S-complements, *wh*-complements, and
       if-complements   91
5.4   The development of Adam's and Sarah's matrix clauses
       including *think*   93
5.5   Subjects of *think, know, mean, bet*, and *guess*   96
5.6   The development of Adam's and Sarah's matrix clauses
       including *know*   97
5.7   Subjects of *wish* and *hope*   99
5.8   Subjects of *see, look*, and *remember*   99
5.9   Subjects of *say, tell*, and *pretend*   103
5.10 Type-token ratio of the most frequent complement-taking
       verbs   104
5.11 S-complements, *wh*-complements, and *if*-complements: mean
       age of their appearance   105
5.12 *See if*-complements   107
5.13 Mean proportions of the various complement-taking verbs of
       S-complements in the mothers' data and the mean age of
       their appearance in the children's data   113
6.1   Mean number of correct responses (out of three) (Sheldon
       1974)   123
6.2   Children's responses to SS-relatives (Tavakolian
       1977)   124
6.3   Children's responses to OS-relatives (Tavakolian
       1977)   124
6.4   Finite and nonfinite relative clauses   129
6.5   Classification of relative constructions   130
6.6   *That-, who-*, and zero-relativizers   137
6.7   Transitive and intransitive subj-relatives   139
6.8   The mothers' relative clauses (external syntax)   145
6.9   The mothers' relative clauses (internal syntax)   146
7.1   Conjoined clauses   156
7.2   Frequency of the children's individual conjoined
       clauses/conjunctions   157

7.3   Intonationally bound and intonationally unbound
        and-clauses   160
7.4   *Because*-clauses that occur in response to a causal
        question   162
7.5   *But*-clauses across and within speaker turns   164
7.6   Mean proportions of the children's initial and final conjoined
        clauses   169
7.7   Mean proportions of the mothers' conjoined clauses and the
        mean age of their appearance in the children's data   172

Acknowledgements

The research for this book was carried out at the Max Planck Institute for Evolutionary Anthropology, Leipzig. I would like to thank the director of the Department of Comparative and Developmental Psychology of the Max Planck Institute, Michael Tomasello, for his encouragement and support.

I am also grateful to the members of the child language research group at the Max Planck Institute: Kirsten Abbott-Smith, Heike Behrens, Franklin Chang, Michael Israel, Kai Kiekhöfer, Elena Lieven, Heide Lohmann, Sabine Stoll, and Angelika Wittek. They offered helpful feedback and discussion. Further, I would like to thank my colleagues from the Linguistics Department of the Max Planck Institute: Lea Brown, Bernard Comrie, Orin Gensler, Tom Güldemann, Martin Haspelmath, Susanne Michaelis, Brigitte Pakendorf, Eva Schulze-Berndt, Donald Stilo and Helma van den Berg. In particular, I would like to thank Brigitte Pakendorf, who carefully proofread the entire manuscript.

A previous version of this book was submitted to the English Department of the University of Leipzig as my Habilitation thesis. I am very grateful to the members of my thesis committee: Adele Goldberg, Susan Olsen, and Michael Tomasello for their comments and suggestions. Further, I would like to thank Sandra Thompson, who read previous versions of chapter 4 and chapter 5, and Kirstin Abott-Smith, Katharina Rohlfing, and Eva Schulze-Berndt, who read previous versions of chapter 2. I am also grateful to Eve Clark and an anonymous referee who reviewed the book for Cambridge University Press.

Finally, I thank my parents, Heidi Diessel and Gustav Diessel, my sister, Carola Diessel, and my brother-in-law Franz Brinker.

Excerpts of this book first appeared, in different form, in the following articles: Holger Diessel and Michael Tomasello 2000, 'The development of relative clauses in English', *Cognitive Linguistics* 11; and Holger Diessel and Michael Tomasello 2001, 'The acquisition of finite complement clauses in English: a corpus-based analysis', *Cognitive Linguistics* 12. I thank the publishers for the permission to include revised materials from these publications in the present monograph.

Abbreviations

ADV-clause	adverbial clause
COMP-clause	complement clause
CTV	complement-taking verb
DET	determiner
gen-relative	relative clause including a genitive relative pronoun
INF	infinitive
IO-relative	relative clause modifying the indirect object
io-relative	relative clause including an indirect object gap
IP	inflectional phrase
MDP	minimal distance principle
NP	noun phrase
N-relative	relative clause modifying an isolated noun (phrase)
OBJ-relative	relative clause modifying the direct object
obj-relative	relative clause including an object gap
OBL-relative	relative clause modifying an oblique element
obl-relative	relative clause including an oblique gap
PL	plural
PN-relative	relative clause modifying a predicate nominal
PP	prepositional phrase
PRO	pronoun
REL-clause	relative clause
S	sentence/clause
S-complement	finite complement clause marked by *that* or zero
SG	singular
SRP	semantic role principle
SUBJ-relative	relative clause modifying the subject
subj-relative	relative clause including a subject gap
to-INF	infinitive marked by *to*
V	verb
V-*en*	past participle

V-*ing*	present participle
VP	verb phrase
WH	question word
wh-complement	finite complement clause marked by a question word
wh-infinitive	infinitive marked by a question word
XP	phrasal category

1 *Introduction*

1.1   The scope and goal of this study

Complex sentences are grammatical constructions consisting of multiple clauses. They are commonly divided into two types: sentences including co-ordinate clauses, and sentences including a matrix clause and a subordinate clause. Three different types of subordinate clauses can be distinguished: complement clauses, relative clauses, and adverbial clauses. In traditional grammar, complement clauses are defined as arguments of a predicate in the superordinate clause; relative clauses are analysed as attributes of a noun or noun phrase; and adverbial clauses are seen as some sort of modifier of the associated matrix clause or verb phrase. All three types of subordinate clauses can be finite or nonfinite. Nonfinite subordinate clauses comprise infinitival and participial constructions. Examples of the various subordinate and coordinate clauses are given in (1)–(7).

(1)	Peter promised **that** he would come.	[finite COMP-clause]
(2)	Sue wants Peter to leave.	[nonfinite COMP-clause]
(3)	Sally bought the bike **that** was on sale.	[finite REL-clause]
(4)	Is that the driver causing the accidents?	[nonfinite REL-clause]
(5)	He arrived **when** Mary was just about to leave.	[finite ADV-clause]
(6)	She left the door open **to** hear the baby.	[nonfinite ADV-clause]
(7)	He tried hard, **but** he failed.	[COOR-clause]

This study examines the development of complex sentences in early child speech. It is based on observational data from five English-speaking children between the ages of 1;8 and 5;1. The data consist of about 12,000 multiple-clause utterances, which is probably the largest database that has ever been used in a study on the acquisition of complex sentence constructions. The literature is primarily concerned with children's comprehension of complex sentences based on data from experiments. There are only a few observational studies examining children's use of complex sentences in spontaneous speech. These are mainly concerned with the early use of complex sentences including adverbial and co-ordinate clauses; the literature on relative and complement clauses is almost entirely experimental. The current investigation is the first observational study systematically to examine the development of *all* multiple-clause structures in English and thus fills an important gap in the literature on the acquisition of complex sentences.[1]

The primary goal of the study is to describe the development of complex sentences and subordinate clauses in spontaneous child speech. When do the first complex sentences emerge? What characterizes the earliest subordinate clauses? How does the development proceed? However, the study also addresses a number of more general questions concerning the organization of grammar and grammatical development.

The theoretical approach taken in this study combines construction grammar with the usage-based model (cf. Fillmore, Kay, and O'Connor 1988; Lakoff 1987; Goldberg 1995; Bybee 1985, 1995; Langacker 1987a, 1988, 1991; Barlow and Kemmer 2000; and Bybee and Hopper 2001). In construction grammar, grammar consists of interrelated symbolic units, combining a specific form with a specific function or meaning. In the usage-based model, grammar is seen as a dynamic system shaped by the psychological mechanisms involved in language use. In order to understand the dynamics of the system, one has to study the development of grammatical knowledge, both historically and in language acquisition. From this perspective, the current study is not just concerned with the acquisition of complex sentences in English but also with the structure and organization of grammar and the emergence of grammatical knowledge.

The investigation proceeds as follows. The remainder of the current chapter presents the central hypotheses of the study and provides an overview of the data. Chapter 2 discusses some central principles of construction grammar and the usage-based model, providing the theoretical background for the study. Chapter 3 gives a short definition of complex sentences and subordinate clauses. Chapters 4–7 present the bulk of the empirical analysis: chapter 4 describes the development of infinitival and participial complement clauses; chapter 5 is concerned with the early use of finite complement clauses; chapter 6 investigates the acquisition of relative clauses; and chapter 7 examines the emergence of co-ordinate and adverbial clauses; finally, chapter 8 provides a summary of the results and discusses the implications of the empirical findings for the theory of grammar and grammatical development.

---

1. For a general overview of the literature, see Bowerman (1979) and O'Grady (1997:chs. 6 and 9). For a review of the literature on the acquisition of subordinate clauses in German, see Rothweiler (1993).

1.2   Hypotheses

The study proposes two major hypotheses:

- First, it is argued that the development of complex sentences originates from simple nonembedded sentences that are gradually 'transformed' to multiple-clause constructions. Two different developmental pathways are distinguished: (i) complex sentences including complement or relative clauses emerge from simple sentences that are gradually expanded to multiple-clause structures; and (ii) complex sentences including adverbial or co-ordinate clauses develop by integrating two independent sentences into a specific biclausal unit.
- Second, it is shown that children's early complex sentences are organized around concrete lexical expressions. More schematic representations of complex sentences emerge only later when children have learned a sufficient number of lexically specific constructions to generalize across them.

In what follows I discuss the two hypotheses in turn.

1.2.1   From simple sentences to complex sentence constructions

The first multiple-clause structures that seem to consist of a subordinate clause and a matrix clause contain a single proposition (i.e. they describe a single situation). Consider the following examples:

(8)	I wanna <u>see it</u>.	[Nina 1;11]
(9)	I think <u>it's a little bear</u>.	[Nina 2;2]
(10)	Here's a rabbit **that** <u>I'm patting</u>.	[Nina 3;0]

Example (8) includes an infinitival construction that one might analyse as an early instance of a nonfinite complement clause. However, the current study shows that the complement-taking verbs of children's early nonfinite complement clauses basically function as quasi-modals that specify the meaning of the infinitive: rather than denoting an independent state of affairs the complement-taking verbs elaborate the semantic structure of the activity expressed by the nonfinite verb.

Example (9) shows a construction that seems to include an early instance of a finite complement clause. However, if we look at children's early finite complement constructions more closely we find that the apparent matrix clauses do not designate an independent state of affairs; rather, they function as epistemic markers, attention getters, or markers of illocutionary force, guiding the hearer's interpretation of the associated complement clause.

The sentence in (10) is characteristic of children's early relative clauses, which tend to emerge a few months after the first complement clauses. The sentence consists of a presentational copular clause and a relative clause that is attached to the predicate nominal. Following Lambrecht (1988), I argue that the presentational copular clause is propositionally empty: rather than denoting an independent state of affairs, it functions to establish a new referent in focus position making it available for the predication expressed in the relative clause.

Although the sentences in (8)–(10) consist of two clauses, or clause-like elements, they designate only a single situation (i.e. they contain only a single proposition) and do not involve embedding. As children grow older, the three constructions become semantically and morphologically more complex. The whole development can be seen as a process of clause expansion: starting from structures that designate a single situation and do not involve embedding, children gradually learn the use of complex sentences in which a matrix clause and a subordinate clause express a specific relationship between two propositions.

Like complement and relative clauses, adverbial and co-ordinate clauses develop from simple nonembedded sentences. However, the development takes a different pathway. It originates from two independent sentences that are pragmatically combined in the ongoing discourse. Two typical examples are given in (11) and (12):

(11)   ADULT: It's not raining today.   [Peter 2;6]
        CHILD: **But** ... it's raining here.
(12)   CHILD: Don't touch this camera.   [Peter 2;7]
        ADULT: Why?
        CHILD: **Cause** it's broken.

Although the clauses in these examples are combined by a connective, they do not constitute a grammatical construction. The two conjuncts are expressed by utterances that are grammatically independent. Starting from such discourse structures, children gradually learn the use of complex sentences in which the matrix clause and the adverbial clause (or two co-ordinate clauses) are tightly integrated in a biclausal construction. Thus, while complement and relative clauses evolve via *clause expansion*, adverbial and co-ordinate clauses develop through a process of *clause integration*.

1.2.2   *From lexically specific constructions to constructional schemas*

The second major hypothesis asserts that children's early complex sentences are lexically specific: they are organized around concrete lexical expressions that are part of the constructions. In studies of adult grammar, constructions including subordinate clauses are defined over abstract grammatical categories. For instance, a relative clause is commonly defined as a subordinate clause modifying a noun or noun phrase in the matrix clause (i.e. [N(P) [REL-clause]$_S$]$_{NP}$), and a complement clause is a subordinate clause functioning as an argument of the matrix clause predicate (i.e. [V [COMP-clause]$_S$]$_{VP}$). However, adult grammar also includes lexically specific constructions, which are often overlooked (or ignored) in the syntactic literature. For instance, the comparative conditional construction (e.g. *The faster you walk the sooner you'll be there*) consists of two comparative phrases that are combined by two concrete lexical expressions: *The— the—* (cf. Fillmore, Kay, and O'Connor 1988). Such lexically specific constructions exist side by side with abstract grammatical representations in adult grammar (cf. chapter 2). However, in child language abstract grammatical representations are initially absent. A number of recent studies have shown that children's early grammatical constructions are organized around concrete lexical material: they are lexically specific constructions consisting of a relational term, usually a verb, and an open slot that can be filled by various elements (cf. Tomasello 1992, 2000a, 2000b, 2003; Tomasello and Brooks 1999; Pine and Lieven 1993; Pine, Lieven, and Rowland 1998; Lieven, Pine, and Baldwin 1997; Diessel and Tomasello 2000, 2001; Dabrowska 2000; Israel, Johnson, and Brooks 2000; Theakston, Lieven, Pine, and Rowland 2001, 2003; Abbot-Smith, Lieven, and Tomasello 2001; Wilson 2003; see also the older works by Braine 1976; MacWhinney 1975; and Bowerman 1976). Consider, for instance, the examples in (13), adopted from a diary study by Tomasello (1992: 285ff.). The sentences were produced by his 2-year-old daughter.

(13)

That's Daddy.	More corn.	Block get-it.
That's Weezer.	More that.	Bottle get-it
That's my chair.	More cookie.	Phone get-it
That's him.	More mail.	Mama get-it
That's a paper too.	More popsicle.	Towel get-it.
That's Mark's book.	More jump.	Dog get-it.
That's too little for me.	More Pete water.	Books get-it.

The formulaic character of these utterances suggests that they are defined upon the occurrence of specific lexical expressions. They consist of a constant part associated with an open slot that is usually filled by a nominal expression: *That's—, More—, — get-it*. Such lexically specific constructions are characteristic of early child speech. Virtually all of the multi-word utterances produced by Tomasello's 2-year-old daughter are organized around specific verbs (or other relational terms).

The current study shows that such lexically specific constructions are not only characteristic of children's early simple sentences but also of their early multiple-clause structures. Like simple sentences, complex sentences are tied to concrete lexical expressions in early child speech. They are associated with a specific conjunction, a formulaic matrix clause, or some other lexical expression providing a frame for the rest of the utterance. Abstract grammatical representations of complex sentences emerge only later when children have learned enough lexically specific constructions to extract a constructional schema from the data.

1.2.3   Determining factors

How do we explain the development of complex sentences from simple item-based constructions? The current study argues that the acquisition process is determined by multiple factors: the frequency of the various complex sentences in the ambient language, the complexity of the emerging constructions, the communicative functions of complex sentences, and the social-cognitive development of the child.

As we will see throughout this book, there is a close correlation between the age at which children begin to use a specific construction and the frequency of this construction in the ambient language. The more frequently a complex sentence occurs in the input data, the earlier it emerges in children's speech. This suggests that input frequency plays a key role in the acquisition process.

However, input frequency alone does not suffice to account for the data; there are various other factors that seem to have an effect on the development. In particular, the complexity of the emerging constructions appears to influence the acquisition process. If we look at children's early complex sentences, we find that they tend to be very simple: although they consist of two clauses (or clause-like elements), they contain only a single proposition and involve very little grammatical marking. More complex constructions denoting a relationship between two propositions in two full-fledged clauses emerge only later. This suggests that the order of acquisition is at least partially determined by the semantic and morphosyntactic complexity of the emerging constructions. Specifically, one might hypothesize that children's early complex sentences are simple (both semantically and formally) because more complex constructions are initially too difficult to plan and to produce.

Since the earliest complex sentences are not only simple but also frequent, complexity and frequency are difficult to disentangle; both correlate very closely with the order of acquisition. However, that complexity is an important factor independent of frequency is suggested by the fact that there are some very complex structures that should have emerged earlier if the development were solely determined by input frequency.

In addition to frequency and complexity, there are several other factors that seem to affect the acquisition process. In particular, the pragmatic functions of complex sentences have an important effect on the development. Most of the complex sentences that children begin to use early are especially well suited for the specific communicative needs of young children. For instance, the earliest relative clauses occur in presentational constructions that are not only frequent and simple but also pragmatically very useful in parent–child speech. Presentational relative constructions consist of a presentational copular clause that identifies a referent in the speech situation and a relative clause that expresses a predication about the previously established referent. Since children tend to talk about elements that are present in the speech situation, presentational relatives are well suited for the particular communicative needs of young children. It is thus a plausible hypothesis that the early appearance of these constructions is partly motivated by their pragmatic functions.

Finally, the development of complement clauses seems to be related to the child's developing 'theory of mind' (cf. Shatz, Wellman, and Silber 1983; see also Lohmann and Tomasello 2003). Complement clauses are commonly used as arguments of 'complement taking verbs' such as *think, know*, and *guess*, which denote mental states and cognitive activities. However, in early child language complement-taking verbs occur almost exclusively in formulaic matrix clauses functioning as epistemic markers, attention getters, or markers of illocutionary force. Since the assertive use of these verbs presupposes a theory of mind that develops only gradually during the preschool years, one might hypothesize that young children do not use assertive matrix clauses because they lack the cognitive prerequisites for this use.

In general, the development of complex sentences seems to be determined by multiple factors. Frequency and complexity appear to be involved in the acquisition of *all* complex sentence constructions, but there are also pragmatic and general cognitive factors that play an important role in the developmental process.

1.3   *Data*

The analysis is based on observational data from five English-speaking children aged 1;8 to 5;1. The data come from 357 computerized transcripts of spontaneous parent–child speech. All data are taken from the CHILDES database (cf. MacWhinney 1995). The transcripts are in the CHAT format, which has

been specifically designed to facilitate the computerized analysis of child language data (cf. MacWhinney 1995: ch. 5). The frequency counts and lists of
examples presented throughout this study have been prepared with the help
of the CLAN computer programs, which are part of the CHILDES system
(cf. MacWhinney 1995: ch. 21).

The five children of this study are well known from the literature: Adam and
Sarah are two of the children that Roger Brown investigated in his classical
study (cf. Brown 1973); Peter is one of the children studied by Lois Bloom
(1973); and the data from Nina and Naomi were provided by Patrick Suppes
(1973) and Jacqueline Sachs (1983), respectively. All five children were born
in the late sixties or early seventies.

Adam was the child of a minister and an elementary school teacher. Although
he was African American, he did not speak African American English (cf.
MacWhinney 2000:28). Adam's data comprise 55 transcripts that cover the
time from age 2;3 to 4;10. The recordings occurred at regular intervals of one
to three weeks. Adam's corpus is the biggest corpus of the study; it includes a
total of 46,498 child utterances.

Sarah was the child of a working-class family (cf. MacWhinney 2000:29).
Her data comprise 139 recordings that were collected at regular intervals from
age 2;3 to 5;1. Although Sarah's corpus includes twice as many files as Adam's
corpus, her database is smaller; it contains a total of 37,021 child utterances.

Peter was the first-born child of an upper middle-class family with college-
educated parents (MacWhinney 2000:21). His corpus comprises 20 transcripts
including a total of 30,256 child utterances. The transcripts are based on recordings that were prepared at regular intervals between the ages of 1;9 and 3;2.

Naomi was the child of the investigator Jacqueline Sachs. Her corpus consists
of 87 files covering the time from age 1;8 to 3;5. In addition to these files,
the CHILDES database includes six other recordings from Naomi that were
excluded from the current investigation because they are temporally separated
from the bulk of her data: two of them are very early recordings from the ages
of 1;3 and 1;6; the four others were prepared after a gap of several months at
the age of 3;8 and between 4;7 and 4;9. The 87 files that have been included
in the current database contain a total of 14,656 child utterances, which is the
smallest corpus of the study.

Finally, Nina's corpus consists of 56 files containing transcripts from the age
of 1;11 to 3;4. There is a gap in Nina's data between the ages of 2;6 and 2;9
during which no recordings were prepared. The recordings before and after the
gap occurred at regular intervals of one to two weeks. Nina's corpus contains a
total of 32,212 child utterances. Table 1.1 provides an overview of the data.

Table 1.1 *General overview of the data*

Children	Age range	Number of utterances	Number of files
Adam	2;3–4;10	46,498	55
Sarah	2;3–5;1	37,021	139
Nina	1;11–3;4	32,212	56
Peter	1;9–3;2	30,256	20
Naomi	1;8–3;5	14,656	87
Total	1;8–5;1	160,643	357

Table 1.2 *MLUs at 2;3 and 3;2*

	MLU at 2;3	MLU at 3;2
Adam	2.11	3.55
Sarah	1.63	2.47
Nina	3.22	3.58
Peter	2.49	3.45
Naomi	2.35	3.34
Mean	2.36	3.28

There are significant individual differences in the development of the five children. Table 1.2 shows the children's mean length of utterances (MLU) at the ages of 2;3 and 3;2. The MLU indicates the average number of morphemes that occur per utterance at a specific time; it is commonly used as a measure for children's level of language development (cf. Brown 1973). The numbers have been automatically computed by the MLU program of the CHILDES system.

As can be seen in this table, at the age of 2;3 Adam, Peter, and Naomi have similar MLUs ranging from 2.11 to 2.49, Nina's MLU is significantly higher, and Sarah's MLU is by far the lowest. At the age of 3;2 the gap between Nina and the other children has become smaller, but Sarah's MLU is still lower than the MLUs of the four other children: while Adam, Peter, Nina, and Naomi produce an average of about 3.5 morphemes per utterance at this age, Sarah's utterances include only an average of 2.47 morphemes. This suggests that Sarah is somewhat lagging behind in her development. As we will see throughout this study, Sarah begins to produce most complex sentences several months after they emerge in the speech of the four other children.

Table 1.3 *Total number of the children's*
multiple-clause utterances

	Total number of multiple-clause utterances
Adam	4,389
Sarah	2,496
Nina	2,545
Peter	1,746
Naomi	802
Total	11,978

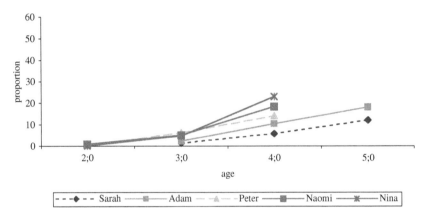

Fig. 1.1 *Mean proportions of complex sentences in the transcripts of the five children*

All 357 computer files have been searched for multiple-clause utterances defined upon the occurrence of at least two verbs (disregarding auxiliaries and modals). Whenever possible, the search was conducted automatically using the CLAN programs of the CHILDES system, but all 357 files have also been searched manually by the investigator and an assistant. Table 1.3 shows the total number of multiple-clause utterances that occur in the transcripts of each child.

The earliest multiple-clause utterances appear around the second birthday. Before the age of 2;0 the children's speech consists almost exclusively of simple nonembedded sentences. Figure 1.1 shows the mean proportions of multiple-clause structures that occurred in the total corpus of all child utterances up to

Table 1.4 *Total number of the children's finite and nonfinite multiple-clause utterances*

	Multiple-clause utterances including two finite clauses	Multiple-clause utterances including a finite and a nonfinite clause
Adam	2,441	1,948
Sarah	1,504	992
Nina	1,638	907
Peter	979	767
Naomi	473	329
Mean	7,035	4,943

Table 1.5 *Total number of the children's nonfinite complement clauses, nonfinite relative clauses, and nonfinite adverbial clauses*

	COMP-clauses	REL-clauses	ADV-clauses	Unclassifiable
Adam	1,770	120	27	31
Sarah	946	36	5	5
Nina	802	71	22	12
Peter	709	44	9	5
Naomi	305	16	4	4
Total	4,532	287	67	57

the age of 4;0 (the numbers on which this figure is based are given in table 1a in the appendix).

As can be seen in this figure, the proportions of complex sentences increases steadily: up to age 2;0 complex sentences are very infrequent; they account for an average of less than 1 per cent of the data (note that there is no data from Adam and Sarah available for this time). However, in the course of the two following years the proportion increases, reaching an average level of 14.3 per cent at the age of 4;0.

The earliest multiple-clause utterances are sentences including nonfinite subordinate clauses; they emerge around the second birthday. Finite subordinate clauses usually appear a few months later during the third year of life. Table 1.4 shows the total numbers of finite and nonfinite multiple-clause utterances that occur in the transcripts of each child.

Table 1.6 *Total number of the children's finite complement clauses, finite relative clauses, and finite conjoined clauses*

	COMP-clauses	REL-clauses	CONJ-clauses
Adam	804	178	1,459
Sarah	474	32	998
Nina	220	62	1356
Peter	266	25	688
Naomi	48	8	417
Total	1,812	305	4,918

As can be seen in this table, multiple-clause utterances including two finite clauses are overall more frequent than multiple-clause utterances including a finite and a nonfinite clause. Both finite and nonfinite multiple-clause utterances have been divided into complement, relative, and adverbial clauses. Table 1.5 shows the number of nonfinite complement clauses, nonfinite relative clauses, and nonfinite adverbial clauses that occur in the transcripts of each child.

As can be seen in this table, the vast majority of the children's infinitival and participial constructions are complement clauses. There are only 287 nonfinite relative clauses and 67 nonfinite adverbial clauses in the entire corpus. In addition the data include 57 nonfinite multiple-clause utterances that could not be classified.

Table 1.6 shows the frequency of the various finite subordinate (and co-ordinate) clauses. Finite complement clauses occur in 1,812 child utterances. Finite relative clauses are much less frequent: the whole corpus includes only 305 finite relative clauses. Since finite adverbial clauses and co-ordinate clauses are closely related (cf. chapter 7), they have been subsumed under a common category called *conjoined clauses*. Conjoined clauses are very frequent: they occur in 4,918 child utterances.

2   A dynamic network model of grammatical constructions

The theoretical framework used by most researchers of child language development is Chomsky's theory of generative grammar. The theory has changed considerably in recent years. The older model, which is still often used in child language research, is called Principles and Parameters Theory, while the newest version is known as Minimalism (cf. Chomsky 1981, 1986, 1995, 2000). Within this framework, it is commonly assumed that children are born with an innate universal grammar consisting of principles and parameters that define the space within which the grammars of individual languages may vary. Grammatical development is seen as a process whereby the parameters of universal grammar are set to a language-specific value by linguistic triggers in the input.

The theoretical framework used in this study is very different; it is based on recent work in functional and cognitive linguistics. The functional–cognitive approach subsumes a variety of related frameworks (cf. Croft 1995; Newmeyer 1998). Two of them are especially important to the current investigation: construction grammar, and the usage-based model. Construction grammar subsumes a family of grammatical theories in which constructions are considered the basic units of grammar (cf. Fillmore, Kay, and O'Connor 1988; Lakoff 1987; Langacker 1987a; Fillmore and Kay 1993; Goldberg 1995; Croft 2001); and the usage-based model comprises various network models in which linguistic knowledge is shaped by language use (cf. Bybee 1985, 1995, 2001; Langacker 1987a, 1991; Barlow and Kemmer 2000; Elman, Bates, Johnson, Karmiloff-Smith, Parisi, and Plunkett 1996). Although construction grammar and the usage-based model are in principle independent of each other, they are often combined in linguistic analyses (e.g. Langacker 1987a; Croft 2001; Morris, Cottrell, and Elman 2000). This chapter discusses the basic principles of the two frameworks in a unified approach.

2.1   Construction grammar

2.1.1   Constructions

In construction-based theories, constructions are the basic units of grammar. They are commonly defined as grammatical assemblies that are characterized by two features: first, constructions combine a specific form with a specific function or meaning (e.g. Lakoff 1987); and second, constructions exhibit both general grammatical properties and idiosyncratic features (e.g. Fillmore, Kay, and O'Connor 1988).

The importance of grammatical constructions has been emphasized in various contemporary theories of grammar, notably in Construction Grammar[1] and Cognitive Grammar (cf. Fillmore, Kay, and O'Connor 1988; Fillmore and Kay 1993; Goldberg 1995; Lakoff 1987; Langacker 1987a, 1988, 1991, 2000; Croft 2001), but also in Head Driven Phrase Structure Grammar (Sag 1997), Role and Reference Grammar (Van Valin and LaPolla 1997), and several other related frameworks (cf. Prince 1978; Zwicky 1987, 1994; Pullum and Zwicky 1991; Wierzbicka 1988; Jackendoff 1990, 1997; Culicover 1998).

The traditional notion of construction refers to specific sentence types such as the passive. The main passive construction in English consists of a subject, the auxiliary *be*, and a verb in the past participle, which may be followed by a *by*-phrase. The whole structure is associated with a particular meaning: in contrast to active sentences, passive sentences express the patient (or undergoer) in the subject NP, whereas the actor is optionally expressed in the postverbal *by*-phrase. What is more, although the passive is defined by common grammatical categories and syntactic relations, it is not sufficiently described on the basis of general grammatical rules; rather, an adequate analysis of the passive must take into account that the whole structure constitutes a specific grammatical unit. It combines general grammatical properties with idiosyncratic features that can only be described by construction-particular rules. For instance, the particular expression of the actor in a *by*-phrase is an idiosyncratic property of the passive that cannot be derived from the meaning of *by* and some general grammatical rules.

In construction grammar the notion of construction has been generalized. It does not only apply to structures such as the passive; rather, construction grammar argues that all grammatical assemblies are constructions, i.e. conventionalized symbolic units consisting of a specific form paired with a specific

---

1. The notion of Construction Grammar, spelled with initial capital letters, refers to a particular construction-based theory developed by Charles Fillmore, Paul Kay, George Lakoff, and Adele Goldberg.

function or meaning (cf. Lakoff 1987; Langacker 1987a; Fillmore et al. 1988; Goldberg 1995). The formal side comprises phonological, morphological, and syntactic features; and the functional side subsumes semantic, pragmatic, and discourse-pragmatic features.

Grammatical constructions can be seen as complex linguistic signs. In the structuralist tradition of linguistics, the notion of sign is used for words but does not apply to grammatical assemblies (cf. Saussure 1916). However, in construction-based theories the notion of sign has been extended to constructions because constructions are like words in that they represent conventionalized form–function pairings: both can be seen as symbols in which a specific form is paired with a specific function or meaning. Strong evidence for the symbolic nature of grammatical constructions comes from recent experimental studies in which it is shown that speakers associate specific meanings with particular morphosyntactic structures (cf. Bencini and Goldberg 2000; Hare and Goldberg 2000; Kaschak and Glenberg 2000).

The notion of construction is incompatible with central assumptions of generative grammar. According to Chomsky (1965), the system of grammatical rules is divided into three major components: the syntactic component, the phonological component, and the semantic component. Similar divisions hold for more recent versions of generative grammar (cf. Chomsky 1981, 1995, 2000). Each component has its own rules that in principle are independent of each other; that is, grammar comprises syntactic, phonological, and semantic rules that apply in separate compartments or 'modules'. Since the modules are more or less 'autonomous' (i.e. encapsulated compartments of grammar; see Croft 1995 and Newmeyer 1998 for discussion), there is no room for complex linguistic signs in the classical version of generative grammar (but see Jackendoff 1990, 1997). The only conventionalized form–function pairings are words. The meaning and structure of grammatical assemblies (i.e. phrases and clauses) can always be decomposed into semantic and syntactic primitives that constitute the building blocks of complex linguistic elements in this approach. Grammar is thus entirely compositional in Chomsky's version of generative grammar and therefore the notion of construction has been abandoned in this approach:

> The notion of grammatical construction is eliminated, and with it, construction-particular rules.   (Chomsky 1995:4)

Note that the elimination of constructions includes structures such as the passive, which have always been treated as constructions in linguistic theory. All complex linguistic expressions are fully compositional in the current version of generative grammar (i.e. Minimalism). They are derived from a small number of linguistic primitives and some general grammatical rules. The only exceptions are idiomatic expressions, which obviously do not abide by general rules. However, since idioms have the status of words in generative grammar, they do not undermine the general principle that grammar is strictly compositional in this approach.

2.1.2   The grammar–lexicon continuum

In the standard version of generative grammar, grammar and lexicon are strictly distinguished: grammar consists of principles and rules that account for the systematic or general properties of language; whereas the lexicon contains all idiosyncratic information, i.e. information that cannot be derived from general rules. Construction-based theories have abandoned the categorial division between lexicon and grammar (cf. Langacker 1987a; Goldberg 1995; see also Hudson 1990; Pollard and Sag 1994; Van Valin and La Polla 1997). Since both words and grammatical constructions are considered symbolic units (i.e. form–function pairings) they are uniformly represented in this approach. Specifically, grammar is seen as a continuum ranging from isolated words to complex grammatical assemblies (cf. Langacker 1987a:25–27; see also Slobin 1997). Idiomatic expressions are part of the grammar–lexicon continuum; in fact, idioms have played a key role in the development of this conception of grammar (cf. Fillmore, Kay, and O'Connor 1988; Nunberg, Sag, and Wasow 1994).

Idioms are obviously conventionalized form–function pairings. Consider, for instance, the idiom *kick the bucket* (cf. Fillmore et al. 1988). It has a nonliteral meaning that is not predictable from the meaning of its components. Moreover, certain syntactic properties of this expression are idiosyncratic. For instance, the structure cannot be passivized (*the bucket was kicked*) and the object NP is restricted to the singular (*kick the buckets*). However, like most idiomatic expressions *kick the bucket* is not entirely idiosyncratic; rather, it involves grammatical properties that are also found in nonidiomatic expressions. For instance, the verb can occur in different tenses (e.g. *kicked/will kick the bucket*) and is followed by an NP that can be analysed as the direct object. Thus, the expression *kick the bucket* combines idiosyncratic properties with general grammatical features. This suggests that idiomatic expressions such as *kick the bucket* are not in principle distinguished from regular expressions such as the passive. In fact, idioms can be seen as grammatical constructions that basically carry the same features as nonidiomatic expressions. Idiomatic and nonidiomatic expressions are commonly defined by both regular grammatical patterns and construction-specific features. Compare, for instance, the previous discussion of *kick the bucket* with Goldberg's analysis of the caused-motion construction.

The form of the caused-motion construction is defined by the following assembly of grammatical categories: '[SUBJ [V OBJ OBL]]' (Goldberg
1995:152). Semantically, the construction expresses the meaning 'X causes Y
to move somewhere'. Examples of the caused-motion construction are given in
(1)–(4) (the examples are adopted from Goldberg 1995):

(1)   She dragged the child into the car.
(2)   He wiped the mud off his shoes.
(3)   She forced the ball into the jar.
(4)   He pushed the book down the chute.

Note that the verbs of these examples have two semantic features that characterize the meaning of the whole structure: first, they are semantically causative
(i.e. an agentive subject is acting on a patient); and second, they indicate some
kind of motion or movement. Based on these examples, one might assume that
the caused-motion interpretation is evoked by the verbs that occur in these constructions, but Goldberg (1995:152–179) shows that the caused-motion reading
is also evoked if the construction includes a semantically different verb such as
sneeze.

(5)   She sneezed the napkin off the table.

Sneeze is neither a causative verb nor is it used to indicate motion, but the sentence in (5) has precisely this meaning, which suggests that the caused-motion
interpretation is not evoked by the verb. Goldberg argues that the caused-motion
reading is a property of the whole structure. In other words, the construction
is associated with a specific meaning independent of the lexical expressions
it includes. The whole structure constitutes a conventionalized symbolic unit,
which cannot be reduced to the properties of its components.

A similar analysis has been proposed for many other constructions such as
comparative conditional clauses (Fillmore et al. 1988), presentational and exis-
tential *there*-constructions (Lakoff 1987), resultative clauses (Goldberg 1995;
Nedjalkov 1983; Boas 2003), verb-initial sentences (Diessel 1997b, 2003b),
verb-particle constructions (Gries 2003), and nominal extrapositions (Michaelis
and Lambrecht 1996). In fact, construction grammar maintains that all grammatical assemblies are constructions; even the most general structures such
as transitive clauses can be seen as conventionalized form–function pairings
(cf. Goldberg 1995:116–119). What distinguishes such general structures from
idioms is that they are more abstract and less idiosyncratic. However, that does
not constitute a principled difference between idiomatic constructions such
as *kick the bucket* and more general constructions such as the caused-motion

construction or the passive. Both idiomatic constructions and nonidiomatic constructions are form–function pairings that combine general grammatical properties with idiosyncratic features.

If grammar consists of symbols (i.e. form–function correspondences), there is no principled difference between lexicon and grammar. The only feature that distinguishes grammatical constructions from words is that constructions generally include at least two meaningful components, whereas words may consist of a single meaningful element (i.e. a single morpheme). However, many words are morphologically complex: they consist of multiple morphemes that are combined to complex expressions, which one might analyse as 'morphological constructions' (Langacker 1987a:83–85). Thus, although words do not generally consist of multiple components, there is no principled difference between words and grammatical constructions, and therefore construction-based theories have abandoned the categorial division between lexicon and grammar.

2.1.3   Schemas and rules

Grammatical constructions vary along two important dimensions (cf. Fillmore et al. 1988; Croft and Cruse 2003). First, they vary in terms of syntagmatic complexity. Some grammatical constructions consist of only two elements while others include multiple components. For instance, a prepositional construction such as *in Berlin* contains two structural elements, a preposition and a noun (phrase), whereas the caused-motion construction comprises four elements, namely a subject, a verb, an object, and an oblique (see above).

Second, constructions vary along a scale of schematicity or abstractness. A construction is schematic if it consists of abstract grammatical categories such as NP or subject, and it is concrete if its components are filled by specific lexical items. For instance, idiomatic expressions such as *kick the bucket* are concrete constructions, in which each element is a concrete lexical expression. Abstract structures such as the caused-motion construction, on the other hand, are highly schematic constructions, which consist of abstract grammatical categories such as NP or subject. Schematic constructions are also called '(constructional) schemas' (Langacker 1987a; Bybee 1995; Ono and Thompson 1995); they account for linguistic generalization, which in other frameworks are described by rules (cf. Rumelhart and McClelland 1986a; Pinker and Prince 1988; Pinker 1999; Bybee 1995; Elman et al. 1996; Marcus 2001; Ramscar 2002).[2]

---

2. Although the notions of schema and construction are closely related they must be kept separate. The notion of construction subsumes both abstract grammatical patterns and lexically specific (or idiomatic) expressions. By contrast, the notion of schema applies only to abstract grammatical patterns, i.e. a schema can be seen as a particular type of construction.

Constructional schemas are like grammatical rules in that they describe the general properties of linguistic structures. In fact, a constructional schema can be seen as a notional variant of a rule if a grammatical rule is defined as a pattern involving variables (or 'placeholders') that can be filled by certain types of elements (cf. Marcus 2001). However, in contrast to traditional grammatical rules, constructional schemas are symbols, i.e. form–function correspondences. They do not only define the way in which elements can be combined but contribute their own (idiosyncratic) properties to grammatical assemblies. In other words, schemas are essentially of the same type as the expressions they combine: both are conventionalized form–function correspondences, whereas traditional grammatical rules (e.g. phrase structure rules such as NP → DET N) are of a different kind than the elements they combine (e.g. words or phrases).

Since schemas are linguistic expressions, they can be related to other linguistic expressions (i.e. other schemas or concrete constructions). The relationship between schemas (or constructions) is based on similarity: two constructions are closely related if they share a significant number of features. For instance, the ditransitive construction (e.g. *Sally gave Peter the ball*) is closely related to the caused-motion construction (e.g. *Sally gave the ball to Peter*) because the two constructions have similar forms and meanings: both include two semantic arguments in addition to the subject and express some kind of transfer (cf. Goldberg 1995:ch. 3).

The similarity between constructions is one important factor determining productivity in this approach (cf. Elman et al. 1996; Diessel and Tomasello 2004). Since the similarity between constructions is gradient, rather than absolute, the productivity of constructional schemas varies along a continuum: in the extreme case a constructional schema applies to all instances of a particular type, but very often the application of a constructional schema is much more limited (i.e. restricted to particular types in certain situations).

Apart from similarity, the productivity of a constructional schema is determined by the number of expressions that are related to a particular schema: the more types of expressions are linked to a constructional schema, the more productive is its use (cf. MacWhinney 1978; Bybee 1985, 1995). The productivity of rules, on the other hand, is not affected by type frequency. Rules are always fully productive; they automatically apply to all linguistic expressions that carry a certain grammatical feature (cf. Pinker and Prince 1988; Marcus 2001; for a detailed discussion of productivity see section 2.2.4).

Finally, the symbolic nature of grammatical constructions explains why many grammatical patterns show prototype effects (cf. Givón 1979, 1984; Hopper and Thompson 1980; Bybee 1995). The prototype effects result from the relationships between a constructional schema and its instances. For example, the transitive construction is a constructional schema that is related to a wide variety of subconstructions (i.e. different instances of transitive clauses). In the transitive schema, subject and object are associated with the semantic roles of a prototypical agent and a prototypical patient, respectively (cf. Hopper and Thompson 1980). If the verb of a transitive clause has a causative meaning, as in *Peter throws the ball*, subject and object express these roles, but if the verb denotes a psychological state, as in *Peter likes bananas*, the semantic roles are only remotely related to the semantic roles of the transitive schema. In other words, *Peter throws the ball* is a better instance of a transitive clause than *Peter likes bananas*. In a construction-based framework, this can be represented by different types of links relating the various types of transitive clauses to the transitive schema. In a rule-based approach, on the other hand, all transitive clauses are licensed by the same rules, i.e. all transitive clauses have equal status in this approach.

2.1.4   Prefabricated formulas

In some varieties of construction grammar, low-level constructions are in general underspecified. They include only information that is not provided by more schematic representations (cf. Fillmore and Kay 1993). For instance, an idiomatic construction such as *kick the bucket* would not include general syntactic information about its structure because this information is 'inherited' from a constructional schema. In this variety of construction grammar, low-level constructions contain only idiosyncratic information that they do not share with other constructions; all general grammatical features are inherited from constructional schemas. The representations are thus minimal in this approach: every piece of information is only represented in one place in mental grammar.

Other varieties of construction grammar posit that lower level constructions are fully specified (cf. Goldberg 1995:ch. 3; Langacker 1987a:87). In this view, constructions contain all the information available at a specific level of schematicity, including information that they share with more schematic representations. Lower level constructions do not inherit information from constructional schemas; rather, they are linked to more schematic representations by instantiation links that indicate the overlap of information. Thus, in this variety of construction grammar, which can be seen as an instance of the 'exemplar model' (cf. Nosofsky 1988), the same information is often stored redundantly at different levels of abstraction.

In generative grammar and many other theoretical frameworks, including certain varieties of construction grammar, the storage of information is maximally economical and nonredundant. Economy and nonredundancy are important criteria for the evaluation of scientific models. However, the application of these criteria presupposes that the proposed models provide an adequate account for the phenomena they describe. Adopting an exemplar-based view of categorization, I contend that generative grammar and many other grammatical theories are psychologically inadequate, precisely because these frameworks posit that grammatical representations are maximally economical and nonredundant. Speakers store frequently occurring word collocations and concrete utterances along with constructional schemas; that is, grammar consists of both abstract grammatical representations and prefabricated chunks of concrete expressions that are frequently used in everyday speech (cf. Pawley and Syder 1983; Langacker 1987a, 1991; Bybee and Scheibman 1999; Gregory, Raymond, Bell, Fosler-Lussier, and Jurafsky 1999; Erman and Warren 1999; Wray and Perkins 2000; Thompson and Hopper 2001; Jurafsky, Bell, Gregory, and Raymond 2001). Some of these 'prefabs' (Erman and Warren 1999) are fully specified utterances; others consist of concrete expressions that are associated with a specific slot. A few illustrative examples are given in (6).

(6)	*Fully specified utterances*	*Concrete utterances including a slot*
	How are you doing?	Why don't you __.
	Thank you, I'm fine.	I don't know __.
	What can I do for you?	Do you mind if __.
	Get the hell out of here!	I am just about to __.
	You can't have it both ways.	Would you please __.
	Either way is fine.	__ is not in the position to __.
	Say that again.	I can't help Ving __.
	I don't believe what's happening.	__ never got around to __.
	You gotta be kidding.	That's just about the __ that __.
	No, I'm dead serious.	I wonder if __.

Every native speaker of English knows a very large number of such prefabricated chunks and word collocations. Some of them are entirely familiar expressions that have been used many times before; others are somewhat less familiar and allow for some variation; however, none of the expressions in (6) is newly created.

The frequent use of prefabricated chunks is one of the features that distinguishes the speech of native speakers from the speech of second language learners (cf. Pawley and Syder 1983). The speech of second language learners often sounds unnatural, even if it is grammatical, because second language learners usually do not have enough communicative experience to know the prefabricated chunks that are characteristic of everyday speech.

Although the expressions in (6) are in accordance with general schematic representations, they are not derived on-line by means of constructional schemas; rather, native speakers access these structures directly without activating the corresponding schemas. Thus, from a psychological perspective, the exclusion of redundant information from grammar seems to be inadequate. Grammar (i.e. the grammar–lexicon continuum) includes both prefabricated chunks and constructional schemas. Rather than being 'minimal' and 'economical', grammar is 'maximal' and 'nonreductive' (Langacker 2000:1). It includes a wide variety of constructions that differ in terms of substance and familiarity. Highly abstract constructional schemas, low-level formulas, and prefabricated chunks coexist in the speaker's mental grammar. What is more, the coexistence is motivated because different types of constructions serve different functions.

Constructional schemas allow for the use of novel expressions; they account for the productivity of grammar, making language a flexible tool in novel situations (see below). However, the production of novel expressions is computationally costly. It involves a series of processing decisions that speakers have to make on-line under enormous time pressure (usually within milliseconds). For that reason, speakers tend to draw on prefabricated chunks and low-level formulas when they are available. Unlike novel expressions, these expressions have been computed so often that processing decisions occur with very little effort. In fact, highly routinized expressions are stored as holophrastic units whose internal structure is no longer computed. Thus, the use of prefabricated chunks and low-level formulas has certain advantages over the use of novel expressions: it reduces the amount of utterance planning and sentence processing so that the interlocutors can concentrate on other aspects of the communicative interaction. Spontaneous speech often abounds with formulaic expressions and semi-productive phrases that are organized around concrete lexical expressions. Highly schematic constructions are only activated if prefabricated chunks and low-level formulas are not available.

In general, while the redundant storage of information increases the memory load, it decreases the computational effort in planning and processing. The more information is stored in multiple places (i.e. at different levels of abstraction), the more likely it is that speakers can draw on prefabricated chunks and utterance formulas, minimizing the mental effort for utterance planning and comprehension. Thus, if we measure economy in terms of computational effort, rather than in terms of storage space, the nonreductive model of construction grammar appears to be more economical and efficient than most other grammatical frameworks after all.

2.2   The usage-based model

2.2.1   The emergence of linguistic structure

One of the central assumptions of generative grammar is that the basic principles of grammar are innate. Specifically, it is assumed that grammar can be divided into an innate 'core' and the 'periphery'. The core consists of universal principles and parameters that are part of our genetic endowment, whereas the periphery comprises those aspects of grammar that are not genetically specified.

Challenging the distinction between the core and the periphery, the usage-based approach posits that linguistic structure emerges from language use (cf. Langacker 1988, 2000; Bybee 1995; Elman et al. 1996). In this approach, grammar is seen as a dynamic system that is constantly changing by virtue of the psychological processes that are involved in language use. For instance, one of the central assumptions of the usage-based approach is that the representation of linguistic elements correlates with frequency of occurrence (e.g. Bybee 1985; Langacker 1988). Linguistic expressions and grammatical patterns that occur with high frequency in language use are more deeply entrenched in mental grammar than expressions that are infrequent. Every time a speaker uses a linguistic expression (or grammatical pattern), it reinforces its mental representation, which in turn facilitates the activation of this expression in language use. Thus, the use of linguistic expressions has an immediate effect on the representation and activation of linguistic knowledge.

What is more, language use can change the meaning and structure of linguistic elements and the organization of grammar. This has been amply demonstrated in the literature on grammaticalization (e.g. Heine, Claudi, and Hünnemeyer 1991; Hopper and Traugott 1993; Bybee, Perkins, and Pagliuca 1994; Lehmann 1995). Linguistic expressions are commonly divided into two general types: symbolic expressions and grammatical markers. Symbolic expressions subsume nouns, verbs, and adjectives, while grammatical markers comprise elements such as prepositions, conjunctions, and auxiliaries. The division between symbolic expressions and grammatical markers is based on two major criteria. First, symbolic expressions and grammatical markers serve different functions. Symbolic expressions denote referents, activities, and other concepts, whereas grammatical markers are structural (or topographic) expressions that function to organize constructions. Second, symbolic expressions and grammatical markers differ in terms of class size. Symbolic expressions are open class (except for adjectives, which may be open or closed class, cf. Dixon 1982), while grammatical markers are always closed-class items (cf. Talmy 1988).

Grammaticalization theory posits that all grammatical markers are derived from symbolic expressions or from other grammatical markers that previously emerged from a symbolic source (cf. Hopper and Traugott 1993:104). Frequency of occurrence plays a key role in this process. Linguistic expressions that are frequently used tend to reduce in structure and meaning (cf. Bybee 1985, 2001; Gregory et al. 1999; Jurasfky et al. 2001). This may lead to the development of new grammatical markers. To mention two well-known examples: the future marker *gonna* developed from the expression *BE going to INF*, and the conjunction *because* emerged from the adpositional phrase *by cause*. Both *BE going to INF* and *by cause* were frequent collocations before they turned into a future auxiliary and a subordinate conjunction. Other grammatical markers that evolved from frequently used symbolic expressions are prepositions such as *in front of* and *inside*, conjunctions such as *in case* and *while*, modals such as *hafta* (i.e. *have to*) and *gotta* (i.e. *got to*), and bound derivational morphemes such as *–hood* and *–ly* (*–hood* evolved from a noun meaning 'person', 'sex', 'quality', and *–ly* developed from a noun meaning 'appearance', 'form', 'body'; *OED*).

Apart from symbolic expressions (i.e. nouns, verbs, and adjectives), demonstratives such as English *this* and *that* and *here* and *there* provide a frequent historical source for the development of grammatical markers (cf. Diessel 1999a:ch. 6; 1999b). Since demonstratives are closed-class items they are commonly analysed as grammatical markers that developed from a symbolic source (i.e. from nouns, verbs, or adjectives); but there is no evidence from any language that demonstratives are historically related to symbolic expressions or any other expressions for that matter that do not include a genuine demonstrative (cf. Diessel 1991a, 2003a). It seems that demonstratives constitute a special class of linguistic expressions that developed very early in the evolution of language.

Demonstratives are commonly used to focus the hearer's attention on entities in the surrounding situation or elements in the ongoing discourse. In the latter use, they serve an important language internal function; specifically, they are used to track discourse participants and to establish links between chunks of the ongoing discourse. Based on such discourse-related uses, demonstratives frequently develop into grammatical markers. Across languages, demonstratives are commonly reanalysed as definite articles, third person pronouns, relative pronouns, complementizers, sentence connectives, focus markers, copulas, and many other grammatical morphemes (cf. Diessel 1997a, 1999a, 1999b). Like

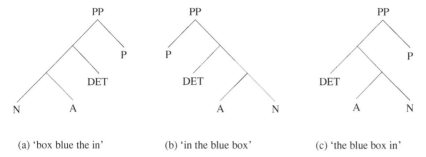

(a) 'box blue the in'   (b) 'in the blue box'   (c) 'the blue box in'

Fig. 2.1 *Left-, right-, and mixed-branching phrase structures.*

symbolic expressions, demonstratives only grammaticalize if they are routinely used in a specific grammatical construction (cf. Diessel 1999b:ch. 6).

Another grammatical phenomenon that is crucially affected by the psychological processes involved in language use is word order. It has been repeatedly argued in the literature that the ordering of linguistic elements is shaped by processing. Specifically, it has been claimed that linguistic elements tend to be arranged in such orders that they are easy to process and easy to produce (cf. Dryer 1992; Hawkins 1994). This concerns both free word-order config-urations in discourse and fixed grammatical word orders. Linguistic typolo-gists have shown that languages tend to be either consistently left-branching (cf. figure 2.1a) or consistently right-branching (cf. figure 2.1b) rather than mixed left- and right-branching (cf. figure 2.1c.) (cf. Dryer 1992).

In generative grammar (notably in Principles and Parameters Theory), the branching directions are assumed to be innate. Languages are either consis-tently left-branching or consistently right-branching because these are the two options (i.e. parameter values) provided by universal grammar (cf. Frazier 1985; Frazier and Rayner 1988). In the usage-based approach, on the other hand, lan-guages are assumed to employ consistent branching directions because such structures carry a lower processing load than structures with inconsistent left- and right-branching (cf. Dryer 1992; Hawkins 1994). In this view, the consistent branching directions are not innate; rather, they emerge in the historical devel-opment of grammar, which is driven by the psychological processes involved in language use. The branching directions can be seen as grammaticalized parsing principles that facilitate the interlocutors' computation of linguistic structures in language use (cf. Hawkins 1990, 1994, 1998).

The psychological mechanism that underlies grammaticalization is 'habituation' (Haiman 1994, 1998). Habituation is a general psychological pro-cess that does not only affect the use of language but also many other activities such as music and sports. It describes the process by which the parts of a complex activity are merged such that the boundaries between the parts are no longer recognized. As a consequence, the complex activity may lose its internal structure and some of its substance, which in turn may lead to the 'emancipation' (i.e. separation) of the restructured activity from its historical source (cf. Haiman 1994, 1998). This is exactly what we find in grammaticalization: linguistic expressions that grammaticalize undergo phonological and semantic changes such that they often lose the connection to their historical source; and free word orders that grammaticalize may become so rigid that grammar requires a specific word order regardless of the factors that motivated its development (cf. Hawkins 1994; Wasow 2002).

In sum, while the generative model posits the existence of innate grammatical principles and parameters, the usage-based model assumes that linguistic structure arises from language use. Grammar is shaped by usage – this is the most fundamental principle of the usage-based approach (cf. Bybee 2001; Bybee and Hopper 2001; Langacker 1988; Hawkins 1994; see also Bresnan and Aissen 2002, who recently expressed a very similar view in the framework of Optimality Theory).

2.2.2   *Network representations*

Linguistic knowledge is commonly represented in an activation network in the usage-based model (cf. Bybee 1985, 1995, 2001; Langacker 1987a, 1991; Bates and MacWhinney 1987, 1989; Barlow and Kemmer 2000; Bybee and Hopper 2001). Network representations have a long tradition in cognitive science. In cognitive psychology and computer science connectionist network models are used to simulate cognitive processes (cf. Rumelhart and McClellend 1986a; Elman, Bates, Johnson, Karmiloff-Smith, Parisi, and Plunkett 1996). Two basic types of connectionist models are commonly distinguished: localist networks, which consist of interconnected symbolic units that are similar to symbolic representations in traditional non-connectionist models; and parallel distributed processing networks (i.e. PDP networks), which constitute a more radical departure from traditional models in cognitive science. Both models are self-organizing in that the processing of data can change the representation of conceptual content. However, PDP models are much more radical in this regard than localist models (cf. Elman et al. 1996:90–97).

In a localist network, each concept is represented by a single node that cannot be decomposed into smaller elements. The specific properties of the nodes are hand-wired by the modeller; that is, the content of each node and its connections

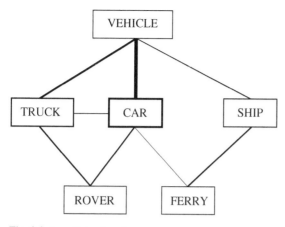

Fig. 2.2 *Localist network.*

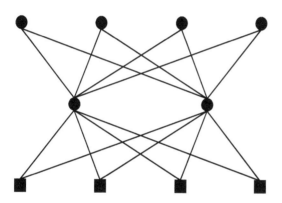

Fig. 2.3 *Distributed network.*

to other nodes are designed prior to the simulation (i.e. prior to the processing of data). An illustrative example of a localist network is given in figure 2.2.

In a distributed network, on the other hand, concepts emerge from processing data, i.e. they are not built into particular nodes. A PDP network consists of several layers of nodes and their connections. Both the nodes and their connections have 'weights', or 'activation values', that change in the course of the simulation.

The network in figure 2.3 has three layers of nodes: the input nodes (represented by the four squares at the bottom), the output nodes (represented by the four circles at the top), and the hidden nodes (represented by the two circles that are connected to both the input nodes and the output nodes). Minimally, a

PDP model has two layers of nodes, the input nodes and the output nodes, but most current PDP models have at least one extra layer of hidden nodes, making them more powerful than two-layer networks, which were often used in earlier PDP models (cf. Rumelhart and McClelland 1986a).[3]

Such networks can learn to match a given input pattern (e.g. the root of English verbs such as *walk, hit, sing*) to a particular output pattern (e.g. the past tense forms of these verbs, i.e. *walked, hit, sang*). During training, the activation values of the nodes and their connections change, based on a particular learning algorithm (cf. Rummelhart, Hinton, and McClelland 1986), such that a given input pattern fits the expected output pattern. At the end of training, the network has assumed a global activation pattern that allows the model to process new data in analogy to the input–output patterns that it has processed during training. The global activation pattern that emerges from processing the data can be interpreted as the representation of conceptual content (e.g. the English past tense schema) (cf. Elman et al. 1996:90–91; see also Rumelhart, Smolensky, McClelland, and Hinton 1986).

PDP models are more flexible than localist representations. In a localist network, the simulation (i.e. the processing of data) can change the activation values of the nodes and their connections, but it cannot alter the content of the concepts. Each concept is represented by a specific node that is designed prior to the simulation. By contrast, the concepts of a PDP model emerge in the course of the simulation – they are immediately grounded in the data that is processed by the network. PDP models are therefore more powerful and more flexible than localist representations.

The network approach has been combined with construction grammar (cf. Langacker 1987a; Lakoff 1987; Goldberg 1995; Croft 2001). Although there are currently no connectionist models of a construction-based grammar (but see Morris, Cottrell, and Elman 2000), most construction grammarians assume that grammatical knowledge is organized in an activation network (e.g. Langacker 2000; Croft 2001). An illustrative example of a construction-based network is given in figure 2.4, adopted from Goldberg (1995:109).

The boxes (or nodes) represent particular constructions that are related to each other. Since each construction is represented by a single node, the network resembles a localist model; however, in principle it could be converted to a distributed representation in which each construction is represented by a global activation pattern. In fact, most functional linguists assume that constructions

---

3. In addition to the hidden nodes, current PDP models often have a fourth layer of 'context nodes', which can simulate the effect of short-term memory in on-line processing. PDP models having context nodes are called 'recurrent networks' (Elman 1990).

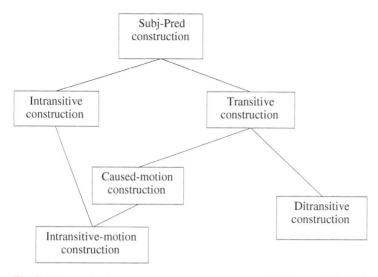

Fig. 2.4 *Network of argument structure constructions (Goldberg 1995:109).*

emerge from the psychological processes that are involved in language use (cf. Hopper 1987; Langacker 1988; Croft 2001; Bybee and Hopper 2001).

2.2.3   Entrenchment

Constructions have an activation value, which Langacker (1987a) calls the 'level of entrenchment'. Entrenchment is a psychological notion that corresponds to the 'activation value' in a connectionist model. It is directly related to frequency: linguistic expressions that are frequently used are more deeply entrenched (i.e. more highly activated) in the speaker's network of grammatical knowledge than linguistic expressions that are infrequent.

Two types of frequencies must be distinguished: token frequency, which refers to the frequency of concrete expressions in the process of language use; and type frequency, which refers to the number of linguistic expressions that instantiate a constructional schema (cf. MacWhinney 1978; Bybee 1985; Plunkett and Marchman 1991). The two types of frequencies have different effects on the storage, activation, and processing of linguistic expressions.

Constructions that are defined upon the occurrence of concrete words (i.e. pre-fabricated utterances and lexically specific constructions) are highly entrenched in mental grammar if they occur with high token frequency in language use. Such frequently occurring constructions function as cognitive routines that can be directly accessed without activating a high-level schema. For instance, Bybee and Scheibman (1999) have argued that expressions such as *I don't know ___, I don't think ___,* and *Why don't you ___* have become cognitive routines due to the fact that they are extremely frequent. Although these expressions seem to abide by general grammatical principles, they are processed (both in production and comprehension) without a constructional schema: all three expressions constitute prefabricated chunks or collocations that are stored as holistic units. The independence of these expressions from a constructional schema is reflected in their particular forms and meanings. All three expressions are slightly different from parallel constructions that are less frequent (cf. Bybee and Scheibman 1999): in casual speech the pronunciation of *don't* is commonly reduced to [rə̃], and although the clauses are formally negated they do not really function to negate a proposition: *I don't know* is either used to express the speaker's uncertainty or to indicate polite disagreement; *I don't think* expresses an epistemic stance towards an associated proposition; and *why don't you* marks a suggestion. Both the phonological reduction of *don't* and the particular meaning of these expressions suggest that they have started a life of their own; they have become cognitive routines, which Bybee and Scheibman characterize as 'storage and processing units'. This is the immediate effect of repetitive language use. In parallel constructions including a less frequent verb and a less common subject (e.g. *we don't eat __*), *don't* is commonly pronounced with an initial stop and a full vowel and serves as a negation marker. In general, what Bybee and Scheibman's analysis shows is that token frequency correlates with the level of entrenchment, which in turn has a significant effect on the storage and processing of lexically specific constructions.

While lexically specific constructions are highly entrenched in mental grammar if they occur with high *token* frequency, constructional schemas are argued to be highly entrenched if they occur with high *type* frequency (cf. Bybee 1985). In a construction-based framework, a type can be defined as a construction that instantiates a particular constructional schema. For instance, *NP pushed NP open* and *NP wiped NP clean* are instances (i.e. types) of the resultative schema (cf. Goldberg 1995:ch. 8). The level of entrenchment of a constructional schema correlates with the number of types that are associated with a constructional schema. Other things being equal, schemas that are instantiated by a large number of types are likely to be more deeply entrenched (i.e. more strongly activated at rest levels) than schemas that are related to only a few types. However, since the activation value of individual types is based on their number of tokens, token frequency is also indirectly involved in the entrenchment of a constructional schema.

Interestingly, very high token frequency can weaken the connection of an expression (i.e. a type) to a constructional schema. As Bybee and Thompson (1997) have shown, linguistic expressions that occur with high token frequency are often resistant to diachronic change. For instance, in Middle English questions were constructed by fronting the tensed verb, and negative sentences were formed by placing *not* immediately after the verb. However, in the fourteenth century the patterns began to change: in both questions and negative sentences *do* appeared as a dummy auxiliary. The change affected all verbs except for *have, be, can, may, need, ought, know*, and a few others (cf. Kroch 1989). With the exception of *know*, all of these verbs still occur without *do* in Modern English. Interestingly, all of the verbs that were not affected by the change were extremely frequent at the time when the *do*-construction emerged. Bybee and Thompson argue that these frequent verbs preserved the old pattern because they were so deeply entrenched in mental grammar that they were not attracted by the new question schema (cf. Tottie 1995). In other words, individual words and constructions may resist analogical change if they are so frequently used that speakers store them independently of a constructional schema.

   In sum, the activation value of a constructional schema is determined by both the number of types that instantiate a schema and the number of tokens that determine the activation value of a specific type (for an insightful discussion of the effects of type and token frequencies on the representation of schemas in a PDP model, see Plunkett and Marchman 1991).

2.2.4   Productivity
One of the central characteristics of human language is the productive use of grammatical patterns. In the usage-based approach, productivity can be defined as the likelihood that a constructional schema will be activated for constructing a novel expression (Langacker 2000:26). Since there are often multiple schemas that are in principle available to construct (or interpret) a novel expression, the activation process usually involves the selection of a specific schema from a set of alternatives (cf. Bock 1977; McClelland and Elman 1986; Bates and MacWhinney 1987, 1989; MacWhinney 1987; Langacker 2000). The selection process is determined by competing factors; two major factors can be distinguished: (i) the level of entrenchment, and (ii) the properties of the competing schemas (cf. Bybee 1995; Hare, Elman, and Daugherty 1995; Langacker 2000).

   Constructional schemas that are highly entrenched in the speakers' network of grammatical knowledge are more likely to be selected for constructing a novel expression than schemas that are not well entrenched. This has been amply demonstrated in connectionist research. For instance, in their well-known work on the acquisition of the English past tense, Rumelhart and McClelland (1986b) showed that the productivity of the *V-ed* past tense results from the high activation value of this schema (which, in turn, is based on high type frequency).

Specifically, they showed that the *V-ed* schema is the most productive past tense pattern functioning as the default because it licenses the use of a very large number of verb types, which outnumber the verb types of all other past tense schemas, i.e. irregular past tense schemas such as *drink-drank-drunk* (cf. Plunkett and Marchman 1991, 1993; see also Bybee and Slobin 1982, who analysed the acquisition of the English past tense in a non-connectionist framework from a usage-based perspective).

However, productivity is not only determined by type frequency. If type frequency were the sole determinant of productivity, it would be impossible to account for so-called 'low-frequency default patterns' (Hare, Elman, Daugherty 1995). A low-frequency default pattern is a morphological schema acting like the default despite the fact that it is based on low type frequency. A good example is the noun plural in Modern Arabic.[4]

Modern Arabic has several classes of irregular noun plurals, the so-called broken plurals, which outnumber the regular plurals by several times (in terms of types). However, when novel nouns are introduced to the language they tend to form the plural on the basis of the regular pattern unless they are phonologically similar to one of the irregular forms. The regular plural acts thus like a minority default schema that is automatically selected if a novel noun does not fit one of the phonological templates that define the irregular forms (cf. McCarthy and Prince 1990).

The Arabic plural suggests that apart from type frequency the productivity of a morphological schema is determined by the phonological properties of the competing schemas. A schema that is defined by specific phonological features can only be selected if the target, i.e. the novel expression, matches these features. If such a narrowly defined schema competes for selection with an 'open schema' (i.e. a schema that is defined by very general features; see Bybee 1995), it is very likely that the open schema will win the competition because the probability that the target will match the features of the open schema is much higher than the probability that it will match the specific features of a narrowly defined schema. Thus, in addition to type frequency, the phonological features of the competing schemas determine the productivity of a morphological pattern in the usage-based approach. Other things being equal (i.e. an equal number of types), an open schema is more likely to be selected for constructing a novel expression than a narrowly defined schema that would be available to construct a parallel expression.

4. Another frequently discussed minority pattern that is very productive, but probably not the default (cf. Behrens 2002), is the German *s*-plural (see Köpcke 1988, 1993, 1998; Clahsen, Rothweiler, Woest, and Marcus 1992; Bybee 1995; Clahsen 1999).

This explains why the regular Arabic noun plural can serve as a low-frequency default pattern. While the broken plurals are defined upon the presence of specific phonological features, the regular plural is basically an open schema, which is selected whenever the target does not match the phonological features of one of the irregular plurals (cf. Plunkett and Marchman 1991, 1993). The reason why the broken plurals are overall more frequent than the default pattern is simply that most existing Arabic nouns match one of the irregular plural schemas. It is thus the specific arrangement of open and narrow schemas that gives rise to a minority default pattern in morphology.

Although low-frequency defaults are relatively rare, they have been discussed extensively in the psycholinguistic literature because they show that productivity is not simply a function of type frequency (cf. Plunkett and Marchman 1991, 1993; Marcus, Ullman, Pinker, Hollander, Rosen, and Xu 1992; Clahsen, Rothweiler, Woest, and Marcus 1992; Prasada and Pinker 1993; Bybee 1995; Hare, Elman, and Daugherty 1995; Elman, Bates, Johnson, Karmiloff-Smith, and Plunkett 1996; Plunkett an Nakisa 1997). While this has never been claimed by the proponents of the usage-based model, some of the early connectionist studies employed two-layer networks in which the productivity of a morphological pattern was, in fact, a direct function of type frequency (e.g. Rumelhart and McClelland 1986b). However, this has changed in recent connectionist models. Using a three-layer network, Hare, Elman, and Daugherty (1995) have shown that a PDP model can in principle account for the existence of a productive morphological pattern that is not backed up by high type frequency. In such a case, it is the overall structure of the similarity space, defined by the features of the competing morphological schemas, that gives rise to the productive use of a minority default pattern (a connectionist model simulating the acquisition of the Arabic noun plural is described in Plunkett and Nakisa 1997).

Like the productivity of morphological schemas, the productivity of syntactic schemas is determined by competing factors. In most situations, there are several syntactic schemas available to realize a specific speech act (or to interpret an utterance). For instance, polar questions can be realized by intonation or by 'auxiliary fronting' (e.g. *It is raining? Is it raining?*), and many declarative sentences can be realized with different word orders (e.g. *He picked up the book – He picked the book up; He gave Peter the book – He gave the book to Peter*). In all of these cases, speakers (and hearers) have to select a specific syntactic schema to produce (or interpret) the utterance. The selection is determined by the level of entrenchment (i.e. by type frequency) and various competing forces. For instance, Diessel (forthcoming) argues that complex sentences including a final adverbial clause constitute two different constructions that speakers select in different situations. The selection process is determined by competing forces from three domains: syntactic parsing, information processing, and semantics. Using Hawkins (1994) parsing theory, Diessel shows that complex sentences including final adverbial clauses are easier to process, and thus more highly preferred, than complex sentences including initial adverbial clauses; but nevertheless the latter are used in certain situations because of semantic and discourse-pragmatic considerations that favour the occurrence of initial adverbial clauses and may override the parsing preference for final occurrence. Similar explanations have been proposed for the productivity of different ordering patterns in verb-particle constructions (cf. Gries 2003; Wasow 2002), ditransitive constructions (cf. Wasow 2002), genitive constructions (cf. Leech, Francis, and Xu 1994), and complex sentences including infinitival purpose clauses (cf. Thompson 1985).

2.3   *Language acquisition*

Concluding this chapter, I discuss some of the major differences between the usage-based approach and the generative approach to language acquisition. I first summarize the major arguments of the debate about innateness and then discuss the different views about grammatical development.

2.3.1   *The innateness hypothesis*

According to generative grammar, children are endowed with innate linguistic knowledge, which crucially determines the process of language acquisition. The initial state of the language faculty is called 'universal grammar' or, from a different perspective, the 'language acquisition device' (Chomsky 1999:43). Universal grammar defines the class of possible languages that children are able to acquire. It consists of grammatical principles and parameters that provide a limited set of binary choices. Chomsky (1999:49) characterizes the parameters as 'switches' that are initially unset or set to a default value (see also Hyams 1986). Grammatical development is seen as a process whereby children determine the parameter values of their language based on specific triggers in the input.

The innateness hypothesis of generative grammar is based on arguments from psychology, neurology, and linguistics. One of the most frequently cited arguments supporting the innateness hypothesis comes from brain function studies (i.e. Project Emission Topography (PET) and functional Magnetic Resonance Imaging (fMRI) studies). These studies have shown that different linguistic functions are located in different areas of the brain. The localization of language functions in specific brain areas is often taken as evidence for the innateness hypothesis (cf. Pinker 1994); however, as Elman et al. (1996:378) have argued convincingly, 'localization and innateness are not the same thing'. While there seem to be specific brain areas that are involved in particular language tasks, the specialization of these areas does not have to be innate; rather, local brain functions might emerge in the process of cognitive development. The brain is a self-organizing organ that develops local specializations as a consequence of processing a specific type of data. Strong support for this view comes from the fact that children with focal brain injuries often develop regional specializations for language in other areas of the brain than normal children (cf. Elman et al. 1996:ch. 5).

Other arguments supporting the innateness hypothesis are based on studies examining SLI children. SLI, which stands for Specific Language Impairment, is usually defined as a cognitive deficit that involves only language, in particular grammatical morphology. Since SLI tends to run in families, some researchers suggested that it is based on a genetic defect affecting grammar (cf. Pinker 1994). However, other researchers are not convinced that SLI is really restricted to language, let alone to grammatical morphology. Challenging the definition of SLI as a specific language impairment, they have shown that SLI children have general difficulties in processing information that occurs in rapid temporal sequences and that SLI children also suffer from deficits in symbolic play and spatial imagery (Tallal, Ross, and Curtis 1989). This suggests that SLI is not caused by a genetic defect affecting only grammar or language (for a review of the literature see Elman et al. 1996:ch. 7).

In addition to the arguments from brain function studies and SLI children, the innateness hypothesis is commonly supported by linguistic arguments. In particular, it has been claimed that the ambient language is not sufficient to learn grammar from experience alone. According to Chomsky (1972:78), there is an enormous discrepancy between the grammatical system that constitutes the speaker's competence and the 'meager and degenerated data' to which a child is exposed. Based on this assumption, Chomsky maintained that the gap between grammar and experience can only be closed if language acquisition is based on innate linguistic knowledge. This argument is known as 'the argument from the poverty of the stimulus' (for a recent discussion of this argument see Crain and Pietroski 2001; see also the articles in the special issue of *The Linguistic Review* 2002).

Challenging this view, Pullum (1996) and Pullum and Scholz (2002) have recently argued that this argument is empirically unfounded. Examining four constructions that, according to generative grammarians, are so rare that their grammatical properties cannot be learned from linguistic experience (i.e. plurals in compounds, auxiliary sequences, anaphoric *one*, and auxiliary-initial clauses), they show that all four types of constructions are quite frequent in both written and spoken language. While this does not refute the innateness hypothesis, it raises considerable doubt about the validity of the argument from the poverty of the stimulus (see also the corpus-based analysis of child-directed speech by Brent and Cartwright 1996; Cartwright and Brent 1997; Redington, Chater, and Finch 1998; Redington and Chater 1998; and Mintz, Newport, and Bever 2002).

Moreover, a number of recent studies suggested that children's ability to determine linguistic patterns is much better than is commonly assumed. For instance, Saffran, Aslin, and Newport (1996) found that infants as young as 8 months are able to segment a complex string of nonsense syllables into word-like components based on their distribution. Similar results, emphasizing the role of distributional learning in early language acquisition, are reported in studies by Jusczyk (1997), Santelman and Jusczyk (1998), Marcus, Vijayan, Rao, and Vishton (1999), Höhle and Weissenborn (1999), and Saffran (2001).

Another linguistic argument that generative grammarians have used to buttress the innateness hypothesis might be called 'the argument from the universality of grammatical features' (cf. Crain 1991). This argument is based on the assumption that all languages have certain grammatical properties in common. For instance, it has been argued that all languages employ the same grammatical categories such as nouns and verb (cf. Pinker 1984). If this is correct, one might ask why these categories are universally attested. Generative grammarians explain the existence of universal categories in terms of innate universal grammar: grammatical categories are universal because they are innate. If they were not innate it would be a complete mystery, according to some generative grammarians, why they are universal (e.g. Crain 1991).

Outside of generative grammar, the existence of universal linguistic categories is highly controversial. Most typologists assume that crosslinguistic generalizations represent tendencies rather than absolute universals (cf. Dryer 1997a). If there are any linguistic categories that exist in all languages, their number is extremely limited. Nouns and verbs are perhaps the only grammatical categories that are truly universal, but even that is controversial (cf. Sasse 1993). However, even if we make the assumption that there are some absolute universals, they would not have to be innate. There are other explanations for the existence of linguistic universals. For instance, nouns and verbs might be universal because all languages need these categories to denote two different types of concepts that are essential to human categorization (cf. Langacker 1987b;

see also Hopper and Thompson 1984). In general, the usage-based approach assumes that linguistic universals are motivated by functional and cognitive pressures (cf. Givón 1995; Dryer 1997b: Croft 2001, 2003). These pressures increase the frequency of particular linguistic patterns so that they may grammaticalize. Since there are usually several pressures competing with each other, linguistic universals tend to be statistical rather than absolute. For instance, although processing (and/or utterance planning) seems to motivate the use of consistent left- and right-branching (see above), the branching directions of most languages are not entirely consistent. The inconsistency can be explained by the competition between processing and other factors affecting word order. There are, for instance, pragmatic word-order principles that can be in conflict with syntactic parsing principles (cf. Diessel forthcoming). In addition, it is well known that language contact can have a significant effect on word order. Since individual languages balance the competing pressures in different ways, the branching directions are similar but not identical across languages. Similar analyses have been proposed for many other linguistic universals (cf. Haiman 1983, 1985; DuBois 1985, 1987; Givón 1984, 1990, 1995; Dryer 1997b; Croft 2001, 2003).

In sum, all of the arguments supporting the innateness hypothesis are controversial. There is no compelling evidence that children are endowed with an innate universal grammar. Of course, language acquisition has certain biological prerequisites, but there is no evidence that these prerequisites involve innate linguistic knowledge. Rather, it is conceivable that language acquisition is based on general cognitive mechanisms that are also involved in the development of other cognitive domains.

2.3.2   *Learning vs. growth*

In the usage-based approach grammatical development is based on (inductive) learning. It involves general psychological mechanisms such as habituation, entrenchment, and analogy. Habituation involves the routinization or automatization of complex verbal (and nonverbal) activities; entrenchment concerns the strength of mental representations; and analogy acts as a mechanism for the derivation of new knowledge. All three mechanisms are affected by frequency of occurrence: linguistic patterns that are frequently processed become routinized and automatized; their level of entrenchment is strengthened in mental grammar; and they are often involved in analogical reasoning.

Learning is crucially distinct from parameter setting and other mechanisms that in generative grammar explain how children 'hook up' their linguistic experience to innate universal grammar. In fact, Chomsky (1999:43) argues that the notion of learning should be eliminated from the study of language acquisition.

> The term learning is, in fact, a very misleading one, and one that is perhaps best abandoned as a relic of an earlier age, and an earlier misunderstanding. (Chomsky 1999:43)

Instead of learning, Chomsky (1999) uses the notion of 'growth' to characterize the acquisition of grammar. Learning and growth are fundamentally distinguished. The remainder of this chapter discusses the most important differences between learning and Chomsky's notion of growth.[5]

The social–cognitive basis of grammatical development

First, learning and growth make very different assumptions about the social–cognitive foundations of language acquisition. According to Chomsky (1999:41), grammatical development 'is something that happens to the child'. In this view, children acquire grammar in a quasi-automatic fashion: if they encounter the appropriate triggers in the input, grammar matures in the same way as the child's body or vision.

In the usage-based approach, grammatical development is considered an active process that crucially involves the use of language. In order to acquire language, including grammar, children have to be involved in social interactions (cf. Tomasello 1999, 2003; Clark 2003). According to Tomasello (1999), human infants are at first exclusively engaged in dyadic situations: they either manipulate objects or focus their intention on other people, whom they do not seem to recognize as a person like themselves. At around 9–12 months the situation changes: human infants begin to engage in triadic situations that involve the child, an object, and another person, who is now seen as an 'intentional agent' (i.e. a person like the self). Triadic situations require a co-ordination of interaction with other people; this provides a crucial prerequisite for language acquisition: children are able to learn the meaning and use of linguistic expressions only because they encounter them in pragmatically meaningful situations. Language is essentially an instrument that children acquire in social interactions with other people.

Thus, while Chomsky characterizes grammatical development as a quasi-automatic process that happens to the child, the usage-based model emphasizes the significance of social interactions for the acquisition of grammar.

---

5. It must be emphasized that Chomsky's notion of growth is not generally assumed in generative studies of language acquisition. Thus, the following discussion characterizes only one position in the generative approach.

The role of the ambient language

Second, learning and growth differ with regard to the data that are needed for acquisition. Learning requires robust data: children will be able to build up representations of grammatical patterns only if they are frequently exposed to the relevant data. In other words, frequency of occurrence plays an important role in learning. By contrast, growth is basically independent of frequency: parameters can be fixed based on very little data: 'The theory predicts that minimal exposure to data should be sufficient for parameter setting. Ideally, a single example encountered in the input could suffice' (Meisel 1994:20).

The time course of grammatical development

Third, inductive learning is a gradual process, whereas growth is, at least in principle, instantaneous (cf. Meisel 1994:14). As soon as the child is able to identify the elements that can act as triggers, a parameter can be set to a specific value. Assuming that most triggers are present in the input data, the theory predicts early and rapid acquisition (see especially Crain 1991 and Crain and Pietroski 2001). Of course, most generative grammarians acknowledge that grammatical development takes a certain amount of time, but this raises the question why triggers do not immediately fix a parameter when children encounter them. Borer and Wexler (1987) call this the 'triggering problem'. They argue that children initially are not sensitive to all triggers encountered in the data because universal grammar is not fully developed at birth; certain innately determined principles mature only later. Borer and Wexler call this the 'maturation hypothesis' (see also Wexler 1999). Based on this hypothesis, they argue that the acquisition of grammar takes time because it follows a 'biological program' that evolves only gradually during the early years of life.

Other generative linguists explain the triggering problem with the architecture of universal grammar (cf. Nishigauchi and Roeper 1987; Roeper and Weissenborn 1990; Roeper and de Villiers 1994; Weissenborn 1992). In their view, grammatical development takes time because parameters are interdependent such that a certain parameter can be set to a specific value only after the value of some other parameter has been determined. In this account, it is the arrangement of parameters in universal grammar that explains why parameters are not always immediately set to a specific value once a child encounters a particular trigger in the input.

Since the usage-based model assumes that language acquisition is based on learning, it is expected that grammatical development is gradual. In contrast to growth, learning requires repeated exposure to data over an extended period of time. From this perspective, the triggering problem is a pseudo-problem that arises from specific theoretical assumptions of generative grammar. In fact, the gradual development of grammar is seen as evidence for the usage-based hypothesis that language acquisition is based on learning.

The relationship between child grammar and adult grammar

Finally, learning and growth make different predictions about the nature of children's grammatical categories. In the generative approach, it is assumed that children have the same grammatical categories as adult speakers. Pinker (1984) called this the 'continuity hypothesis'. It is a logical consequence of the innateness hypothesis: children have adult-like categories because the categories they acquire are predetermined by innate universal grammar.

In the usage-based approach, it is assumed that children's grammatical representations are distinct from the grammatical categories of adult speakers (cf. Tomasello 2000a). Children develop representations of grammatical categories by analysing and systematizing the input data. The development is based on distributional analysis. Based on the distributional patterns that children detect in the ambient language, they construct abstract grammatical representations or schemas. The construction of schemas, which Langacker (2000) calls 'schematization', is based on a specific type of analogy that involves the extraction of common features from the ambient language. The extracted features reinforce each other, giving rise to constructional schemas and other abstract representations of linguistic knowledge (see chapter 8 for a more detailed discussion of this process). Since the extraction of common features from the data is a continuous process, one has to assume that the categories of early child grammar are constantly changing. As children attempt to organize the data, they gradually build up a network of interrelated constructions that successively become more complex and schematic. From this perspective, it is expected that children's grammatical categories are distinct from the categories of adult grammar.

3 Towards a definition of complex sentences and subordinate clauses

3.1   Towards a definition of complex sentences

In this study complex sentences are defined as grammatical constructions that express a specific relationship between two (or more) situations in two (or more) clauses. The definition involves three important notions: (i) construction, (ii) situation, and (iii) clause. The notion of construction has been discussed in detail in the previous chapter; here I concentrate on the two other notions, situation and clause. My definition of these terms is based on Langacker's notions of process, which I call situation, and relational predicate (cf. Langacker 1991:chs. 5–7).

A situation is a conceptual unit that has two important properties: situations are *relational* and *temporal*. They can be seen as conceptualized scenes involving a set of entities that are arranged in a specific constellation or engaged in an activity. Situations can be divided into several types: (i) situations that are stative vs. situations that involve a change of state (e.g. *The cat is sitting on the table* vs. *The cat is running*); (ii) situations that are conceptually bound vs. situations that are conceptually unbound (e.g. *The ball hit the wall* vs. *The ball is rolling*); and (iii) situations that are punctual vs. situations that are temporally extended (e.g. *He recognized the mistake* vs. *He learned how to play the guitar*) (cf. Vendler 1967; Van Valin and LaPolla 1997). Situations must be distinguished from things. Things are *nonrelational* and *atemporal*. Like situations, they can be divided into several types, e.g. objects, persons, and places.

The distinction between things and situations corresponds to the distinction between nouns and clauses. Following Langacker (1987b), I assume that nouns and clauses are linguistic categories that construe or profile concepts in different ways:[1] nouns construe concepts as atemporal and nonrelational entities, whereas clauses construe concepts as being temporal and relational. In other words, the linguistic categories of nouns and clauses are characterized by the

---

1. Note that Langacker speaks of nouns and verbs rather than of nouns and clauses, but since verbs function as the profile determinant of a clause, clauses have basically the same conceptual properties as verbs according to his proposal.

same conceptual features as the prelinguistic (i.e. conceptual) categories of things and situations. This explains why things are commonly expressed by nouns and situations are usually encoded in clauses. However, nouns do not always designate a thing, and clauses do not always denote a situation. For instance, a noun such as *destruction* makes reference to a situation rather than a thing. In such a case, a situation (i.e. a relational and temporal concept) is linguistically construed as a nonrelational and atemporal entity. Similarly, presentational clauses such as *That's the man who*. . . do not designate a situation; rather, they present an isolated referent: presentational clauses are pseudo-clauses that function to establish a nonrelational and atemporal entity in focus position making it available for the predication expressed in the following clause (cf. Lambrecht 1988). Thus, although things are commonly expressed by nouns and situations are usually encoded in clauses, the linguistic construal of things and situations is not entirely predetermined by the concepts they encode.

Moreover, the division between nouns and clauses is fluid. English has a number of constructions that share certain properties with both nouns and clauses. For instance, while gerunds function syntactically as nouns (or noun phrases), they share several properties with clauses: like clauses they designate a situation and may include semantic arguments that are selected by the head noun (e.g. *Driving a car can be dangerous*). A number of studies have therefore suggested that nouns and clauses should be seen as the two ends of a continuum rather than two discrete categories (cf. Lehmann 1988). What makes this proposal especially interesting in the context of the current investigation is that certain types of subordinate clauses have an intermediate status between nouns and clauses. Specifically, nonfinite subordinate clauses share properties with both categories. According to Langacker (1991:ch. 10), nonfinite subordinate clauses construe a situation as an atemporal structure. In contrast to finite clauses, infinitival and participial clauses are temporally unspecified; they are marked by the infinitive marker *to* or the – *ing* suffix, which are incompatible with grammatical tense markers. If we follow this line of reasoning, nonfinite subordinate clauses can be seen as some kind of nominalization (cf. Lehmann 1988). They are linguistic entities that share properties with both prototypical clauses and prototypical nouns.

3.2   *Towards a definition of subordinate clauses*

Complex sentences are traditionally divided into two basic types: (i) sentences including co-ordinate clauses, and (ii) sentences including subordinate clauses. The former consist of two (or more) clauses that are functionally equivalent and symmetrical, whereas the latter consist of two (or more) clauses that constitute an asymmetrical relationship: a subordinate clause and a matrix clause do not have equal status and equal function (cf. Foley and Van Valin 1984:239). In what follows, I suggest that prototypical subordinate clauses carry the following features: they are (i) syntactically embedded, (ii) formally marked as a dependent clause, (iii) semantically integrated in a superordinate clause, and (iv) part of the same processing and planning unit as the associated matrix clause. The four features will be discussed in turn.

3.2.1   The syntactic features of subordinate clauses

First, subordinate clauses are commonly defined as embedded structures. More precisely, it is assumed that subordinate clauses are syntactically embedded within the matrix clause. In this view, complement clauses serve as subjects or objects of the matrix clause predicate, relative clauses function as attributes of a noun or noun phrase, and adverbial clauses are seen as sentential modifiers or adjuncts of the associated matrix clause (or verb phrase). One central piece of evidence supporting this analysis comes from the substitution test, which shows that all three types of subordinate clauses can be paraphrased by nonclausal expressions.

(1)	a.	I noticed <u>that the building was destroyed</u>.	[COMP-clause]
	b.	I noticed <u>the destruction of the building</u>.	[paraphrase]
(2)	a.	The police found the car <u>that was stolen</u>.	[REL-clause]
	b.	The police found the <u>stolen</u> car.	[paraphrase]
(3)	a.	She left <u>after the train arrived</u>.	[ADV-clause]
	b.	She left after <u>the arrival of the train</u>.	[paraphrase]

However, since the paraphrases are not entirely equivalent to the subordinate clauses, the evidence of the substitution test has been disputed. In particular, the substitution of adverbial clauses by prepositional phrases is controversial (cf. Matthiessen and Thompson 1988:280–281). A number of studies have argued that the substitution test alone does not suffice to demonstrate that adverbial clauses are modifiers or adjuncts of the matrix clause. In fact, these studies claim that there is no evidence for the hypothesis that adverbial clauses are embedded (cf. Halliday 1985:ch. 10; Matthiessen and Thompson 1988; Givón 1990:ch. 19).

In my analysis (cf. chapter 7), I argue that one has to distinguish between different types of adverbial clauses. While some adverbial clauses are only loosely adjoined to a neighbouring clause, others are tightly integrated in a specific composite structure. The latter type can be seen as some kind of modifier or adjunct of the matrix clause, whereas the former type is basically indistinguishable from co-ordinate clauses. Thus, although adverbial clauses are not generally embedded, there are at least some structures that one might analyse as embedded adverbial clauses. In general, while embedding is an important concept of subordinate constructions, it does not characterize all structures that are traditionally classified as subordinate clauses.

3.2.2   *The morphological features of subordinate clauses*
Second, subordinate clauses are often marked as dependent structures. A dependent structure is an expression that is formally incomplete in isolation. For instance, subordinate clauses including a nonfinite verb form are dependent structures because they do not constitute a complete utterance without the associated matrix clause. Consider examples (4) and (5).

(4)   <u>To open the door</u> you have to push this button.
(5)   <u>Walking down the street</u> I noticed that all the stores were closed.

To open the door and *walking down the street* are nonfinite adverbial clauses that need to be integrated in a larger construction. Since they are incomplete without the matrix clauses, they are considered dependent structures.

   Like nonfinite subordinate clauses, finite subordinate clauses are dependent structures if they include a complementizer, a subordinate conjunction, or a relative pronoun, as in the following examples.

(6)   I regret **that** I didn't come.   [COMP-clause]
(7)   I left **when** he started talking.   [ADV-clause]
(8)   I asked the man **who** was waiting outside.   [REL-clause]

The clauses in (6)–(8) are dependent structures because they are formally incomplete without the associated matrix clauses. However, unlike nonfinite subordinate clauses, finite subordinate clauses are not generally dependent structures. A finite complement clause, for instance, is formally independent if it does not include a complementizer as in (9), where the subordinate clause could function as a complete utterance without the associated matrix clause (cf. *We should leave*).

(9)   I think <u>we should leave</u>.   [COMP-clause]

3.2.3   *The semantic features of subordinate clauses*
Third, subordinate clauses have a specific meaning or function that sets them apart form nonsubordinate clauses. In the discourse-oriented literature, complex sentences are often described in terms of foreground and background information (cf. Tomlin 1985; Thompson 1987). The notions of foreground and background characterize the content and pragmatic function of clauses

in narrative discourse (cf. Hopper 1979; Hopper and Thompson 1980). Foreground information is significant and central information that contributes to the actual storyline; it provides the 'backbone' of the narration. Background information, on the other hand, provides supportive material that elaborates the main events but does not itself narrate the story. A number of discourse-oriented studies have argued that the distinction between foreground and background information correlates with the distinction between matrix clauses and subordinate clauses: while matrix clauses code foreground information, subordinate clauses function as backgrounded clauses that support, enrich, or comment on the events of the main narrative (cf. Tomlin 1985; Thompson 1987; Matthiessen and Thompson 1988).

The discourse-pragmatic distinction between foreground and background is related to the semantic distinction between figure and ground (cf. Reinhart 1984). According to Talmy (2000:ch. 5), complex sentences including subordinate clauses make reference to two situations that one can analyse as figure and ground. Specifically, Talmy argues that adverbial clauses function to encode the ground for the figure event encoded in the matrix clause (see also Talmy 1978; Reinhart 1984; and Croft 2001). This explains, according to Talmy, why the complex sentence in (10b) is not acceptable.

(10a)   He dreamed <u>while he slept</u>.
(10b)   *He slept <u>while he dreamed</u>.

Sleeping and *dreaming* are in a specific figure–ground relationship: since *dreaming* is contingent on *sleeping*, while *sleeping* is independent of *dreaming*, *dreaming* must be regarded as the figure and *sleeping* can only be seen as the ground. In example (10a) the adverbial clause encodes the ground (i.e. *sleeping*) for the figure (i.e. *dreaming*) encoded in the matrix clause. The sentence is acceptable because the semantic relationship between *sleeping* and *dreaming* matches the figure–ground organization of the complex sentence: the ground event is encoded in the ground clause (i.e. the adverbial clause) and the figure event is encoded in the figure clause (i.e. the matrix clause). Example (10b), on the other hand, is unacceptable because the semantic relationship between *sleeping* and *dreaming* does not conform with the figure–ground organization of complex sentences: the ground (i.e. *sleeping*) is encoded in the figure clause (i.e. the matrix clause) and the figure (i.e. *dreaming*) is encoded in the ground clause (i.e. the adverbial clause). If the two events that are encoded in matrix and adverbial clauses are not biased towards a particular interpretation, like *sleeping* and *dreaming*, it is the conventionalized meaning of the complex sentence that evokes a specific figure–ground interpretation, as in examples (11a) and (11b).

(11a)   He was eating <u>while he was watching TV</u>.
(11b)   He was watching TV <u>while he was eating</u>.

Unlike *sleeping* and *dreaming*, *eating* and *watching TV* do not predetermine a specific figure–ground analysis: either one of them can serve as the figure or as the ground. This explains why both sentences in (11) are acceptable. In (11a) *watching TV* is encoded in the ground clause and *eating* serves as the figure, whereas in (11b) *eating* occurs in the ground clause and *watching TV* serves as the figure. The specific interpretation of these examples is evoked by the conventionalized figure–ground structure of matrix and adverbial clauses.

Both the discourse-oriented approach and the gestalt-semantic approach have been concerned mainly with adverbial clauses. There are no systematic studies of the discourse-pragmatic or gestalt-semantic properties of complement and relative clauses. However, Langacker (1991:ch. 10) proposed an account for all subordinate clauses that is closely related to the gestalt-semantic approach. In his analysis, subordinate clauses are defined as structures 'whose profile is over-ridden by that of the matrix clause' (Langacker 1991:436). Langacker defines the notion of profile as the 'focal point' of a composite semantic structure. The profile is usually determined by a specific element that lends its schematic semantic properties to a larger construction. For instance, in an expression such as *the tall man*, the noun *man* is the 'profile determinant' of the noun phrase construction (cf. Langacker 1987a:492). Using this notion of profile, Langacker argues that the profile of a complex sentence is determined by the matrix clause, whose semantic properties override the profile of the subordinate clause. According to this analysis, a sentence such as '*I know she left* designates the process of knowing, not of leaving' (Langacker 1991:436).

While Langacker is able to support his analysis by convincing examples, it is not difficult to find examples challenging his proposal. In particular, in spoken discourse the matrix clause is not always the profile determinant of a complex sentence (cf. Verhagen 2001; Thompson 2002). However, that does not invalidate Langacker's proposal. In my view, his analysis is appropriate if we take it as the description of a prototypical subordinate clause.

3.2.4   Processing of subordinate clauses

Finally, I suggest that subordinate clauses can be characterized from a processing (or planning) perspective. A prototypical subordinate clause occurs together with the associated matrix clause within the same viewing frame. Consider for instance examples (12)–(14).

(12)   Peter knew <u>that they would come</u>.   [COMP-clause]
(13)   The book <u>I bought</u> cost 28 Dollars.   [REL-clause]
(14)   <u>After we left</u> it began to rain.   [ADV-clause]

In all three examples, the interpretation of the initial clause cannot be completed before the whole sentence has been processed. In example (12), the final clause, i.e. the complement clause, fills an obligatory position in the initial clause, i.e. the matrix clause, so that the interpretation of the initial clause is incomplete until the final clause has been computed. In example (13), the initial clause, i.e. the matrix clause, is interrupted by a relative clause, so that the interpretation of the matrix clause, i.e. the initial clause, must be continued after the relative clause has been processed. Finally, in (14) the initial clause, i.e. the adverbial clause, is a dependent structure that needs the final clause, i.e. the matrix clause, to form a complete sentence; the processor knows therefore from the very beginning (i.e. as soon as it encounters the subordinate conjunction) that the initial clause will be followed by another clause in which the initial clause is integrated (see chapter 7). In all three examples, the matrix clause and the subordinate clause are held together in working memory until the parser has reached the end of the sentence. Although the whole structure consists of two clauses, it functions as a single processing unit. Compare the sentences in (12)–(14) with example (15).

(15)   The whole discussion is pointless ... and I don't wanna talk about it anymore.

Example (15) consists of two co-ordinate clauses that are intonationally unbound and separated by a pause. In contrast to the clauses in (12)–(14), the clauses in (15) are processed successively. The construction of the first clause is completed before the second clause moves into the viewing frame; there is no indication in the first clause that it will be continued by a co-ordinate clause.

Like the three other criteria, the processing criterion does not establish a clear-cut division between subordinate and nonsubordinate clauses. Two co-ordinate clauses may be planned and processed as a single grammatical unit, and a subordinate clause may function as an independent processing unit if it is added to a matrix clause that constitutes a formally complete sentence. Consider, for instance, examples (16) and (17).

(16)   I met his colleague, **who** is really <u>very nice</u>.
(17)   I will be working tonight, **because** I have <u>to finish this paper</u>.

The subordinate clause in (16) is a (nonrestrictive) relative clause that is adjoined to the final noun (phrase) of the matrix clause. Since the matrix clause is syntactically and intonationally complete without the associated relative clause, the processor will construct the matrix clause as a simple sentence, which is continued by the relative clause after the interpretation of the matrix clause has been completed. Thus, although the relative clause is linked to a noun (phrase) in the previous clause, it is computed as a separate processing unit. Similarly, the two clauses in (17) are processed separately. Again, since the matrix clause is a formally complete sentence and since there is no indication that a subordinate clause will follow (disregarding possible intonational cues) the parser will complete the construction of the matrix clause after *tonight*. While the following adverbial clause is semantically linked to the matrix clause, it is processed as a separate linguistic unit after the matrix clause has been computed. Thus, in contrast to the complex sentences in (12)–(14), the parser constructs the sentences in (16) and (17) successively, computing one clause at a time.

The same argument can be constructed from the speaker's point of view: while the sentences in (12)–(14) presuppose a complex utterance plan, including both the matrix clause and the subordinate clause, the sentences in (16) and (17) can be planned successively, i.e. the speaker can plan the subordinate clause after the matrix clause has been produced.

3.2.5   Summary

To summarize, there are a number of features that are characteristic of subordinate clauses, but none of them applies to the whole range of constructions that are traditionally considered subordinate clauses, and some of them also apply to co-ordinate clauses. It seems that there are no necessary and sufficient criteria defining the notion of subordinate clause. I suggest therefore that the notion of subordinate clause has a prototype structure (cf. Haiman and Thompson 1984; Lehmann 1988). Specifically, I propose that prototypical subordinate clauses carry the following features:

    (i)   they are syntactically integrated (i.e. embedded) in the matrix clause;
   (ii)   they are marked as dependent structures that are formally incomplete without the matrix clause;
  (iii)   they are semantically integrated in a matrix clause that determines the profile of the composite structure; and
  (iv)   they are part of the same processing and planning unit as the associated matrix clause.

Like the notion of subordinate clause, the notions of complement clause, relative clause, and adverbial clause have a prototype structure. The specific features of these structures and their relationships to the notion of subordinate clause will be discussed in the following chapters.

4 Infinitival and participial complement constructions

The earliest multiple-clause utterances that all five children produce include a finite verb and an infinitive that one might analyse as a nonfinite complement clause (e.g. *I wanna eat*). The occurrence of these constructions is initially restricted to a small number of complement-taking verbs such as *want, have,* and *like* that indicate volition or obligation. The present chapter shows that, although these verbs behave grammatically like matrix verbs, semantically they function like modals: rather than denoting an independent state of affairs, they indicate the child's desire or obligation to perform the activity denoted by the nonfinite verb. The whole utterance contains a single proposition and thus does not involve embedding. Other early infinitival and participial complements occur with aspectual verbs such as *start* and *stop*. Like the early quasi-modals, the aspectual verbs do not make reference to an independent state of affairs; rather, they elaborate the temporal structure of the activity denoted by the nonfinite verb. As children grow older, these constructions become increasingly more complex. Many of the complement-taking verbs that emerge later describe activities that are semantically more independent of the nonfinite verb than the early quasi-modals and aspectual verbs. Moreover, while children's early nonfinite complement clauses are always controlled by the matrix clause subject (e.g. *I wanna sing*), later nonfinite complements are often controlled by the direct object, which occurs between the finite verb and the infinitive or participle (e.g. *He told **him** to leave*). Based on these findings, I argue that the development of nonfinite complement constructions can be seen as a process of clause expansion. Starting from structures that denote a single situation, children gradually learn the use of complex sentences in which a nonfinite complement clause and a matrix clause express a specific relationship between two states of affairs.

The analysis proceeds as follows. Section 4.1 reviews the previous literature on the acquisition of infinitival and participial complement clauses; section 4.2 discusses the various nonfinite complement constructions in adult English; Section 4.3 provides a general overview of the data; section 4.4 presents my analysis of children's early nonfinite complement clauses; finally, section 4.5 summarizes the main results of the chapter and considers the factors that might account for the described development.

4.1   Literature

The acquisition of nonfinite complement clauses has been subject to numerous investigations over the past thirty years (cf. Chomsky 1969; Menyuk 1969; Limber 1973; Maratsos 1974; Tavakolian 1977; Lederberg and Maratsos 1981; Goodluck 1981, 1987; Bloom, Tackeff, and Lahey 1984; Hsu, Cairns, and Fiengo 1985; Chipman and Gerard 1987; Sherman 1987; Sherman and Lust 1986, 1993; Kim 1989; Hsu, Cairns, Eisenberg, and Schlisselberg 1989; McDaniel and Cairns 1990; Gerhardt 1991; Cairns, McDaniel, Hsu, and Rapp 1994; Eisenberg and Cairns 1994; Gawlitzek-Maiwald 1997). Most of these are experimental studies that examine children's interpretations of the unexpressed subject (or actor) of the nonfinite verb. Consider, for instance, the following examples (the blank space indicates the unexpressed actor of the infinitive):[1]

(1)   He$_i$ forgot [__$_i$ to buy the newspaper].
(2)   He told the boy$_i$ [__$_i$ to buy the newspaper].

In both examples the infinitival complement does not have a grammatical subject. The unexpressed actor is identified by an element in the matrix clause, which is commonly called the 'controller'. In example (1) it is the matrix clause subject that controls the activity denoted by the nonfinite verb; and in example (2) it is the matrix clause object that functions as the controller. If the infinitive is separated from the matrix verb by a nominal complement as in (2), it is almost always the matrix clause object that serves as the controller. There are only a few verbs that involve subject control in this case; the best known example is *promise*:

(3)   The boy$_i$ promised the girl [__$_i$ to give her the ball].

Although the infinitive in (3) is separated from the matrix verb by a nominal complement (i.e. the direct object *the girl*), it is controlled by the matrix clause subject (i.e. *the boy*). There are only a few other complement-taking verbs that involve subject control in this type of construction.

The first systematic investigation of children's comprehension of control structures was a study by Carol Chomsky (1969). She conducted a series

---

1. Following Van Valin and LaPolla (1997), I use the notions of 'actor' and 'undergoer' for the semantic subject and semantic object, respectively.

of experiments with 40 5-to-9-year-old children, testing their comprehension of various infinitival complement constructions. In one of these experiments Chomsky used sentences in which the unexpressed object (i.e. the undergoer) of a nonfinite verb was coreferential with the matrix clause subject, as in (4):

(4)   The doll$_i$ is easy [to see ___$_i$].

In order to determine children's comprehension of this construction, Chomsky showed her subjects a blindfolded doll and then asked them 'Is the doll easy to see or hard to see?' Since the doll was in plain sight of the children, the correct response would have been 'The doll is easy to see'. However, many of the younger children responded 'The doll is hard to see'. When these children were asked 'Could you make her easy to see?' they took off the blindfold, suggesting that they interpreted the doll as the unexpressed subject of the infinitive. Chomsky's experimental design was criticized because the blindfold covering the doll's eyes might have led the children to focus on the doll's inability to see. However, when subsequent studies repeated the experiment without blindfolding the doll, children misinterpreted the *easy-to-see* construction in the same way (cf. Cromer 1974; Cambon and Sinclair 1974; Fabian-Kraus and Ammon 1980).

   In another experiment Chomsky asked the same children to act out the meaning of two other constructions including an infinitival complement clause: in one of these constructions the unexpressed actor of the infinitive was controlled by the matrix clause object as in (5); in the other construction the unexpressed actor was controlled by the matrix clause subject as in (6).

(5)   Bozo tells Donald$_i$ [___$_i$ to hop up and down].
(6)   Bozo$_i$ promises Donald [___$_i$ to hop up and down].

What Chomsky found is that many children interpret the matrix clause object as the controller regardless of the matrix verb; that is, many children interpret the *promise*-construction in the same way as most other constructions including a nominal complement and a nonfinite complement clause: they select the matrix clause object (i.e. *Donald*) rather than the subject NP (i.e *Bozo*) as the actor of the activity described by the nonfinite verb. Based on this finding, Chomsky suggested that children tend to interpret the NP that occurs in minimal distance to the nonfinite verb as the unexpressed actor (or subject) of the complement clause. This strategy has become know as the 'Minimal Distance Principle' (abbreviated henceforth as MDP), a term that Chomsky adopted from Rosenbaum (1967).

While Chomsky's empirical findings were confirmed in subsequent studies (cf. Hsu, Cairns, and Fiengo 1985; Sherman and Lust 1986; Eisenberg and Cairns 1994), several researches suggested that the MDP does not adequately explain how children interpret control constructions (cf. Maratsos 1974; Goodluck 1981; Sherman and Lust 1986, 1993; Sherman 1987; Chipman and Gerard 1987). In one of these studies, Maratsos (1974) argued that children's interpretations of the unexpressed subject are based on a semantic principle rather than the MDP, which Chomsky defined as a surface strategy based on linear order. Maratsos observed that the controller of an infinitival complement is not only the NP that usually occurs in minimal distance to the nonfinite verb but also the goal of the event denoted by the matrix verb. Based on this observation, Maratsos proposed the 'Semantic Role Principle' (abbreviated henceforth as SRP), which posits that children select the goal (or a participant with a similar semantic role) as the controller of the nonfinite verb. In order to test this hypothesis, Maratsos designed an experiment in which 40 4 to 5-year-old children were asked to act out the meaning of control constructions in which the matrix clause was passivized, as in (7).

(7)   The bear$_i$ is told by the elephant [__$_i$ to get in].

In this case, the MDP (i.e. the Minimal Distance Principle) and the SRP (i.e. the Semantic Role Principle) make different predictions. Since *the elephant* occurs in minimal distance to the nonfinite verb, the MDP predicts that children interpret *the elephant* as the controller. However, since *the elephant* is the actor (rather than the goal) of the activity denoted in the matrix verb, it cannot be the controller according to the SRP. Rather, if children's interpretation of control is determined by the Semantic Role Principle, the matrix clause subject (i.e. the goal) will serve as the controller despite the fact that *the elephant* occurs in closer distance to the nonfinite verb.

In accordance with the SRP, Maratsos found that if children understand the passive construction correctly they usually interpret *the bear* as the controller. In 50 responses there were only two instances in which *the elephant* was chosen as the implicit actor of the infinitive; in all other instances the children selected *the bear* as the controller. This provides strong evidence against the MDP and seems to support Maratsos's hypothesis that children's interpretations of control constructions are based on semantic roles (see also Lederberg and Maratsos 1981).

While Maratsos's empirical results could be replicated in later studies (e.g. McDaniel, Cairns, and Hsu 1991), Goodluck (1981) suggested an alternative account for these data. According to her analysis, children interpret the subject

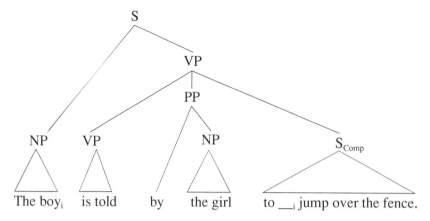

Fig. 4.1 *Phrase structure of a complex sentence including a passive matrix clause and a nonfinite complement clause.*

of a passive sentence as the controller of an infinitival complement clause because the NP that occurs in minimal distance to the infinitive is embedded in a prepositional phrase and thus does not c-command the nonfinite clause. The notion of c-command denotes a specific relationship between two constituents in a tree structure. While there are several versions of c-command, the classical formulation is 'a node A c-commands another node B iff the lowest branching node which properly dominates A also properly dominates B' (Trask 1993:39). Since the demoted actor of a passive sentence is dominated by two branching nodes, PP and VP (see figure 4.1), it does not c-command the unexpressed subject (or actor) of the subordinate clause.

Both Maratsos's semantic role principle and Goodluck's syntactic analysis account for the data; however, Goodluck maintained that her analysis is preferable because it is based on principles of innate universal grammar.

While Chomsky and Maratsos were only concerned with infinitival complement clauses, Goodluck (1981) also examined children's interpretations of nonfinite adverbial clauses (see also Goodluck and Behne 1992; Goodluck 2001). Interestingly, Goodluck found that many children still misinterpret nonfinite adverbial clauses when they have mastered the interpretation of nonfinite complement clauses. In contrast to nonfinite complement clauses, nonfinite adverbial clauses involve subject control if the matrix clause includes a direct object. As can be seen in figure 4.2, the object does not c-command the subordinate clause in this case. However, Goodluck's experiments showed that children tend to interpret the matrix clause object as the controller of the adverbial clause.

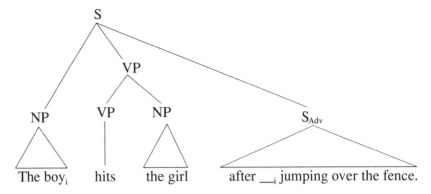

Fig. 4.2 *Phrase structure of a complex sentence including an active matrix clause and a nonfinite adverbial clause.*

In order to account for this finding, which seems to challenge her analysis of nonfinite complement clauses, Goodluck argued that younger children often attach nonfinite adverbial clauses to VP rather than S: if the adverbial clause is attached to VP, the matrix clause object c-commands the unexpressed subject just like the matrix clause object of a nonfinite complement clause. In other words, Goodluck maintained that, in both cases, the child's interpretation of the controller is based on c-command, but children sometimes misinterpret these structures because they attach the subordinate clause to the wrong node. Goodluck's analysis was later adopted by McDaniel, Cairns, and Hsu (1991), who proposed a stage model providing a unified account for children's interpretations of nonfinite complement clauses and nonfinite adverbial clauses (see also Hsu, Cairns, and Fiengo 1985; Hsu, Cairns, Eisenberg, and Schlisselberg 1989; McDaniel and Cairns 1990; Eisenberg and Cairns 1994).

While children's comprehension of control constructions has been studied extensively, there have been only a few studies that have investigated the production of these constructions in spontaneous child speech. Two studies are especially relevant to the current investigation: Limber (1973) and Bloom, Tackeff, and Lahey (1984).[2]

Limber (1973) described the emergence of finite and nonfinite subordinate clauses in the speech of 12 English-speaking children aged 1;6–3;0. The first

---

2. Apart from Limber (1973) and Bloom et al. (1984), there are two other observational studies that merit mention: Kim (1989), who investigated children's use of finite and nonfinite complement clauses in Korean; and Gawlitzek-Maiwald (1997), who examined the use of infinitival complements in the speech of bilingual children learning English and German. See also Eisenberg and Cairns (1994), who examined children's production of infinitival complements in a story completion task.

subordinate constructions that appeared in his data were infinitival complement clauses of the verb *want*, which, according to Limber (1973: 177), provide 'an important model' for the development of a wide variety of infinitival
complement constructions. Apart from *want*, there were several other early
complement-taking verbs in Limber's data, which he divided into two major
classes: the 'wants' (e.g. *want, need, like*) and the 'watches' (e.g. *watch, see*).
These verbs occurred with both simple infinitives (e.g. *I wanna go*) and infinitives that were separated from the complement-taking verb by a nominal complement (e.g. *Watch me draw circles*). Note that in both constructions the nonfinite verb was generally controlled by the NP that occurred in minimal distance
to the infinitive; infinitival complements that are controlled by the matrix clause
subject across an intervening NP did not occur in Limber's data.

Bloom, Tackeff, and Lahey (1984) examined the early use of infinitival complements in the speech of 4 English-speaking children aged 1;10–3;2. They
were especially interested in the occurrence of the infinitive marker *to*. Among
other things they found that children's early use of *to* is determined by the matrix
verb. While some matrix verbs were commonly used with the infinitive marker,
others appeared primarily with bare infinitives. In particular, the earliest matrix
verbs, *want, got*, and *have*, did not occur with the infinitive marker, whereas the
matrix verbs that children learned later were usually marked by *to*. Based on
these findings, Bloom et al. suggested that children's early use of the infinitive
marker is not determined by a general rule; rather, children seem to learn the
use of *to* in combination with particular matrix verbs. In other words, children's
early use of the infinitive marker *to* appears to be lexically specific. Moreover,
Bloom et al. found that infinitival *to* emerged at around the same time as prepositional *to*, with which it 'shared the meaning direction toward' (Bloom et al.
1984:304): the vast majority of the children's early *to*-infinitives occurred in
constructions in which the infinitive marker expressed some kind of movement
towards the activity denoted by the nonfinite verb. Based on this observation,
Bloom et al. suggested that there is a close connection between infinitival and
prepositional *to* in the child's grammar (see also Pinker 1984:226).

4.2   *Infinitival and participial complement clauses in adult grammar*

In adult grammar, nonfinite complement clauses are commonly defined as sentential arguments of the main clause predicate (cf. Quirk, Greenbaum, Leech,
and Svartvik 1985). They comprise both infinitival and participial constructions. Both types of constructions occur with a variety of complement-taking
verbs, which can be divided into several semantic classes: (i) volitional verbs

(e.g. *want, like*), (ii) aspectual verbs (e.g. *start, stop*), (iii) perception verbs (e.g. *see, hear*), (iv) causative verbs (e.g. *make, have*), (v) communication verbs (e.g. *tell, ask*); and several others (cf. Quirk et al. 1985:ch. 16; Noonan 1985). Many of these verbs impose idiosyncratic restrictions on the type of complements with which they occur. For instance, although *cease* and *stop* have basically the same meaning, *cease* can take either an infinitive or a participle while *stop* may occur only with participles (cf. *He ceased smoking/to smoke* vs. *He stopped smoking/*to smoke*). However, despite such lexically specific characteristics, nonfinite complement clauses can be grouped into some general construction types.

To begin with, nonfinite complement clauses occur in two different word order constructions: (i) NP-V-VP constructions, in which the nonfinite complement is the only complement of the complement-taking verb (e.g. *I wanna eat*); and (ii) NP-V-NP-VP constructions, in which the complement-taking verb selects for a nominal complement (i.e. an object) in addition to the nonfinite complement clause (e.g. *I want Peter to come*). Both constructions may include infinitival or participial complements.

The infinitival complements can be divided into *to*-infinitives, bare infinitives, and *wh*-infinitives. *To*-infinitives and bare infinitives are distinguished by the presence or absence of the infinitive marker *to*. *Wh*-infinitives include a *wh*-adverb or *wh*-pronoun in addition to the infinitive marker (e.g. *I don't know what to do*). All three infinitives occur in both NP-V-VP and NP-V-NP-VP constructions; however, when bare infinitives occur in NP-V-VP constructions they are commonly classified as the main verb of a modal rather than a complement-taking verb (see example (9a)).

(8)	a. I tried to convince Mary.	NP-V-*to*.INF
	b. I told John to help Mary.	NP-V-NP-*to*.INF
(9)	a. I can leave.	NP-V-bare.INF (modal)
	b. I saw him come.	NP-V-NP-bare.INF
(10)	a. I know how to do it.	NP-V-WH-*to*.INF
	b. I showed you how to do it.	NP-V-NP-WH-*to*.INF

The complement-taking verbs are commonly divided into control and raising predicates. The term raising, which was coined in early transformational grammar (cf. Chomsky 1965), is supposed to suggest that the underlying (or semantic) subject of the embedded clause is 'raised' to a syntactic position in the matrix clause. Although raising constructions are superficially similar to control constructions (or 'equi constructions' as they were called in transformational grammar), they have different grammatical properties. For instance,

Table 4.1 *Infinitival and participial complements*

Infinitival constructions			
NP-V-VP	*to*-INF	control	*Peter tried to work.*
		raising	*Peter seemed to work.*
	Bare-INF	(modal)	*Peter can work.*
	wh-INF	control	*Peter knows how to work.*
NP-V-NP-VP	*to*-INF	control	*Peter told Bill to work.*
		raising	*Peter expects Bill to work.*
	Bare-INF	control	*Peter helped Bill work.*
		raising	*Peter saw Bill work.*
	wh-INF	control	*Peter showed Bill how to work.*
Participial constructions			
NP-V-VP	V-*ing*	control	*Peter finished working.*
NP-V-NP-VP	V-*ing*	control	*Peter helped Bill working.*
		raising	*Peter saw Bill working.*

while the object of a raising construction can be a semantically empty element
(e.g. *it* in *It is raining*), it must be a referential element in a control construction (cf. (11a–b)), and while the infinitival complement of a raising construction can be passivized without changing the (referential) meaning, passivizing
the infinitival complement of a control construction *does* change its meaning
(12a–b).

(11)   a. I expect it to rain.   [raising]
       b. *I convinced it to rain.   [control]
(12)   a. I expect Peter to kiss Sue.   [raising]
          = I expect Sue to be kissed by Peter.
       b. I convinced Peter to kiss Sue.   [control]
          ≠ I convinced Sue to be kissed by Peter.

Table 4.1 provides an overview of the various infinitival and participial complement constructions in English.[3]

While infinitival and participial complement constructions are lexically
specific, they exhibit a systematic relationship between the meaning of a
complement-taking verb and the type of complement(s) they include. Following

---

3. In addition to the infinitival and participial complements shown in table 4.1, there are *for*-
   infinitives in which the controller of the nonfinite verb is expressed in a *for*-phrase (e.g. *I am
   anxious for you to arrive on time*). *For*-infinitives do not occur in the child language data I
   examined.

Givón (1980), I assume that constructions in which the complement clause is semantically closely related to the matrix clause tend to be syntactically more tightly integrated in the matrix clause than complement clauses that are semantically relatively independent. In other words, I assume that the semantic bond between matrix clause and complement clause is reflected in the syntactic relationship between the two clauses: the stronger the semantic bond between the two clauses, the tighter the degree of syntactic integration (see also Van Valin and LaPolla 1997:477–484). The semantic relationship between matrix clause and complement clause is crucially determined by the meaning of the complement-taking verb. Givón (1980) divides the complement-taking verbs into three major semantic classes: (i) modality verbs, (ii) manipulative verbs, and (iii) cognition-utterance verbs (see also Givón 1984:117–125):

  (i)   modality verbs elaborate the semantic structure of the activity denoted by the nonfinite verb (e.g. *want, try, begin*);
  (ii) manipulative verbs describe activities that bring about the activity denoted by the embedded verb (e.g. *make, force, cause*);
  (iii) cognition-utterance verbs provide a viewing frame for the situation in the complement clause (e.g. *know, see, say*).

Givón argues that modality verbs and manipulative verbs are semantically more closely associated with the activity denoted in the complement clause than cognition-utterance verbs. This would predict that if the strength of the semantic bond between matrix clause and complement clause is reflected in the degree of syntactic integration, complement clauses of modality verbs and complement clauses of manipulative verbs are syntactically more tightly integrated in the matrix clause than complement clauses of cognition-utterance verbs.

I agree with Givón's general approach, but in contrast to his specific proposal I suggest that modality verbs and manipulative verbs should also be distinguished. In my view, modality verbs are semantically more closely associated with the complement clause than manipulative verbs. Manipulative verbs describe activities that bring about the activity expressed in the complement clause (e.g. in *Peter made Bill leave*, 'Peter' and 'Bill' perform two separate activities); whereas modality verbs basically function to elaborate the meaning of the nonfinite verb (e.g. in *Peter tried to sleep*, 'trying' and 'sleeping' describe one complex activity). In other words, I suggest that the three verb classes form a cline, as shown in (13).

(13)   modality verbs > manipulative verbs > cognition-utterance verbs

Modality verbs are semantically more closely associated with the complement clause than manipulative verbs, which in turn exhibit a closer semantic relationship to the complement clause than cognition-utterance verbs. If this is correct, one would expect that complement clauses of modality verbs are syntactically more tightly integrated in the matrix clause than complement clauses of manipulative verbs.

The degree of syntactic integration is reflected in the linguistic encoding of the complement clause: the more explicitly the complement clause is morphologically marked (for person, tense, aspect, mood, and subordination) the more tightly integrated it is in the matrix clause (cf. Givón 1990:538).

- Complement clauses that consist of a bare infinitive are syntactically more tightly integrated in the matrix clause than complement clauses that are marked by a subordinating morpheme (e.g. *to, –ing, wh-*pronoun/adverb).
- Complement clauses that do not contain a separate actor (i.e. complement clauses of NP-V-VP constructions) are syntactically more tightly integrated in the matrix clause than complement clauses that include a separate actor (i.e. complement clauses of NP-V-NP-VP constructions).
- Complement clauses including a nonfinite verb form are syntactically more tightly integrated in the matrix clause than complement clauses including a verb marked for tense, aspect, and mood.

In what follows, I show that the development of nonfinite complement clauses originates from tightly organized NP-V-VP constructions in which a modality verb elaborates the activity denoted by a bare infinitive. In the earliest nonfinite complement constructions, the complement-taking verb and the complement clause are semantically so closely associated that they together describe a single situation. Starting from such simple sentences, children gradually learn the use of constructions in which the complement-taking verb and the complement clause are semantically more independent and syntactically less integrated. In contrast to the earliest nonfinite complements, these constructions include manipulative or cognition-utterance verbs, are marked by subordinating morphemes, and often contain a nominal complement in addition to the complement clause.

4.3   Data

There are 4,532 utterances including a nonfinite complement clause in the data. These utterances comprise all constructions containing a complement-taking verb and an infinitive or a participle. Precluded are utterances in which an infinitive or participle occurs with an auxiliary or modal. Table 4.2 shows the

Table 4.2 *Nonfinite complement clauses*

	Age range	Number of nonfinite complement clauses
Adam	2;3–4;10	1,770
Sarah	2;3–5;1	946
Nina	1;11–3;4	802
Peter	1;9–3;2	709
Naomi	1;8–3;5	305
Total	1;8–5;1	4,532

total number of nonfinite complement clauses that occur in the transcripts of each child.

All nonfinite complement clauses were coded for two features: first, I indicated the type of complement (e.g. *to*-infinitive, bare infinitive etc.), and second, I marked the occurrence of a nominal complement after the complement-taking verb (i.e. the distinction between NP-V-VP and NP-V-NP-VP constructions).

Overall, the data include 33 complement-taking verbs that occur with infinitival or participial complement clauses; however, many of them have just a few tokens. Table 4.3 shows the mean proportions of the most frequent complement-taking verbs in the data.[4]

As can be seen in this table, an average of 62.5 per cent of the children's nonfinite complement clauses occur with the complement-taking verb *want* (or *wanna*). Overall, there are 2,679 utterances including *want* and an infinitival complement in the data. Apart from *want*, 7 other complement-taking verbs are quite common: *have* (or *hafta*), *got* (or *gotta*), *make, know, like, try,* and *see.* Note that these verbs occur with different types of complements: *want, have,* and *got* occur both with and without a nominal complement (in addition to the infinitive or participle). Although these verbs may include the infinitive marker *to,* young children tend to use them with bare infinitives: in the

---

4. Throughout this study I report mean proportions rather than percentages. Mean proportions are calculated by summing the scores from each child and then dividing the sum by the number of children. For instance, in table 4.3 I first calculated the percentages of each verb in the corpus of complement-taking verbs produced by each child (for example, *want* accounts for the following percentages: Naomi 74.1%, Peter 65.9%, Nina 59.1%, Sarah 59.8%, Adam 53.4%). Then I added the percentages of each verb from each child and divided the sum by five (i.e. the number of children). The resulting score (i.e. 62.5% in the case of *want*) indicates the mean proportion of a specific verb in the entire corpus of complement-taking verbs. Mean proportions are more representative than percentages because they factor out the differences in corpus size between the corpora of individual children.

Table 4.3 *Complement-taking verbs of the children's nonfinite complement clauses*

	Naomi	Peter	Nina	Sarah	Adam	Total	Mean
want	226	467	474	566	946	2,679	62.5
have	35	46	131	94	234	540	11.5
got	0	117	8	77	38	240	5.5
make	3	19	56	21	41	140	3.0
know	2	1	5	65	85	158	2.6
like	4	4	37	13	79	137	2.5
try	8	7	17	29	66	127	2.5
see	7	11	12	14	48	92	1.9
need	5	0	13	1	37	56	1.1
watch	0	3	6	10	30	49	0.8
stop	2	1	4	0	28	35	0.6
show	2	8	1	1	17	29	0.6
others	11	25	38	55	121	250	4.9
Total	305	709	802	946	1,770	4,532	

NP-V-VP construction they primarily use the colloquial forms *wanna, hafta,* and *gotta,* which do not occur with an overt subordinating morpheme (e.g. *I wanna eat, I hafta run, I gotta go*), and in the NP-V-NP-VP construction they simply omit the infinitive marker (e.g. *Do you) want me open it*; Adam). *Make* and *see* occur with a nominal complement followed by a bare infinitive or, less frequently, a participle (e.g. *I make him go; See it coming*). *Like* and *try* always occur with *to*-infinitives (e.g. *I like to swim*). Finally, *know* and *show* occur with *wh*-infinitives (e.g. *I know how to do it*). Figure 4.3 shows the mean proportions of the various types of complements that are included in the whole corpus of nonfinite complement clauses (cf. table 4a in the appendix).

As can be seen in this figure, an average of 77.8 per cent of the children's nonfinite complements are bare infinitives (i.e. infinitives that do not occur with a separate subordinating morpheme). *To*-infinitives are also quite common: they account for an average of 15.5 per cent of the data. *Wh*-infinitives and participial complements are less frequent: on average, they occur in 3.6 and 3.0 per cent of all nonfinite complement clauses, respectively. Note that virtually all participial complements are present participles (marked by *–ing*); utterances including a past participle are almost entirely absent from the data.

The vast majority of the children's infinitival and participial complements occur in NP-V-VP constructions. As can be seen in table 4.4, a mean proportion

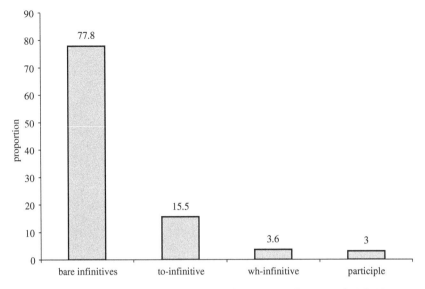

Fig. 4.3 *Mean proportions of bare infinitives,* to-*infinitives,* wh-*infinitives, and participial complements.*

Table 4.4 *Mean proportions of the children's NP-V-VP constructions and NP-V-NP-VP constructions*

	Naomi	Peter	Nina	Sarah	Adam	Total	Mean
NP-V-VP	282	642	633	806	1,284	3,647	83.9
NP-V-NP-VP	23	67	169	140	486	885	16.1
Total	305	709	802	946	1,770	4,532	

of 83.9 per cent of all nonfinite complement clauses occurs in this type of construction.

In what follows, I first describe the general development of infinitival and participial complement clauses and then take a closer look at the development of *want*-constructions.

4.4   Analysis

4.4.1   *Infinitival and participial complement constructions*
The earliest nonfinite complement clauses appear in NP-V-VP constructions. The occurrence of these constructions is initially restricted to a small group of complement-taking verbs. Table 4.5 shows the most frequent

Table 4.5 *The most frequent complement-taking verbs of the children's NP-V-VP constructions and the mean age of their appearance*

	Complement type	Mean proportions	Mean age of appearance
wanna	bare INF	64.8	2;1
hafta	bare INF	13.8	2;3
like	*to*-INF	2.9	2;5
gotta	bare INF	6.1	2;6
try	*to*-INF	3.1	2;6
be hard	*to*-INF	0.7	2;9
stop	*to*-INF + V-*ing*	0.7	3;0
need	*to*-INF	1.2	3;1
start	*to*-INF + V-*ing*	0.6	3;4
know	WH-INF	3.3	3;4

Others: *forget, finish, begin, help, love, mean, pretend, learn, promise, say, hear, wonder, seem, be ready, be easy, be glad, be happy.*

complement-taking verbs in the order in which they emerge in NP-V-VP constructions (cf. table 4b and table 4c in the appendix).

As can be seen in this table, the earliest and most frequent complement-taking verbs are *wanna* and *hafta*. They occur at first in highly formulaic matrix clauses consisting of the first person pronoun *I* and the complement-taking verb in the present tense. The infinitive follows the matrix verb without *to*. The occurrence of bare infinitives is characteristic of modals such as *can* and *must*, with which *wanna* and *hafta* are semantically closely related. Like modals, these two verbs 'function to express the child's mood of wish or intention' (Bloom, Tackeff, and Lahey 1984:297): rather than denoting an independent state of affairs, they indicate the subject's desire or obligation to carry out the activity denoted by the nonfinite verb. Note, however, that *wanna* and *hafta* are grammatically distinguished from ordinary modals. In contrast to modal verbs such as *can* and *must*, *wanna* and *hafta* cannot be fronted in questions (e.g. *Can I have that?* vs. **Wanna you have that?*) and they cannot be negated without *do* (e.g. *We cannot go* vs. **We wanna not go*). Thus, from a syntactic point of view, *wanna* and *hafta* are matrix verbs, but semantically and morphologically they are similar to modals: they occur with bare infinitives and express intentions or obligations.

Most of the complement-taking verbs that emerge after *wanna* and *hafta* occur with *to*-infinitives. Like *wanna* and *hafta*, these verbs do not describe an independent state of affairs; rather, they elaborate the semantic structure of the activities denoted by the nonfinite verb. For instance, *try* indicates the subject's intention to perform the activity described by the infinitive, and *start* and *stop* are aspectual verbs that specify the temporal structure of the event expressed by the embedded verb. Similarly, *be hard* does not denote an independent activity; rather, it functions to evaluate the situation that is denoted by the nonfinite verb. In general, all of the verbs in table 4.5, except for *know*, are modality verbs (in Givón's sense of the term): they do not denote an independent state of affairs; rather, they modify, specify, or evaluate the activity denoted by the nonfinite verb. The whole utterance makes reference to a single situation and thus does not involve embedding.

As the children grow older, more complex structures emerge. The development involves a number of interrelated changes. First, children begin to use complement-taking verbs that are semantically more independent of the activity expressed by the nonfinite verb than the semi-modals and aspectual verbs that occur in the earliest NP-V-VP constructions. For instance, *forget* and *say*, which emerge at a mean age of 3;4 and 4;0, respectively, denote situations that are semantically independent of the activities denoted by the nonfinite verb.

(14)   I forgot to buy some soup.   [Adam 3;6]
(15)   The doctor said to stay in bed all day.   [Sarah 4;7]

The 'forgetting' in (14) does not elaborate the sales event described by the infinitive; rather, it makes reference to an independent state of affairs. Similarly, the doctor's communicative act (i.e. 'saying') in (15) is semantically independent of the activity denoted by the nonfinite verb. While the earliest complement-taking verbs are modality verbs, *forget* and *say* are cognition-utterance verbs providing a viewing frame from the rest of the utterance; they are semantically delimited from the activities denoted by the nonfinite verb.

Second, while the earliest nonfinite complements are accompanied by short and formulaic matrix clauses (e.g. *I wanna, I hafta*), later examples are often embedded in structures that are more diverse: they occur with a variety of subjects including lexical NPs (cf. (16)–(17), they contain complement-taking verbs in the past and future (cf. (18)–(19)), and they are sometimes negated (cf. (20)).

(16)   Dolly wanna drink that.   [Nina 2;5]
(17)   Children have begin to sing.   [Sarah 3;8]
(18)   I tried to get under.   [Adam 3;2]
(19)   I gon try to fight dem with dis.   [Adam 3;8]
(20)   I don't like to do all this work.   [Peter 3;1]

Third, nonfinite complements emerge that are marked by a *wh*-adverb or, less frequently, a *wh*-pronoun (cf. (21)–(22)). While *wh*-infinitives are almost entirely absent before the third birthday, they soon become very common. In particular, the use of *know-how-to*-INF is very frequent in the transcripts of the two older children, Adam and Sarah.

(21)   I know how to drive.   [Sarah 4;1]
(22)   I know what to do.   [Adam 4;7]

Like *forget* and *say, know* is a cognition-utterance verb. It denotes a mental state providing a viewing frame for the situation described in the embedded clause. The weaker semantic bond between the complement-taking verb and the complement clause is reflected in the morphological marking: *wh*-infinitives are marked by two subordinating morphemes, the question word and the infinitive marker *to*.

Finally, while children's early nonfinite complement clauses always occur in NP-V-VP constructions, later instances frequently include a nominal complement in addition to the nonfinite complement clause. In the latter case, the nonfinite verb is controlled by the matrix clause object rather than the subject NP (unless the construction includes one of the few *promise*-type verbs, which do not occur in the data). In other words, if the construction includes a nominal complement in addition to the nonfinite complement clause, the complement-taking verb and the infinitive (or participle) are controlled by different actors, which makes the two verbs semantically more independent of each other than in the earlier NP-V-VP construction, in which the complement-taking verb and the infinitive are controlled by the same referent (i.e. the matrix clause subject).

Table 4.6 shows the most frequent complement-taking verbs that occur with a nominal complement and an infinitive (or participle) in the data (cf. table 4d and table 4f in the appendix).

The earliest complement-taking verbs that the children use in NP-V-NP-VP constructions are *see, want, make*, and *help*. Interestingly, two of these verbs, *see* and *make*, take bare infinitives like the earliest complement-taking verbs that occur in NP-V-VP constructions. Thus, in both types of constructions, nonfinite complement clauses are at first often morphologically unmarked (cf. Bloom, Tackeff, and Lahey 1984).

Apart from *see* and *make*, most of the other verbs in table 4.6 occur with *to*-infinitives and participles; *wh*-infinitives appear only later. The earliest complement-taking verbs that occur with *wh*-infinitives in NP-V-NP-VP constructions are *tell* and *show*; they appear at a mean age of 3;5 and

Table 4.6 *The most frequent complement-taking verbs of the children's NP-V-NP-VP constructions and the mean age of their appearance*

	Complement type	Mean proportions	Mean age of appearance
see	bare INF + V-*ing*	14.9	2;5
want	*to*-INF	40.8	2;7
make	bare INF	19.5	2;7
help	*to*-INF + V-*ing*	2.7	2;7
watch	bare INF + V-*ing*	4.3	2;9
got	*to*-INF + V-*ing*	1.9	2;9
have	bare INF + V-*ing* + V-*en*	1.0	3;0
hear	*to*-INF + V-*ing*	2.0	3;5
tell	*to*-INF + WH-INF	0.9	3;5
show	WH-INF	5.1	3;6

Others: *like, need, ask, learn, teach, put, stop, start.*

3;6, respectively. Thus, the different types of nonfinite complements basically emerge in the same order as in the NP-V-VP construction: bare infinitives appear before *to*-infinitives (and –*ing* participles), which, in turn, emerge before *wh*-infinitives.

(23)   bare infinitives > *to*-infinitives > *wh*-infinitives

The order of acquisition correlates with the formal complexity of the construction. The more morphological marking is involved in a construction, the later it appears in the transcripts: nonfinite complements that do not include a subordinating morpheme (i.e bare infinitives) occur before nonfinite complements marked by *to* or –*ing*, which, in turn, emerge prior to nonfinite complements marked by two subordinating morphemes (i.e. a *wh*-adverb or *wh*-pronoun and the infinitive marker *to*).

Semantically, the complement-taking verbs of NP-V-NP-VP constructions can be divided into two classes: manipulative verbs and cognition-utterance verbs; modality verbs do not occur in NP-V-NP-VP constructions. Manipulative verbs are more closely associated with the activity expressed by the embedded verb than cognition-utterance verbs (cf. Givón 1980): the latter designate a viewing frame that is semantically independent of the activity denoted by the infinitive (or participle); manipulative verbs, on the other hand, describe activities that bring about the activity denoted by the nonfinite verb.

Most of the complement-taking verbs that the children use in early NP-V-NP-VP constructions are manipulative verbs such as *make, want,* or *help*. There are only two cognition-utterance verbs that appear in NP-V-NP-VP constructions before the mean age of 3;0, *see* and *watch*. If we take a closer look at these two verbs we find that they occur in particular constructions. Some typical examples are given in (24–29).

(24)   See George do it?   [Naomi 2;1]
(25)   See that monkey crying?   [Nina 2;1]
(26)   See me hop?   [Adam 3;0]
(27)   Watch me do horsie.   [Sarah 2;11]
(28)   Watch it go?   [Adam 2;9]
(29)   Watch me do it.   [Adam 2;5]

As can be seen from these examples, the children use *see* and *watch* primarily in imperatives and reduced questions. In my view, *see* and *watch* do not serve as perception verbs in these examples (i.e. they do not denote an act of perception); rather, they function to mark a specific type of speech act in which the sentence initial verb draws the hearer's attention to the activity denoted by the nonfinite verb. In other words, *see* and *watch* do not describe an independent state of affairs; rather, they function as attention getters or markers of illocutionary force (for a more detailed discussion of this use of perception verbs see chapter 6).

If this is correct, the earliest complement-taking verbs denoting an independent state of affairs in NP-V-NP-VP constructions are manipulative verbs such as *want, make*, and *help*; cognition-utterance verbs emerge only later. The first complement-taking verb that truly functions as a cognition-utterance verb in an NP-V-NP-VP construction is *tell*, which appears at a mean age of 3;5; all earlier complement-taking verbs are manipulative verbs. Thus, like children's early NP-V-VP constructions, their early NP-V-NP-VP constructions describe activities that semantically are especially closely related. As the children grow older, they begin to use nonfinite complement constructions in which the complement-taking verb and the infinitive (or participle) denote activities that are semantically more independent.

In general, the development of nonfinite complement clauses originates from structures in which the matrix clause and the complement clause are semantically closely related and syntactically tightly organized. Starting from such *dense constructions*, children gradually learn the use of sentences in which the

Table 4.7 *Frequency of the children's want-constructions and the mean age of their appearance*

	Naomi	Peter	Nina	Sarah	Adam	Total	Appearance (mean age)
NP-want-NP	361	309	402	372	515	1,959	2;0
NP-want-INF	220	452	404	492	649	2,217	2;1
NP-want-NP-XP	15	24	122	20	48	229	2;3
NP-want-NP-INF	6	15	70	76	298	465	2;7
Total	602	800	998	960	1,510	4,870	

matrix clause and the complement clause are syntactically more independent and semantically less tightly bound to each other.

4.4.2   Want-constructions

In order to examine the acquisition of nonfinite complement constructions more closely, let us take a look at children's *want*-constructions, which seem to be characteristic of the whole class of children's nonfinite complement clauses (cf. Limber 1973). *Want* is generally the first and most frequent complement-taking verb in the transcripts of the five children. Overall there are 2,682 utterances including *want* and an infinitive in the data. The vast majority of these utterances are instances of the NP-V-VP construction: 2,217 utterances include *want* and a simple infinitive; and 465 utterances are of the type NP-*want*-NP-VP. In addition to these constructions, *want* appears in two other structures: in simple transitive clauses, in which *want* takes a direct object; and in sentences in which *want* is followed by a nominal complement and some other element: a particle (e.g. *I want it up*), a prepositional phrase (e.g. *I want the ball on the ground*), an adjective (e.g. *I want it big*), or a noun phrase (e.g. *I want it dat color*). Examples of the various *want*-constructions are given in (29)–(32).

(29)	I wanna bag.	NP-*want*-NP
(30)	I wanna ride.	NP-*want*-INF
(31)	I want my book here.	NP-*want*-NP-XP
(32)	I wan Daddy to help me.	NP-*want*-NP-INF

Table 4.7 shows when and how frequently the four constructions appear in the data.

The first *want*-constructions are simple transitive clauses in which *want* occurs with a direct object (i.e. NP-*want*-NP). Soon after this construction appears, the children begin to use *want* with infinitival complements (i.e. NP-*want*-INF). Both constructions are at first highly formulaic: they include a first or, less frequently, a second person pronoun as subject, they are never negated, and *want* always appears in the present tense. Moreover, both constructions take bare complements, either a bare noun or a bare infinitive. The examples in (33) show Sarah's first 15 *want*-constructions included in the transcripts.

(33)   Sarah's first 15 *want*-constructions
Wan Bobo.	2;3
I wan a bottle.	2;3
Want bag, Mommy.	2;3
Want bag.	2;3
I wanna bag.	2;3
I wanna ride.	2;3
I wanna ride my horse.	2;3
I wan milk.	2;4
I wan ride, ride . . . two doll.	2;4
I wan ride a horsie.	2;4
I want ribbon.	2;4
I wan two ribbon head.	2;4
I want my dolly.	2;4
I want celery.	2;4
Want talk.	2;6

The parallelism between NP-*want*-NP and NP-*want*-INF suggests that the two constructions are closely related in the child's grammar. Both consist of a formulaic matrix clause (i.e. *I wanna, I want*, or *I wan*) and an open slot that is filled by a nominal expression in one case and an infinitive in the other. Note, however, that the formulaic matrix clauses have different meanings in these constructions. In the NP-*want*-NP construction, *I want* expresses the child's desire to obtain an object, whereas in the NP-*want*-INF construction, *I want* indicates the child's intention to perform an activity. Thus, although the two constructions involve the same formulaic matrix clauses, the child must keep them separate because the formulas have different meanings with different types of complements.

A few months after the children begin to use *want* with nominal and infinitival complements, a new construction emerges in which *want* occurs with a nominal complement and a locational expression, either a locational particle (cf. (34)) or a prepositional phrase with locational meaning (cf. (35)):

(34)   I want a bandaid on.   [Nina 2;4]
(35)   I want ice cream in the refrigerator.   [Sarah 2;10]

Closely related to these structures are the examples in (36) and (37) in which *want* occurs with a pronominal complement and an adjective in one case and a noun phrase in the other.

(36)   I want it big.   [Adam 4;9]
(37)   I don't want it dat color. [Adam 4;9]

What makes the constructions in (34)–(37) particularly interesting in the context of the current investigation is that they share certain properties with both the early use of *want* in sentences including a nominal complement (i.e. NP-*want*-NP) and the later use of *want* in sentences including an object and an infinitive (i.e. NP-*want*-NP-INF). Similar to the nominal complement of *want* in NP-*want*-NP clauses, the nominal complements in (34)–(37) denote an undergoer. In the NP-*want*-NP-INF construction, on the other hand, the nominal complement typically denotes an actor or agent, i.e. it expresses a different semantic role. However, like the NP-*want*-NP-INF construction, the NP-*want*-NP-XP construction (i.e. the construction exemplified in (34)–(37)) involves a complex semantic argument consisting of two elements: NP-INF in one case, and NP-XP in the other. In both cases the postverbal elements constitute a semantic unit that designates an independent state of affairs: in the NP-*want*-NP-INF construction the postverbal elements describe an activity (e.g. *I want Mommy to sing*); and in the NP-*want*-NP-XP construction they describe the location or quality of a thing (i.e. *I want it there; I want it big*). Since the NP-*want*-NP-XP construction shares properties with both children's early NP-*want*-NP clauses and their later use of NP-*want*-NP-INF constructions, it is a plausible hypothesis that this construction helps the child to bridge the gap between the early use of *want* with simple nominals (e.g. *I want milk*) and the later use of *want* with a nominal complement and an infinitive (e.g. *I want Peter to leave*).

Interestingly, the NP-*want*-NP-INF construction includes the same formulaic matrix clauses as the earlier *want*-constructions. Four of the five children, Naomi, Peter, Nina, and Sarah, used the NP-*want*-NP-INF construction primarily with the formulaic *I want*; the fifth child, Adam, used *want*-plus-NP-INF at first only in questions: between the age of 2;9, when Adam's first NP-*want*-NP-INF construction occurred, and the age of 3;1 there are 148 instances of this construction in Adam's transcripts; all of them are questions of the type *(do you) want*-NP-INF:

(38)   Adam's first 10 utterances including *want* in NP-V-NP-VP constructions
        Want me open it?   2;9
        Want me get out?   2;9
        Want car go, go dat way?   2;10
        Want me get it?   2;10
        Want me see it?   2;10
        Do you want me get in?   2;10

Do want he walk?	2;10
Do want me ride it?	2;10
Do you want me drink hot coffeee?	2;10
Do want wheel come off?	2;10

The exclusive use of the NP-*want*-NP-INF construction in *(do-you)-want* questions suggests that Adam learned this expression as a prefabricated chunk of a lexically specific utterance frame.

Note that *want* does not serve as a modality verb in the NP-*want*-NP-INF construction; rather, if it is interpreted as an indirect request, it serves as a manipulative verb (cf. (39)), and if it is *not* interpreted as a request (usually when it occurs with a third person subject) it functions as a cognition-utterance verb providing a frame for the rest of the utterance (cf. (40)).

(39)	I want Paul to play with this.	[Adam 3;5]
(40)	He wants somebody to play with him.	[Adam 4;0]

Interestingly, the NP-*want*-NP-INF construction includes a number of errors that reflect the sentential character of the postverbal elements. As can be seen in (41)–(47), there are several utterances in the data in which the postverbal NP occurs in nominative case (cf. (41)–(45)) and in which the infinitive is replaced by a finite verb form (cf. (46)–(47)).

(41)	Do want he walk?	[Adam 2;10]
(42)	Do want he walk like dis?	[Adam 2;11]
(43)	You want . . . I finish my milk?	[Adam 3;0]
(44)	You want I do a cartwheel?	[Sarah 3;11]
(45)	I want she visit for a while.	[Peter 2;10]
(46)	I want my doll's waking up.	[Nina 2;5]
(47)	I want dat came out.	[Sarah 2;10]

The occurrence of these errors suggests that children do not fully understand the syntactic structure of this construction. Specifically, they do not realize that the postverbal NP functions as the direct object of *want*. Instead they interpret the NP-*want*-NP-INF construction as a combination of *I want* (or *(do) you want*) and a sentential argument realized by a finite complement clause.

To summarize, *want* occurs in four constructions that children learn in an incremental fashion. Starting with simple sentences in which the formulaic *I want* occurs with a nominal or infinitival complement, they gradually learn the use of more complex constructions in which the complement of *I want* functions as a clause-like element that designates an independent state of affairs. Figure 4.4 summarizes the described development.

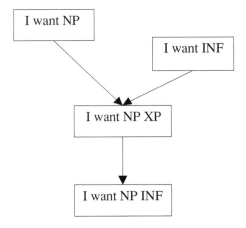

Fig. 4.4 *The development of want-constructions.*

4.5   Discussion

4.5.1   Summary

This chapter has shown that the development of infinitival and participial complement clauses originates from simple lexically specific constructions. The earliest nonfinite complement clauses occur with a small number of highly frequent complement-taking verbs that elaborate the semantic structure of the activity denoted by the nonfinite verb. The whole construction makes reference to a single situation and thus does not involve embedding. As the children grow older, they begin to use more complex constructions in which the complement-taking verb and the complement clauses are semantically more independent and structurally less tightly bound to each other. The development involves a number of interrelated changes, which are summarized in (i)–(iv):

(i) modality verbs   > manipulative verbs > cognition-utterance verbs
(ii) NP-V-VP   > NP-V-NP-VP
(iii) bare infinitives   > *to*-infinitives   > *wh*-infinitives
(iv) nonfinite complement > finite complement

First, the earliest nonfinite complement clauses occur with modality verbs that elaborate the semantic structure of the nonfinite verb. As children grow older, they begin to use manipulative verbs and cognition-utterances verbs that are semantically more independent of the activity denoted by the nonfinite verb than the early modality verbs.

Second, the earliest nonfinite complements occur exclusively in NP-V-VP constructions, in which the matrix clause subject serves as the controller of both the complement-taking verb and the infinitive or participle. As children grow older, the first instances of the NP-V-NP-VP construction emerge, in which the complement-taking verb and the infinitive/participle are controlled by different NPs.

Third, the earliest nonfinite complements are morphologically unmarked: they are bare infinitives that do not include a subordinating morpheme. As the children grow older, they begin to use infinitival complements that are separated from the rest of the clause by the infinitive marker *to* and/or a *wh*-adverb/pronoun.

Finally, the earliest nonfinite complement clauses include a nonfinite verb. As we will see in the next chapter, the first finite complement clauses appear several months after the children begin to use infinitival and participial complement constructions.

The whole development can be characterized as a process of clause expansion. Starting from simple lexically specific constructions in which the complement-taking verb elaborates the situation denoted by the infinitive or participle, children gradually learn the use of more complex constructions in which the matrix clause and the complement clause express a specific relationship between two independent states of affairs.

4.5.2   Discussion

Let us finally ask what motivates the described development. How do we account for the order of acquisition? I suggest that the development of nonfinite complement constructions is crucially determined by two factors: the frequency of the various complement-taking verbs in the ambient language, and the complexity of the emerging constructions.

Table 4.8 shows the mean proportions of the various complement-taking verbs in the mothers' NP-V-VP constructions and the mean age of their appearance in the children's data (cf. table 4f and table 4c in the appendix).

The statistical analysis shows a significant correlation between input frequency (i.e. the frequency of the various complement-taking verbs in the mothers' data) and the age of appearance (Spearman: $r = .799$, $p = .006$, $N = 10$). This suggests that the order of development is crucially determined by (token) frequency in the ambient language: the earliest nonfinite complement constructions occur with complement-taking verbs that are frequent in the input.

However, children do not just imitate adult speakers; they also analyse and organize the input data. If we look at the development of infinitival and participial complement constructions more closely, we find that the earliest nonfinite complement clauses occur in very simple structures: they denote a single

Table 4.8 *Mean proportions of the mothers' NP-V-VP constructions and the mean age of their appearance in the children's data*

	Mothers' data (mean proportions)	Children's data (mean age of appearance)
wanna	43.0	2;1
hafta	26.1	2;3
like	12.7	2;5
try	5.5	2;6
gotta	2.9	2;6
hard	2.2	2;9
stop	1.2	3;0
need	2.0	3;1
start	1.4	3;4
know	3.3	3;4

situation and are morphologically unmarked. As the children grow older, these constructions become increasingly more complex. This suggests that the complexity of the emerging constructions has a significant effect on the development.

Since the most frequent structures tend to be the ones that are semantically simple and morphologically unmarked, the two factors, frequency and complexity, are difficult to disentangle. However, if we take a closer look at table 4.8, we find one structure that should have emerged earlier if the order of acquisition were solely determined by input frequency: although the complement-taking verb *know* appears more often in the input data than *gotta, be hard, need, stop*, and *start* (on the average *know* is 65 per cent more frequent than each of the five other verbs), it emerges after them. This might be due to the fact that *know*-plus-*wh*-infinitive is more complex than the earlier constructions including *gotta, be hard, need, stop*, and *start*. The latter are modality verbs taking bare infinitives or infinitives/participles marked by a single subordinating morpheme (i.e. the infinitive marker *to* or the *–ing* suffix), whereas *know* is a cognition-utterance verb taking *wh*-infinitives, which are double-marked by a *wh*-pronoun/adverb and the infinitive marker *to*. Thus, *know*-plus-*wh*-infinitive is semantically and morphologically more complex than the five other verbs.

Table 4.9 shows the proportions of the various complement-taking verbs in the mothers' NP-V-NP-VP constructions and the mean age of their

Table 4.9 *Mean proportions of the mothers' NP-V-NP-VP*
constructions and the mean age of their appearance in the
children's data

	Mothers' data (mean proportions)	Children's data (mean age of appearance)
see	7.7	2;5
want	50.0	2;7
make	16.8	2;7
help	5.9	2;7
watch	1.1	2;9
got	1.2	2;9
have	2.4	3;0
hear	5.1	3;5
tell	5.4	3;5
show	1.6	3;6

occurrence in the children's transcripts (cf. table 4g and table 4c in the appendix).

As can be seen in this table, the correlation between input frequency and age of appearance is much weaker in this case. Although *want* is by far the most frequent complement-taking verb in the mothers' data it appears after *see*, and although *hear* and *tell* are more frequent than *watch, got,* and *have* they emerge several months later. Interestingly, all complement-taking verbs that emerge before other more frequent complement-taking verbs occur in less complex construction.

The earliest complement-taking verb that the children use in NP-V-NP-VP constructions is *see*, which takes bare infinitives and functions as some sort of attention getter or speech act marker; that is, *see* does not denote an independent state of affairs in the children's early NP-V-NP-VP constructions. Following *see*, several manipulative verbs emerge: *want, make, help, get,* and *have*. The only other verb that appears before the age of 3;5 is the cognition-utterance verb *watch*. However, like *see, watch* initially does not function as a perception verb; rather, it serves, similar to *see*, as some kind of attention getter or speech act marker. The first cognition-utterance verbs that children really use to describe a communicative act or a mental activity are *hear* and *tell*. Interestingly, both verbs are much more frequent in the mothers' data than some of the earlier verbs; notably *watch, got,* and *have* are less frequent. Once again, the late appearance of *hear* and *tell* can be explained in terms of the complexity of the emerging constructions: *watch, got,* and *have* are manipulative verbs that are semantically more tightly associated with the activity described by the nonfinite verb than the cognition-utterance verbs *hear* and *tell*.

In sum, the development of nonfinite complement clauses seems to be determined by two factors: the frequency of the various complement-taking verbs in the ambient language, and the complexity of the emerging constructions. The following chapters show that the same factors are also relevant to the development of other types of complex sentences.

5 Complement clauses

A few months after the first nonfinite complement clauses emerge, the children begin to produce utterances like the ones in (1)–(3):

(1)   (I) think it's a cow.   [Peter 2;2]
(2)   Know what that is?   [Nina 2;3]
(3)   Let's see if we can fix them.   [Peter 2;3]

Utterances of this type have been analysed as complex sentences including the first instances of a finite complement clause. Specifically, it has been argued that these utterances consist of two clauses: a matrix clause (i.e. *I think . . .* , *(Do you) know . . .* , *Let's see . . .*) and a subordinate clause functioning as a sentential complement (cf. Pinker 1984; Bloom, Rispoli, Gartner, and Hafitz 1989). In this chapter, I argue that most of the utterances that seem to include a finite complement clause in early child speech are simple nonembedded sentences containing a single proposition. More precisely, I claim that the apparent matrix clauses are nonassertive: rather than denoting a mental state or an act of perception, they function as epistemic markers, attention getters, or markers of illocutionary force.

The nonassertive use of matrix clauses is also frequently found in adult conversational English. For instance, Thompson and Mulac (1991) have argued that in spoken discourse *I think* and *I guess* commonly function as parenthetical epistemic markers rather than as independent assertions. The current chapter shows that the parenthetical use emerges long before the matrix clauses of finite complements are used to express an assertion. Specifically, it is argued that the development of finite complement clauses originates from structures in which the apparent matrix clause serves as a clausal operator of the associated complement clause, which is really a simple nonembedded sentence.

5.1   *Literature*

There are only a few studies examining the acquisition of finite complement clauses in English.[1] The most comprehensive observational study dealing with the development of finite complement clauses is Bloom, Rispoli, Gartner, and Hafitz (1989). Their investigation is based on data from four English-speaking children aged 2;0 to 3;2. It concentrates on the analysis of four common verbs that children frequently use with finite complement clauses: *think, know, look,* and *see.* Interestingly, Bloom et al. already noticed the nonassertive use of early matrix clauses. According to their analysis, children employ *think* and *know* 'in order to qualify the degree of certainty–uncertainty of the complement proposition'. Similarly, *look* and *see* primarily function to indicate the speaker's assessment of the information expressed in the complement clause: while *look* suggests 'an attitude of definiteness', *see* signals the speaker's lack of certainty, notably when it occurs with an *if*-complement clause (Bloom et al. 1989:330–331). However, since Bloom et al.'s analysis is limited to only four verbs, it remains unclear how general their findings are. Is the nonassertive use of matrix clauses restricted to *think, know, look,* and *see,* or does it also occur with other complement-taking verbs? Moreover, the analysis that Bloom et al. proposed appears to be somewhat inconsistent. Although they argue that children use *think, know, look,* and *see* to qualify the information expressed in the complement clause, they seem to assume that the composite structure is really a complex sentence consisting of two full-fledged clauses (cf. Bloom et al. 1989:332).

The nonassertive use of early matrix clauses has also been noticed in a study by Limber (1973), in which he surveyed the emergence of a wide variety of complex sentence constructions. Limber (1973:185) observed that one of the most frequent complement-taking verbs, namely *think,* does not denote a cognitive activity in early child language; rather, children seem to use *(I) think* as a parenthetical formula that they attach to a simple utterance to qualify its information. However, like Bloom et al., Limber did not indicate how often the parenthetical use occurs in early child speech. In fact, his analysis suggests that the parenthetical use is restricted to *(I) think* and perhaps a few other mental state verbs.

In accordance with Bloom et al. (1989) and Limber (1973), Shatz, Wellman, and Silber (1983) observed that children's early use of *think* and other mental state verbs does not always involve 'mental reference'. According to their analysis, the earliest uses of mental state verbs such as *think, know,* and *wish* serve

---

1. For the acquisition of finite complement clauses in German, see Rothweiler (1993).

various 'conversational functions': they may modulate an assertion, express the speaker's desire, or co-ordinate the interaction between the interlocutors (see also Wellman 1990; Bartsch and Wellman 1995). The results of Shatz et al.'s analysis are consistent with the empirical findings of the current investigation; however, since Shatz et al. were primarily interested in children's cognitive development, they did not consider the implications of their findings for the acquisition of grammar; in fact, grammar plays only a minor role in their study, which considers children's use of mental verbs across a wide variety of grammatical constructions (i.e. not just in complex sentences, including finite complement clauses).

In addition to these corpus-based analyses, there are a number of experimental studies testing children's comprehension of sentences including finite complement clauses (e.g. Phinney 1981; de Villiers, Roeper, and Vainikka 1990; Roeper and de Villiers 1994; Vainikka and Roeper 1995; de Villiers 1999; de Villiers and de Villiers 1999; Schulz 2000). However, most of these studies are not specifically concerned with the acquisition of complement clauses; rather, they use complement clauses in order to investigate the development of more general grammatical phenomena. For instance, in one series of experiments complement clauses were used to study children's comprehension of long-distance dependencies. The example in (4) shows a complex sentence in which the question word at the beginning of the construction is coreferential with the unexpressed object in the embedded clause.

(4)   What did the girl say she bought __?

Although such sentences are extremely rare in the speech of young children, they can provide crucial insights into children's comprehension of complement clauses. For instance, de Villiers (1999) showed that when children under 4 years are asked to answer the question in (4), they usually name the thing that the girl actually bought rather than what she said she bought, which might be different. In other words, young children do not understand that 'the question concerns the joint effect of two verbs: both saying and buying' (de Villiers 1999:103); instead, they concentrate on the verb in the complement clause, which, according to de Villiers, suggests that they have not yet fully mastered the syntax and meaning of sentential complements (cf. de Villiers, Roeper, and Vainikka 1990; Roeper and de Villiers 1994). While this conclusion is open to various interpretations, it is in any case compatible with the analysis I propose: children might ignore the complement-taking verb in sentences like (4) because the matrix clauses of sentential complements are usually nonassertive in early child speech.

In what follows, I show that the development of finite complement clauses originates from constructions in which the apparent complement clause is really a simple nonembedded sentence that is accompanied by a nonassertive matrix clause. However, before presenting the data, I consider the structure and meaning of finite complement clauses in adult English, providing the background for the following analysis.

5.2   *Finite complement clauses in adult grammar*

Complement clauses are commonly defined as subordinate clauses functioning as an argument of the matrix clause predicate (for a critique of this view, see Thompson 2002). While the matrix clause predicate is usually a verb, it can also be an adjective or a noun (cf. Noonan 1985). Examples (5) and (6) show that the complement clause may serve as the subject or object of the matrix clause.

(5)   <u>That Bill wasn't in class</u> annoyed the teacher.
(6)   The teacher noticed <u>that Bill wasn't in class</u>.

The complement clause in (5) functions as subject of the verb *annoyed*; it could easily be replaced by a subject noun phrase (cf. *Bill's absence in class annoyed the teacher*), which is sometimes used to demonstrate the subjecthood of the subordinate clause. However, such subject complement clauses do not occur in the data (see also Limber 1973:175). The complement clause in (6) serves as the direct object of the verb *noticed*; it could also be replaced by a simple noun phrase (cf. *The teacher noticed Bill's absence in class*). Note also that example (6) can be passivized (*That Bill wasn't in class was noticed by the teacher*), providing additional support for the assumption that the complement clause serves as the direct object in the superordinate clause. Unlike subject complement clauses, object complement clauses are very common in early child speech (cf. Limber 1973; Bloom et al. 1989). They can be divided into three basic types: (i) S-complements marked by *that* or by zero; (ii) *if*-complements marked by *if* (or *whether*); and (iii) *wh*-complements introduced by a *wh*-pronoun or *wh*-adverb. Examples of each type are given in (7)–(9):

(7)   Sally thought **that** he was crazy.
(8)   Peter asked Bill **if** that was true.
(9)   Mary didn't understand **what** Bill was saying.

S-complements either include a *that*-complementizer or they are morphologically unmarked (i.e. structurally independent). *If*-complements are introduced by the complementizers *if* or *whether*, which in contrast to *that* qualify the mean-ing of the complement clause: unlike S-complements, *if*-complements have a hypothetical meaning. Finally, *wh*-complements have a specific syntactic struc-ture, setting them apart from both S-complements and *if*-complements. They are introduced by a *wh*-word serving as an argument or adjunct in the subor-dinate clause; that is, while the complementizers of S- and *if*-complements are grammatical operators, the *wh*-pronouns (or *wh*-adverbs) of a *wh*-complement serve a semantic and syntactic role in the embedded clause.

The three types of complement clauses occur with a limited number of complement-taking verbs. Some of them are compatible with all three types of complement clauses, while others take only one or two of them. For instance, while *see* may occur with S-, *if*-, and *wh*-complements, *think* only occurs with S-complements, and *ask* is restricted to *if*- and *wh*-complement clauses. The co-occurrence restrictions are partially motivated by the meaning of the complement-taking verbs (cf. Quirk, Greenbaum, Leech, and Svartvik 1985: ch. 16); they can be divided into various semantic classes: utterance verbs (e.g. *say, tell, ask*), mental state verbs (e.g. *think, believe, assume*), perception verbs (e.g. *see, hear, notice*), desiderative verbs (e.g. *wish, desire, hope*), and several others (cf. Noonan 1985:110–133). While these verbs are commonly used to denote a mental state or a verbal activity, this is by no means their only usage. In what follows, I distinguish between two different uses of the matrix clause (i.e. clauses including the complement-taking verb): (i) the *assertive* use, and (ii) the *performative* use. The two uses differ with regard to both their pragmatic func-tions and the semantic relationships between matrix and complement clauses.

In the assertive use, the matrix clause denotes the central situation lending its profile to the composite structure (cf. chapter 3.2). Consider, for instance, the examples in (10)–(12).

(10)   Peter remembered clearly that he had seen this guy before.
(11)   Peter told Mary that he would not come to the party.
(12)   Peter saw that Mary was coming.

The utterances in these examples express a specific relationship between two situations denoted by the matrix clause and the complement clause: the proposi-tion of the complement clause functions as an element of the matrix proposition. The latter determines the profile of the entire utterance, overriding the profile of the embedded clause: example (10) describes a cognitive activity (i.e. 'remem-bering'); (11) refers to a communicative act (i.e. 'telling'); and (12) denotes the perception of an event (i.e. 'seeing'). Thus, the central state of affairs is expressed in the proposition of the matrix clause. The complement clause is only of secondary interest; it does not present an independent object of thought; rather, it provides background information that is only relevant within the situation denoted in the matrix clause. In other words, the complement clause is semantically embedded in the matrix clause.

In the performative use, the relationship between matrix clause and complement clause is very different. The matrix clause does not contain the basic proposition (i.e. the proposition functioning as the profile determinant); rather, it serves primarily to co-ordinate the interaction between the interlocutors. As a starting point, let us consider Austin's (1962) analysis of 'explicit performative utterances'. Noticing that utterances are not only used to *describe* some state of affairs but also to *perform* an action, Austin introduced the well-known distinction between meaning and (illocutionary) force. The meaning of an utterance is its propositional content (i.e. the description or denotation of some state of affairs), whereas the illocutionary force is what speakers *do* with an utterance (e.g. to make a promise, to apologize, to express regrets, etc.). Interestingly, Austin used sentences including finite complement clauses in order to illustrate aspects of his analysis. Specifically, he argued that the illocutionary force of a speech act can always be expressed in an explicit performative utterance, which is basically a complex sentence in which the matrix clause includes a speech act verb in 'the first person singular present indicative active' (Austin 1962:61–62).[2] Some typical examples are given in (13)–(16).

(13)   I promise that I will help you with this work.
(14)   I (want to) ask you whether you could do me a favour.
(15)   I maintain that your hypothesis is invalid.
(16)   I suggest that we leave before it begins to rain.

While Austin was not interested in the analysis of complex sentences, his discussion of explicit performative utterances reveals an interesting aspect of the relationship between matrix clause and complement clause. It shows that the two clauses of this construction are at different speech act levels if they constitute an explicit performative utterance: while the complement clause describes some state of affairs, the matrix clause basically serves to indicate the illocutionary force of the utterance. Since matrix clause and complement clause concern different speech act levels they are semantically less tightly integrated in the performative use than in the assertive use (in which both clauses together describe a complex state of affairs). This is easily demonstrated by the fact that a performative matrix clause can always be omitted if the illocutionary force of the utterance is sufficiently determined by the discourse context (or by

2. In addition to these features, the word *hereby* may serve as a 'useful criterion that the utterance is performative' (Austin 1962: 57) (e.g. *I hereby promise that I will come*).

linguistic means such as a modal adverb or a discourse particle). In fact, it is probably much more common to express the speech acts in (13)–(16) without the associated matrix clauses, as in the following examples:

(13′)   I will (definitely) help you with this work.
(14′)   Would you do me a favour?
(15′)   Your hypothesis is invalid.
(16′)   We had better leave before it begins to rain.

In contrast to the performative use, the assertive use involves information that cannot be so easily omitted. If we consider the examples in (10)–(12) above, for instance, it appears to be impossible to express the (referential) meaning of the whole utterance without the matrix clause, given that the complement clause functions as an argument of the matrix verb. In contrast to performative matrix clauses, assertive matrix clauses contribute crucially to the expression of the propositional content, which is not so easily inferable from the discourse context as the illocutionary force.[3]

While Austin analysed the performative use of speech act verbs in great detail, he did not consider the use of other verbs that may occur in the matrix clause of a sentential complement. In what follows, I argue that there are many other complement-taking verbs, notably mental verbs and perception verbs, that can be used in a similar way as performative speech act verbs. While most of them do not (immediately) indicate the illocutionary force of an utterance, they are generally concerned with the interaction between the interlocutors: they may express the speaker's mental stance regarding the situation expressed in the complement clause (which is sometimes called the 'propositional attitude', Searle 1979); they may indicate the knowledge source of the information expressed in the complement clause; or they may instruct the hearer in various other ways as to how to interpret the propositional content of the complement clause. Like performative speech act verbs, these complement-taking verbs are immediately concerned with the speaker–hearer interaction, and therefore I subsume them under the performative use.

On formal grounds, two major types of performative matrix clauses can be distinguished: first, matrix clauses including a verb in the first person singular

---

3. That does not mean that parts of the propositional content cannot be implicit; in fact, implicatures, entailments, and presuppositions concern the implicit expression of meaning (i.e. the propositional content). However, I would contend that the illocutionary force of an utterance is more directly determined by the discourse context than its propositional content. One piece of evidence supporting this hypothesis comes from the study of language acquisition. As Bruner (1983), Tomasello (1992), and others have shown, children are able to comprehend the speaker's intention for an utterance (i.e. the illocutionary force) long before they are able to understand its meaning (i.e. the propositional content) as expressed by the words it includes.

present indicative active. This type subsumes both the performative use of speech act verbs and many other verbs expressing a mental state or an act of perception.

(17)   I believe that this is a mistake.
(18)   I find that these conditions are unfair.
(19)   I (can) hear that Paul is coming.
(20)   I see that Jack is leaving.

While the matrix clauses in these examples do not include a speech act verb indicating the illocutionary force, they address other aspects of the interaction between the interlocutors: the matrix clauses in examples (17) and (18) expresses the speaker's propositional attitude, and the ones in examples (19) and (20) indicate the knowledge source for the information expressed in the complement clause. In all four examples, the matrix clauses denote a mental state or an act of perception, i.e. they describe some state of affairs, as in the assertive use. However, this is not their sole function; rather, they also serve to instruct the hearer as to how to interpret the utterance. In fact, I maintain that the propositional content of the matrix clause is secondary in these constructions; its primary function is to guide the hearer in his/her interpretation of the complement clause. This is suggested by the fact that the propositional content of the whole construction can be expressed without the matrix clause:

(17′)   This is probably a mistake.
(18′)   These conditions are unfair.
(19′)   Paul is coming.
(20′)   Jack is leaving.

While the constructions in examples (17′)–(20′) are not as explicit as their counterparts in (17)–(20), they basically convey the same (referential) meaning. Thus, as in the case of explicit performative utterances, the central state of affairs is expressed in the complement clause rather than in the matrix clause. What distinguishes the matrix clauses in examples (17)–(20) from performative speech act verbs is that they concern the propositional attitude or knowledge source for the complement proposition rather than the illocutionary force; that is, they do not indicate what the speaker *does* with the utterance, rather they guide the hearer in his/her interpretation of the propositional content expressed in the complement clause.[4]

---

4. This is, of course, an idealized description of their function. The expression of the propositional content and the indication of the illocutionary force are not independent of each other: the way in which speakers denote a state of affairs has an effect on the illocutionary force, and conversely

Apart from first person performatives (i.e. performatives including a first person subject), performative matrix clauses can be expressed by questions, imperatives, and hortatives. While the verbs of these constructions also occur in the present indicative active (as in all other performative uses), they involve different subjects: the subject of a question is the second person pronoun *you*; the hortative involves the first person plural accusative pronoun *us*; and the imperative usually occurs with no overt subject. The following examples illustrate the performative use of these constructions.

(21)   What do you think happened last Friday?
(22)   Show me what you got from Peter.
(23)   Let us assume that this is right . . .

Like first person performatives, these matrix clauses concern the performative dimension of the utterance: the matrix clause in (21) indicates that the hearer should answer the question based on his/her beliefs (which might not be true); the one in (22) induces the hearer to demonstrate an action; and in example (23) the matrix clause opens a mental space for the situation described in the complement clause. Again, the matrix clauses do not primarily serve to *denote* some state of affairs; rather, they function to co-ordinate the interaction between the interlocutors. Since the performative dimension is usually inferable from the discourse context, the matrix clauses are easily omitted, as in all previous examples of the performative use:

(21')   What happened last Friday?
(22')   What did you get from Peter?
(23')   If this is right . . .

To summarize the discussion so far, we have seen that the matrix clauses of sentential complements can be used in two ways: either they express the main situation of a complex state of affairs, or they address a specific aspect of the interaction between the interlocutors. I have called these two uses the assertive and performative uses, respectively. In the assertive use, the matrix clause and the complement clause denote some complex state of affairs; the matrix clause includes the main proposition, in which the complement clause is embedded.

---

the expression of the illocutionary force affects the interpretation of the propositional content contained in an utterance. However, that does not mean that the linguistic expression of the propositional content and the illocutionary force cannot be distinguished. What I suggest is that in the performative use some matrix clauses primarily function to indicate the illocutionary force (notably clauses including performative speech act verbs), while others primarily function to qualify the propositional content (notably clauses including mental state and perception verbs).

In the performative use, the matrix clause and the complement clause concern different speech act dimensions. While the complement clause expresses the main proposition, the matrix clause serves primarily to co-ordinate the interaction between the interlocutors: it may indicate the illocutionary force, the speaker's propositional attitude, the knowledge source for the complement proposition, or some other aspect that is relevant to the interpretation of the complement clause. Since the matrix clause and the complement clause concern different speech act dimensions, they are less tightly integrated in the performative use than in the assertive use. In fact, I maintain that in the performative use the complement clause is not semantically embedded in the matrix clause: rather than being viewed as a semantic element of the matrix clause (as in the assertive use), the complement clause expresses the main proposition, while the matrix clause provides some instructions as to how to interpret the utterance.[5]

The assertive use and the performative use can be seen as the two major uses of the matrix clause. In addition to these two uses, there is at least one other use, which I will call the *formulaic use* of matrix clauses. It is historically related to the performative use, from which it developed through grammaticalization. The following examples illustrate the formulaic use of a matrix clause:

(24)   Suppose we do it this way.
(25)   You're right, I guess.
(26)   She left, I think.
(27)   I bet you missed the bus, didn't you?
(28)   You know, we've been here before.

While examples (24)–(28) include both a matrix clause and a complement clause, they are not really biclausal. Unlike the matrix clause in the assertive and performative uses, the matrix clause of the formulaic use is not a full-fledged main clause; rather, it constitutes a holistic formula functioning as an epistemic marker or attention getter that is only loosely adjoined to the complement clause, which is really an independent assertion. In other words, the examples in (24)–(28) are monoclausal constructions in which the matrix clause has been

---

5. A similar analysis has been suggested by Verhagen (2001:16): 'In a sense, we have thus turned the traditional notion of dependent clause upside down, by showing that it is the matrix clause that is actually conceptually dependent on a subordinate one [i.e. a COMP-clause].' However, since Verhagen does not distinguish the performative use form the assertive use, he seems to overgeneralize his conclusion.

demoted to some kind of clausal operator.[6] This is evidenced by a number of features that characterize the formulaic use (cf. Hooper and Thompson 1973; Hooper 1975; Thompson and Mulac 1991; Thompson 2002).

  (i)   The matrix clauses are always short and formulaic (suggesting that they are stored as holistic expressions).
 (ii)   The subject of the matrix clause is either implicit or it is expressed by a first or second person pronoun.
(iii)   The complement-taking verb itself occurs in the present indicative active.
 (iv)   There are no auxiliaries, modals, adverbs, or prepositional phrases in the matrix clause.
  (v)   The complement clause tends be much longer and more diverse.
 (vi)   Since the complement clause is not embedded (neither syntactically nor semantically) it does not include a *that*-complementizer.
(vii)   The order of matrix clause and complement clause is variable: the matrix clause may precede or follow the complement clause or may even be inserted into it.

Note that some of the features in (i)–(vii) are also characteristic of the performative use. Like formulaic matrix clauses, performative matrix clauses occur in the present indicative active and include either a first or second person pronoun as subject (unless they are imperative clauses). The performative use shares these features with the formulaic use because the two uses are historically related. As pointed out above, the formulaic use derives historically from the performative use through grammaticalization. In fact, in many cases the development is not yet completed so that it is often difficult to distinguish the two uses. However, some formulaic matrix clauses are easily identified. Consider the examples in (29)–(34) (the historical sources are indicated in square brackets):

(29)   She's a doctor y'know.   [> (did/do) you know]
(30)   Y'mean you won't come tomorrow?   [> (did/do) you mean]
(31)   Guess you are right.   [> I guess]
(32)   Remember you promised to help me. [> do you remember]
(33)   Suppose we do it this way.   [> let us suppose]
(34)   Say we leave at eight o'clock, ... [> let us say]

---

6. Although a formulaic matrix clause is not really a clause, I will use the term 'matrix clause' for this usage in order to indicate its relationship to the matrix clauses in the performative and assertive uses.

Since the matrix clauses in examples (29)–(34) are formally distinguished from their historical sources (i.e. the performative matrix clauses in square brackets), they can only be interpreted as epistemic markers or attention getters (i.e. as formulaic matrix clauses). However, there are many utterances in which the matrix clause is equivocal between the performative use and the formulaic use. This suggests that there is no clear-cut borderline between the two uses. One can think of the formulaic use as a performative matrix clause in which the propositional content has been bleached or demoted. Since this is a continuous process, the distinction between the performative use and the formulaic use is fluid. In the extreme case, the matrix clause has entirely lost its referential meaning, as in examples (29)–(34), but very often it still has a referential interpretation, despite the fact that it basically functions as some kind of clausal operator. I assume, therefore, that the performative use and the formulaic use form a cline including many intermediate cases.

Below I summarize the previous discussion, highlighting three important aspects of the three different uses: (i) the function of the matrix clause, (ii) the function of the complement clause, and (iii) the relationship between matrix clause and complement clause.

(i) Function of the matrix clause

    (a) In the assertive use, the matrix clause expresses the main proposition and lends its profile to the composite structure.

    (b) In the performative use, the matrix clause has some (propositional) meaning; however, its primary function is to co-ordinate the interaction between the interlocutors.

    (c) In the formulaic use, the matrix clause is propositionally empty: rather than denoting an independent state of affairs, it serves as some kind of clausal operator (e.g. epistemic marker, attention getter).

(ii) Function of the complement clause

    (a) In the assertive use, the complement clause denotes a situation whose profile is overridden by the profile of the complement clause; that is, the complement proposition is semantically an element of the matrix clause proposition.

    (b) In the performative use, the complement clause expresses the core proposition of the composite structure and determines its own profile.

    (c) In the formulaic use, the complement clause contains the only proposition that is expressed in the composite structure; the matrix clause is propositionally empty.

(iii) Relationship between matrix clause and complement clause
    (a) In the assertive use, the complement clause is both syntactically and semantically embedded in the matrix clause.
    (b) In the performative use, the complement clause is syntactically subordinated but semantically not embedded in the matrix clause.
    (c) In the formulaic use, the complement clause is neither syntactically nor semantically embedded in the matrix clause.

We are now in a position to state the hypothesis regarding children's acquisition of complement clauses more precisely: the earliest and most frequent complement clauses that English-speaking children learn occur in highly formulaic matrix clauses. These clauses do not designate an independent state of affairs; rather, they function as epistemic markers, attention getters, or markers of illocutionary force. Thus, the whole utterance expresses only a single state of affairs and does not involve embedding. As children grow older, they begin to use performative and assertive matrix clauses. However, while these uses are semantically and structurally more complex than the early formulaic uses, they are restricted to a few complement-taking verbs. This suggests that children's early performative and assertive matrix clauses are isolated constructions organized around particular verbs.

5.3   *Data*

The corpus includes 1,812 complex sentences containing a finite complement clause. There is considerable variation as to the amount of data that is available for each child. As can be seen in table 5.1, the most comprehensive corpus exists for Adam; it includes 804 finite complement clauses. The corpora for Sarah, Peter, and Nina are significantly smaller; they consist of a few hundred complement clauses each. Finally, Naomi's corpus contains only 48 finite complement clauses. Note that the figures in table 5.1 subsume all three uses of the matrix clause; that is, the assertive, performative, and formulaic uses were not distinguished at the initial stage of the analysis. The database includes all utterances in which a finite clause seems to function as a sentential complement.

All complex sentences including finite complement clauses were coded for the following features:

(i) the subject of the matrix clause (e.g. 1SG.PRO, lexical NP, etc.)
(ii) the tense features of the complement-taking verb (e.g. present, past, etc.)

Table 5.1 *Finite complement clauses*

	Age range	Number of complement clauses
Adam	2;3–4;10	804
Sarah	2;3–5;1	474
Nina	1;11–3;4	220
Peter	1;9–3;2	266
Naomi	1;8–3;5	48
Total	1;8–5;1	1,812

(iii) the occurrence of modals and negation markers in the matrix clause
(iv) the occurrence of a complementizer or *wh*-pronoun/adverb in the complement clause (e.g. *that, if, what*)
(v) the order in which matrix clause and complement clause appear

Overall the data include 35 different complement-taking verbs. Many of them are found only in the transcripts of some of the children. *See, look, think, know, say, tell, pretend*, and *show* are the only complement-taking verbs that occur in the data of all five children. Table 5.2 shows the mean proportions of the most frequent complement-taking verbs within the entire corpus of finite complement clauses.

The majority of the children's complement clauses are S-complements. As can be seen in table 5.3, they account for nearly two-thirds of all finite complement clauses (mean proportion of 61.5 per cent). *Wh*-complements are also quite common, accounting for an average of about 35 per cent of the data. However, *if*-complements are relatively infrequent; they occur in only 69 utterances in the entire corpus (mean proportion of 3.3 per cent).

In what follows, I show that the vast majority of the children's early matrix clauses are instances of the formulaic use: they function as epistemic markers, attention getters, or markers of the illocutionary force. The performative and assertive uses are less common and emerge only later. In particular, the assertive use is rare and initially restricted to a few complement-taking verbs.

5.4   Analysis

5.4.1   S-complements
The earliest complement clauses are S-complements; they emerge a few months after the second birthday. Overall, the children used 18 different complement-taking verbs with S-complements; however, many of them had just a few tokens.

Table 5.2 *Complement-taking verbs of the children's finite complement clauses*

	Naomi	Peter	Nina	Sarah	Adam	Total	Mean
know	14	85	30	107	138	374	22.9
see	8	49	53	113	156	379	20.5
think	12	48	21	89	191	361	19.0
say	7	17	30	46	38	138	9.8
look	2	18	44	20	72	156	8.8
tell	2	17	6	10	16	51	3.5
pretend	1	3	19	2	9	34	2.7
guess	1	8	1	18	19	47	2.4
wonder	0	1	6	4	50	61	2.0
mean	0	2	2	20	14	38	1.5
bet	0	1	3	14	18	36	1.4
show	1	9	1	1	6	18	1.4
wish	0	0	0	5	28	33	0.9
hope	0	1	0	6	10	17	0.6
others	0	7	4	19	39	69	2.7
Total	48	266	220	474	804	1,812	

Table 5.3 *S-complements,* wh-*complements, and* if-*complements*

	Naomi	Peter	Nina	Sarah	Adam	Total	Mean
S-complement	28	131	154	335	477	1,125	61.5
wh-complement	20	112	63	128	295	618	35.2
if-complement	0	23	3	11	32	69	3.3
Total	48	266	220	474	804	1,812	

The following analysis concentrates on S-complements that occur at least five times with a particular complement-taking verb. These verbs have been divided into four classes, which will be discussed in turn.

Epistemic markers: *think, guess, bet, mean,* and *know*
There are five verbs in the data that the children primarily used as parenthetical epistemic markers: *think, guess, bet, mean,* and *know*. About one-third of all S-complements occurred with one of these five verbs. The following examples show the first 15 utterances that Sarah produced with the complement-taking verb *think*.

(35)   Sarah (first 15 utterances including *think* plus S-complement)
           I think I'm go in here.   3;1
           And I think (pause) we need dishes.   3;2
           Think some toys over here too.   3;3
           I think I play jingle bells . . . with the record player.   3;5
           I think he's gone.   3;5
           Oh (pause) I think it's a ball.   3;5
           It's a crazy bone (pause) I think.   3;5
           I think it's in here.   3;5
           I think it's in here . . . Mommy.   3;5
           Think it's in there.   3;5
           I think I don't know that one.   3;6
           I'm get my carriage (pause) I think.   3;6
           Think it's in this.   3;6
           I think that your hands are dirty.   3;6
           I think my daddy took it.   3;7

At first glance, the utterances in (35) seem to denote two situations, a mental process (i.e. thinking) and some other activity (expressed in the complement clause). However, if we look at the constructions more closely, we find good evidence that the matrix clauses do not really denote a mental process. In all 15 examples, the matrix clause is short and formulaic: *think* always occurs in the present indicative active, taking the first person singular pronoun *I* as subject. Note that in three utterances *I* is omitted, yielding a matrix clause with no overt subject. Apart from the pronominal subject, there is no other element that co-occurs with *think* in the matrix clauses: *think* is never accompanied by an auxiliary or modal and never modified by an adverb or prepositional phrase.

The complement clauses are longer and more diverse. Some of them include an auxiliary, a negative marker, a prepositional phrase, or a verb in the past tense. None of the complement clauses in (35) is marked by a *that*-complementizer and, with one exception, there are also no complementizers in Sarah's later complement clauses of *think*. Finally, although the complement clause usually follows the matrix clause, there are two examples in which the complement clause precedes *(I) think*.

All of this suggests that the matrix clauses function as prefabricated formulas; they serve as parenthetical epistemic markers that indicate the speaker's degree of certainty towards the associated proposition, somewhat similar to an epistemic adverb such as *maybe* (cf. Thompson and Mulac 1991; Thompson 2002).

As Sarah grows older, a few other patterns emerge. At the age of 3;7 she uses *think* for the first time in an interrogative clause with a second person pronoun as subject (cf. example (36)), which from then on occurs quite frequently. Five months later, there is an utterance in which *think* appears in the past tense

Table 5.4 *The development of Adam's and Sarah's matrix clauses including* think

Age	Adam	Sarah
2;11	I think __ (108)	
3;0		
3;1		I think __ (68)
3;2		
3;3	Do you think __ (9), Does he think __ (1)	
3;4		
3;5	You don't think __ (1)	
3;6	What/where do you think __ (3)	
3;7		Do you think __ (5)
3;8	I don't think __ (4)	
3;9		
3;10	Why do you think __ (3)	
3;11		
4;0		I thought __ (7)
4;1		
4;2		I'm thinking __ (1)
4;3		They think __ (1)
4;4		What do you think __ (2)
4;5		
4;6	One think __ (1)	
4;7		
4;8		I don't think __ (2)
4;9		
4;10	Paul think __ (1)	I'll think __ (1)

(cf. example (37)), and at the age of 4;3 she uses *think* for the first time with the pronoun *they* as subject (cf. example (38)):

(36)	<u>You think</u> it does?	3;7
(37)	<u>(I) thought</u> it was in the house.	4;0
(38)	I will sing along with them . . . then <u>they think</u> I . . . will . . . have . . .	4;3

While the formulaic *I think* remains the dominant type of matrix clause in Sarah's data, the examples in (36)–(38) illustrate that some of her later uses of *think* are more substantial.

Table 5.4 shows all matrix clauses (i.e. all types) that Sarah and Adam produced with *think* and an S-complement clause. The data from Nina, Peter, and Naomi are not shown in this table because they are too sparse to show significant developmental changes.

As can be seen in this table, both Adam and Sarah use *think* initially in the parenthetical formula *I think*, which is very frequent: Adam produced 108 utterances including *I think*, and Sarah used 68 tokens of this expression. As Adam and Sarah grow older, they begin to use *think* in other types of matrix clauses, which occur much less frequently (the numbers in parentheses indicate the number of tokens of each clause type in the child's entire corpus). In these later matrix clauses, *think* occurs in different tenses, with auxiliaries and negation markers, and with other subjects: apart from the first person pronoun *I*, the second person pronoun *you* is quite common, notably in questions. There are also a few utterances in which *think* occurs with a third person subject, but they are very rare.

Together, these features suggest that the children's use of *think* becomes increasingly more substantial. Adam and Sarah begin with the formulaic use of *(I) think* as a parenthetical epistemic marker (which is also the first use of *(I) think* in the transcripts of the three other children). The formulaic use is later supplemented by the performative use in questions; however, the assertive use remains rare throughout the entire time period of the study. There are only a few later examples in which the matrix clause expresses the main proposition.

Like *think*, the four other complement-taking verbs are primarily used in formulaic matrix clauses. The examples in (39) and (40) illustrate the use of *guess* and *bet*. They show the first 10 utterances in Sarah's corpus.

(39)   Sarah (first 10 utterances including *guess* plus S-complement)

I guess I better come. . . .	3;5
Guess I'll write some more white.	3;9
Guess I lay it down.	3;10
I guess saw me break them.	3;10
I guess I have one more.	4;4
That goes right here but it don't fit . . . I guess.	4;4
Now . . . I guess that goes right there . . . doesn't it?	4;4
Because it have both lines . . . I guess.	4;5
I guess this is a hill . . . like this.	4;9
I guess this is . . .	5;0

(40)   Sarah (first 10 utterances including *bet* plus S-complement)

Bet can't . . . it.	3;4
I bet I can't do that.	3;4
That will be me bet you. . . .	3;6
I bet the other one's Shaggy.	3;8
I bet I can.	3;9
I bet I can try with a spoon.	4;1
I bet you he'll eat one of the birds up.	4;1

I bet you can't make a. . . .	4;3
I bet you don't know this.	4;4
I bet I can win this time.	4;6

The sentences in (39) and (40) have basically the same structure as the constructions including *think*: the complement-taking verbs always occur in the present indicative active; they are never accompanied by an auxiliary, modal, or adverb; and their subject is always the first person singular pronoun *I* (which is sometimes omitted). The complement clauses are longer and more diverse; they are never introduced by a *that*-complementizer; and in some utterances they precede the matrix clause. Thus, like *I think*, *I guess*, and *I bet* can be seen as parenthetical epistemic markers adjoined to an independent utterance. The composite structure is thus monoclausal. However, while the use of *think* is later extended to other types of matrix clauses, the use of *guess* and *bet* does not change: their occurrence remains restricted to the parenthetical formulas *(I) guess* and *(I) bet* throughout the time period of this study.

The examples in (41) show the first 10 utterances including *mean* and a S-complement clause in Adam's data.

(41)   Adam (first 10 utterances including *mean* plus S-complement)

Does lion crawl (pause) I mean.	3;5
I mean (pause) make another airplane	3;6
You mean dat's on there?	3;11
You mean Paul says that?	3;11
I mean I'm a police driver.	4;1
What do you mean (pause) I'm not afraid?	4;3
What do you mean about play with it?	4;3
What do you mean (pause) that's all?	4;7
What do you mean (pause) they'll last a long time?	4;9
What do you mean (pause) it's going to be one?	5;2

Adam uses *mean* either in the declarative matrix clause *I mean* or in questions, where it occurs with a second person pronoun as subject. Both uses are formulaic: *I mean* can be seen as a parenthetical epistemic marker, while the interrogatives function as question formulas: *You mean . . .?* is used to ask for confirmation that the speaker understood the hearer correctly, and *what do you mean (pause) . . .?* signals that the speaker disagrees with the hearer's previous utterance unless s/he can provide some reason to explain it. Both questions can be regarded as some sort of speech act marker.

While Adam's use of *mean* is restricted to matrix clauses including a first or second person pronoun as subject, some of the children use *mean* also with a third person subject.

Table 5.5 *Subjects of* think, know, mean, bet, *and* guess

	1SG	2SG	3SG	PL	Lex NP
think	297	55	5	3	1
know	27	45	2	0	4
mean	13	12	12	1	0
bet	36	0	0	0	0
guess	33	0	0	0	0

As can be seen in table 5.5, the first person pronoun *I* is by far the most frequent subject; second person subjects are also quite common, but third person subjects are rare. The only complement-taking verb that occurs with a significant proportion of third person subjects is *mean*. There are 12 utterances (in the entire corpus) in which *mean* occurs either with *it* or *that*; but these are not assertive matrix clauses. While *it means*, and *that means* do not function as epistemic markers, they do not denote an independent state of affairs; rather, they indicate a specific link between two utterances (similar to a conjunctive adverb such as *therefore* or a linking phrase such as *in other words*). Thus, like *I think, it means*, and *that means* are formulaic matrix clauses: rather than denoting an independent state of affairs, they serve to organize the transition between two clauses.

Like *mean*, *know* occurs in two types of matrix clauses: in the expression *I know*, and in questions. The sentences in (42) show Adam's first 10 utterances including *know* and an S-complement clause.

(42)   Adam (first 10 utterances including *know* plus S-complement)
        <u>I know</u> this piece go.   2;6
        <u>I know</u> (pause) soldier marching.   2;8
        <u>How do you know</u> it going eat supper?   3;0
        <u>How do you know</u> dat a duck?   3;0
        <u>How do you know</u> dat convertible?   3;0
        <u>How do you know</u> (pause) I saw ducks   3;0
        <u>How do you know</u> (pause) put my cup up?   3;0
        <u>How do you know</u> (pause) doesn't hurt me?   3;1
        Mommy (pause) <u>how do you know</u> dat's Harvard Square bus?   3;1
        <u>Do you know</u> de lights went off?   3;2

Like *I think*, *I guess*, and *I bet*, I *know* basically functions as an epistemic marker. However, compared to the three other uses, *I know* is somewhat more substantial and less grammaticalized: in contrast to other early matrix clauses, it always precedes the complement clause and is often negated (like performative

Table 5.6 *The development of Adam's and Sarah's matrix clauses including* know

Age	Adam	Sarah
2;6	I know __ (12)	
2;7		
2;8		
2;9		
2;10		
2;11		
3;0	How do you know __ (9)	
3;1		
3;2	Do you know __ (3)	I know __ (4)
3;3		
3;4		
3;5		
3;6	I want to know __ (1)	
3;7	You know__ (4)	I didn't know __ (3), She knows __ (1)
3;8	How did you know __ (2)	
3;9		
3;10		
3;11		
4;0		Do you know __ (2)
4;1		Did you know __ (1)
4;2		You know __ (1)
4;3		
4;4		
4;5	I didn't know __ (3)	
4;6		How do you know __ (1)
4;7		
4;8		You won't even know __ (1)
4;9		
4;10	Mommy don't know __ (1)	I knew __ (1)
4;11		You knew __ (1)

and assertive matrix clauses). Adam's early use of *know* in questions is largely restricted to the interrogative formula, *How do you know . . .?*, which does not ask for the source of the hearer's knowledge; rather, it functions to elicit an explanation. In other words, *How do you know . . .?* is used to mark a specific type of question.

As the children grow older, *know* appears in a wider variety of matrix clauses. Table 5.6 presents a list of all matrix clauses (i.e. a list of all types) in which *know* occurs with an S-complement clause in Adam's and Sarah's transcripts.

Again, the data of the three other children are not included because they are too sparse to observe any significant developmental changes.

As can be seen in this table, Adam and Sarah begin to use *know* in the formulaic expression *I know*. As they grow older, the use of *know* becomes somewhat more substantial. *Know* is especially common in questions where it often functions as an interrogative formula marking a specific type of speech act. The assertive use of *know* remains rare throughout the study: there is only one relatively early example in Sarah's data in which *know* appears with a third person subject and a few later examples that might include an assertive matrix clause.

Deontic modality markers: *wish* and *hope*

W*ish* and *hope* occur only in Sarah's and Adam's corpus.[7] The examples in (43) and (44) show the first ten utterances in Adam's transcripts.

(43)   Adam (first 10 utterances including *wish* plus S-complement)

I wish I could play with dis [= a Christmas present].	3;5
I wish I can keep it (pause) for writing on.	3;5
I wish I can keep dat so I can tick (pause) tick it.	3;5
I wish we can eat . . .	3;8
I wish we could eat that.	3;8
I wish I could have a tractor to drive in them.	3;8
I wish (pause) could (pause) make some more just like dat.	3;8
I wish you could color all dese.	3;9
I wish I could have a picnic.	3;11
Momma (pause) I wish I could come back here.	3;11

(44)   Adam (all utterances including *hope* plus S-complement)

Hope he tipped again.	3;6
I hope he won't bother you.	4;0
I hope my cat friends are alright.	4;4
I hope dey alright.	4;4
I hope I can knock dese pretty bowling balls down with only one strike.	4;9
I hope de house won't be on fire.	4;9
I hope dat kitty's not getting into trouble.	4;9
I hope I put my sponge in here.	4;9
I hope they are not in my group.	4;10

The examples in (43) and (44) are very similar to the constructions that we have seen in the previous section. *Wish* and *hope* occur exclusively in the present indicative active, they are never accompanied by an auxiliary or modal, they

---

7. There is one isolated example of *hope* in Peter's transcripts.

Table 5.7 *Subjects of* wish *and* hope

	1SG	2SG	3SG	PL	Lex NP
wish	32	0	0	0	1
hope	14	3	0	0	0

Table 5.8 *Subjects of* see, look, *and* remember

	1SG	2SG	3SG	PL	Lex NP	ZERO
see	18	4	1	6	1	182
look	0	0	0	0	0	93
remember	1	0	0	0	0	8

are never negated, and their subject is almost always the first person pronoun *I*. Table 5.7 shows that there are only four utterances in the entire corpus in which *wish* and *hope* occur with a different subject.

The formulaic character of the matrix clauses suggests that they are nonassertive: rather than denoting the child's hope or desire, *I wish* and *I hope* can be seen as deontic modality markers, serving basically the same function as a modal adverb such as *hopefully*.

In contrast to *think* and *know*, which show at least some developmental changes (see above), *wish* and *hope* occur in the same formulaic matrix clauses throughout the entire time period of this study. While it is conceivable that the children recognize at some point that *I wish* and *I hope* can literally denote the speaker's hopes or desires, this is not evident from the data: the use of *wish* and *hope* remains formulaic until the end of the study.

Discourse directives: *see, look*, and *remember*

There are three other verbs in the sample that are commonly used as parentheticals: *see*, *look*, and *remember*. Table 5.8 shows that these three verbs usually do not occur with an overt subject. *See* is either used in the imperative or in an intonational question; *look* always appears in the imperative; and *remember* occurs in reduced questions. The examples in (45) and (46) illustrate the early uses of *see* and *look*.

(45)   Peter (first 10 utterances including *see* plus S-complement)
         Got to make them bigger . . . see?   2;3
         See this is empty.   2;3
         Let's see we fix them.   2;3

See these are stamps.	2;4
See Daddy's on the grass.	2;5
See boat has sails on it.	2;5
See the peoples going.	2;6
Mommy write it . . . see?	2;6
See I'm writing	2;6
See you do it?	2;7

(46)   Adam (first 10 utterances including *look* plus S-complement)

Look birdie fly.	2;5
Look (pause) Mommy (pause) cowboy reach.	2;6
Look (pause) Daddy put it on a wall.	2;8
Fell down (pause) look.	2;9
Look (pause) dat man doing.	2;10
Look (pause) see new wheel.	2;10
Look (pause) dat me talking.	2;11
We (pause) all (pause) look (pause) mail come out.	2;11
Look I did to mailbox.	3;0
It's got something . . . look.	3;0

See and *look* are common perception verbs, but in these examples they serve a pragmatic function. *See* has two distinct uses that are sometimes difficult to distinguish: it serves either as an attention getter (e.g. *See Daddy's on the grass*) or as some kind of question marker (e.g. *See, it works?*). The two uses are intonationally distinguished and derived from different historical sources. The attention getter is based on the imperative, whereas the question marker developed from an interrogative matrix clause (i.e. *(do) you see . . . ?*). In addition, *see* occasionally occurs in the hortative formula *let's see*, which draws the interlocutors' attention to the activity denoted in the complement clause. *Look*, which does not really take finite complement clauses, has been included in the data because it serve a similar function as the imperative *see*. While the use of *look* does not change in the data, *see* is later also used in other types of matrix clauses; notably the use of *I see* is quite common:

(47)   I see you bought some babies too.   [Adam 4;4]
(48)   I see you have bought new toys.   [Adam 4;6]
(49)   I see you carried the book with you.   [Adam 4;9]

While *I see* is more substantial than the earlier uses of *see* in imperatives and questions, it is not clear whether *I see* is a performative matrix clause: in most examples *I see* is equivocal between an interpretation as parenthetical epistemic marker and perception/cognition verb (cf. Johnson 1999). While *I see* and a few other matrix clauses including *see* can be seen as performative uses, the assertive use of *see* is almost entirely absent; there are only a few later examples in Adam's transcripts in which *see* might be analysed as a perception verb.

Children's early use of *remember* is illustrated in (50) with examples from Nina, Adam, and Sarah. These are all examples included in the corpus in which *remember* serves as the complement-taking verb of an S-complement clause.

(50) Nina, Adam, and Sarah (all utterances including *remember* plus S-comp)

Remember we played with Samantha?	3;0
Remember you reading de puzzle . . . I put it in there?	3;2
(You) remember I broke my window?	4;0
You have to put it in the barn . . . remember?	4;0
Remember it was Halloween and you had a mask on too?	4;2
I remember the bee bite me in the belly. . . .	4;5
Remember I don't had to go to the doctors?	4;5
Remember last year I knew how to make a two?	4;11
Hey . . . remember that I hanged them on like dat?	5;0

In its basic use *remember* describes a cognitive activity, but in these examples it functions to qualify the information expressed in the associated clause. As pointed out above, *remember* occurs in reduced questions (*do you remember [that] . . .? > remember . . .?*). In this usage it indicates that the associated proposition contains information that is familiar to the interlocutors from shared experience. Like *see* and *look*, *remember* basically serves a pragmatic function. There is only one example in the entire corpus in which *remember* seems to function as a cognition verb: *I remember the bee bite me in the belly* . . . (Sarah 4;5). In this case, *remember* occurs in a performative matrix clause that indicates the knowledge source for the information expressed in the complement clause.

Say, tell, and *pretend*

Finally, there are three other complement-taking verbs that we need to consider: *say, tell*, and *pretend*. These three verbs have more semantic weight and a less abstract meaning than all other complement-taking verbs in the sample. *Say* and *tell* refer to a verbal activity, an act of speaking, and they are always used in this sense. *Pretend* seems to have a more abstract meaning. In adult language, *pretend* is commonly used to indicate a distinctive mental state, but children use *pretend* in a more concrete sense, denoting a game in which somebody adopts the role or character of somebody else. In this use, *pretend* means something like 'acting' or 'staging' and thus is not a cognition verb as in adult language (Perner 1991).[8] Although *say, tell*, and *pretend* are semantically more concrete

---

8. Indirect support for this analysis of *pretend* comes from a study by Custer (1996), who found that 3 to 5-year-olds have little difficulty in interpreting complex sentence including *pretend* (e.g. *He*

than cognition or perception verbs, they appear after *think, know, look,* and *see* in matrix clauses. The sentences in (51)–(53) illustrate the children's use of these three verbs.

(51)   Nina (first 10 utterances including *say* plus S-complement)

The cowboy say (pause) 'I'm angry at you'.	2;9
He sayed he has something to play with for me.	2;9
That means peoples say 'put the kitty down'.	2;10
She gonna say I have a pretty dress on.	2;10
The kitty says he wants to come in.	2;10
He say the alligator's gonna bite him up.	2;10
You make a rabbit and a bear I said.	2;10
He said yes he will give you a cow.	2;11
She said she is gonna give me a pillow . . .	2;11
Dolly said 'yes she (pause) she's a witch.	2;11

(52)   Nina and Sarah (first 10 utterances including *tell* plus S-complement)

She told me she forget the doll carriage for me.	2;10
He told me . . . me don't scream again.	3;0
Tell me . . . I would like to come to your house again.	3;0
I'm gonna tell him I wanna go to his house.	3;3
I tell her . . . 'no . . . no . . . baby that's my stuff'.	3;3
I told you I could make a carrot.	4;2
I told you you're cuckoo.	4;6
I wanna tell the kids 'do you heard of this kind of water?'	4;9
Tell Daddy I'm sick.	4;10
I told you I need the (. . .) to do it.	4;11

(53)   Nina (first 10 utterances including *pretend* plus S-complement)

Pretend it's Ernie.	2;3
We will pretend there's play dough for something to eat.	2;10
Just pretend you have a hurt.	3;10
I pretending fish were coming.	3;0
I pretending whales were coming.	3;0
Oh. . this . . . pretend this is a blanket.	3;0
I gonna pretend this is a sleeping bag.	3;0
But . . . but just pretend that's his name.	3;1
Let's pretend that's name.	3;1
Now you pretend this is Spencer's Mommy.	3;1

The utterances in examples (51)–(53) are different from those that we have seen before. The complement-taking verbs occur in different tenses and are

is pretending that his puppy is outside), while they often misunderstand sentences including the complement-taking verb *think* (e.g. *He thinks that his puppy is outside*). I take this as additional evidence for my hypothesis that *pretend* has a more concrete meaning in the speech of young children than in the speech of adults and that *pretend* must be distinguished from other cognition verbs such as *think* or *know* in early child speech (see also Lillard 1993).

Table 5.9 *Subjects of* say, tell, *and* pretend

	1SG	2SG	3SG	PL	Lex NP	ZERO
say	39	15	33	2	30	19
tell	9	3	5	0	0	4
pretend	5	2	1	16	0	10

frequently accompanied by a modal or adverb: 50 per cent of all matrix clauses including *say, tell,* or *pretend* occur in the past tense, and 15 per cent include either a modal or an adverb. By contrast, only 7 per cent of all other complement-taking verbs occur in the past and fewer than 2 per cent are accompanied by a modal or adverb. Furthermore, while the complement-taking verbs that we considered in the previous sections occurred almost exclusively with a first or second person pronoun as subject, the use of *say, tell,* and *pretend* is much more flexible in this regard. Table 5.9 shows that they occur with a wide variety of subjects, including third person pronouns and, in the case of *say,* lexical NPs, which are extremely rare with most other complement-taking verbs.

Finally, *say, tell,* and *pretend* are much more likely to occur with a *that*-complementizer than all other complement-taking verbs that appear with a S-complement clause (cf. Diessel and Tomasello 1999). The vast majority of the S-complements does not include a complementizer; there are only 22 complement clauses in the entire corpus that are marked by *that* (i.e. an average of 2.0 per cent). However, more than half of them (13 tokens) occur with *say, tell,* or *pretend,* although these verbs account for only 17 per cent of all complement-taking verbs in the corpus. Put differently, the children use the complementizer *that* seven times more often with *say, tell,* and *pretend* than with other complement-taking verbs. Moreover, with one exception all of the *that*-complement clauses occur after the third birthday; that is, the earliest S-complement clauses are virtually never marked by *that.*

In contrast to the complement-taking verbs that we have seen in the previous sections, *say, tell,* and *pretend* do not occur in parenthetical formulas. As can be seen in table 5.10, they appear in matrix clauses that are much more diverse than the matrix clauses of other complement-taking verbs. The table shows the average number of tokens with which a specific type of matrix clause occurs in the data, where 'type of matrix clause' is defined as a structure having at least one formal feature (e.g. a specific tense form or a specific pronoun) that distinguishes it from all other matrix clauses including the same verb. For

Table 5.10 *Type-token ratio of the most frequent complement-taking verbs*

	Total number of tokens	Total number of types (i.e. matrix clause types)	Average number of tokens per type
look	93	2	46.5
bet	36	1	36.0
guess	33	1	33.0
think	361	16	22.6
see	212	15	14.1
wish	33	3	11.0
hope	17	2	8.5
know	78	15	5.2
mean	38	8	4.8
pretend	34	12	2.8
say	138	59	2.3
tell	21	16	1.3

instance, the verb *wish* has 33 tokens (in the entire corpus) distributed over three different types of matrix clauses: (i) *I wish . . .?*, (ii) *I could wish . . .*, and (iii) *Paul wish . . .?*, which yields a type-token ratio of 11.

As can be seen in this table, *say, tell*, and *pretend* have the lowest type-token ratios (*pretend* 2.8, *say* 2.3, *tell* 1.3). The greater degree of diversity suggests that they are not parenthetical formulas but full propositions. Specifically, *say* and *tell* occur in assertive matrix clauses, as suggested by the high percentage of third person subjects and past tense forms. *Pretend*, on the other hand, is primarily used in performative matrix clauses; it occurs in three different constructions: (i) in declarative clauses with a first person singular subject (e.g. *I pretending fish were coming*), (ii) in imperative clauses (e.g. *Pretend it's Ernie*), and (iii) in hortatives (e.g. *Let's pretend it's raining*).

Although *say, tell*, and *pretend* appear in full-fledged matrix clauses, it is unclear whether children are able to acquire a general complement clause schema based on these three verbs. There are two reasons why this seems to be unlikely. First, a constructional schema can only be extracted from the data if the child has learned a certain number of types (cf. chapter 2). Though it is unclear how many types are needed, three different verbs do not seem to be sufficient to extract a general complement clause schema from the data. Second, the first matrix clauses are so diverse that one might doubt that the children conceive of them as instances of the same grammatical construction. While *say* and *tell* denote an act of speaking, *pretend* refers to an activity in a game. The

Table 5.11 *S-complements,* wh-*complements, and*
if-*complements: mean age of their appearance*

	S-complement	*wh*-complement	*if*-complement
Adam	2;3	2;4	3;7
Sarah	2;9	2;11	3;8
Nina	2;1	2;3	2;10
Peter	2;0	2;11	3;8
Naomi	2;6	2;8	–
Mean age	2;4	2;7	3;5

semantic difference correlates with several structural differences. Unlike *say* and *tell*, *pretend* is frequently used in the progressive tense and accompanied by a modal adverb; moreover, while *say* and *tell* primarily occur in declarative matrix clauses, *pretend* is also commonly used in imperatives and hortatives. If we compare the use of *say* and *tell*, we find that although both denote an act of speaking, they take different types of complements: while *say* is commonly used with a direct quote, *tell* takes complement clauses that paraphrase the content of a previous utterance. Moreover, while *say* usually occurs with a simple S-complement, *tell* takes in addition an indirect object denoting the addressee (e.g. *I am gonna tell Mommy I want paper*). Given that *say, tell,* and *pretend* occur in rather different constructions and that the early use of matrix causes is largely restricted to these three verbs, it appears to be unlikely that children are able to form a general complement clause schema at this stage. Rather, what they seem to have learned are isolated complement clause constructions that are organized around specific complement-takings verbs.

5.4.2   If-*complements and* wh-*complements*
If- and *wh*-complement clauses appear several months after the first S-complements. As can be seen in table 5.11, S-complements emerge at a mean age of 2;4, *wh*-complements emerge three months later at a mean age of 2;7, and *if*-complements appear at the age of 3;5.

If-complements and *wh*-complements require a co-occurring matrix clause to form a complete utterance. This distinguishes *if-* and *wh*-complements from S-complements. The latter are formally indistinguishable from independent utterances (unless they are marked by a *that*-complementizer). Since *if-* and *wh*-complements are structurally incomplete without the associated matrix clause, they cannot be interpreted as parentheticals. However, that does not mean that the composite structure is necessarily biclausal. In what follows I show that the matrix clauses of *if*- and *wh*-complements basically serve the same pragmatic functions as the matrix clauses of S-complements: they may serve as epistemic markers, attention getters, or markers of illocutionary force. However, while the matrix clauses of S-complements are parentheticals, the matrix clauses of *if*- and *wh*-complements function as an integral part of a lexically specific utterance frame that is associated with a particular pragmatic function.

If-complements

The data include seven complement-taking verbs that occur with an *if*-complement clause: *see, tell, wonder, ask, care, watch,* and *happen.* Most of them have just a few tokens. The only verb that is frequently used with an *if*-complement clause is *see*: 44 of the 63 *if*-complements occur with *see* in the data. Apart from *see, tell* is the only other complement-taking verb that has a significant number of tokens. However, since 13 of the 14 utterances including *tell* and an *if*-complement clause were produced in a single session by the same child, the following discussion concentrates on *see*. The examples in (54) show the earliest utterances including *see* and an *if*-complement clause in Nina's and Sarah's transcripts.

(54)   Nina and Sarah (first 10 utterances including *see* plus *if*-complement)
     ... and <u>see</u> if I'm tall.   2;10
     Now <u>let's see</u> if it fits on this little boy.   3;1
     <u>Let me see</u> if there's something else in her bag.   3;3
     <u>I want to see</u> if you ...   3;8
     <u>Let me see</u> if I can touch you.   4;2
     <u>See</u> if I can make a kite.   4;8
     <u>See</u> if I can make you wink.   4;9
     <u>See</u> if I can pour it like this.   4;9
     <u>See</u> if it smells.   4;11
     <u>Let me see</u> if you get anymore.   5;1

While *see* does not only occur in one specific formula, its occurrence is restricted to a few types of matrix clauses. Table 5.12 shows all matrix clauses (i.e. all types) that Adam, Sarah, Nina, and Peter produced with *see* and an *if*-complement clause (Naomi's data do not include *if*-complements).

   In more than half of the utterances in which *see* occurs with an *if*-complement, the matrix clause consists solely of *see*. In such a case, *see* does not serve as

Table 5.12 See if-*complements*

	Adam	Sarah	Nina	Peter	Mean
See if__	15	4	1	6	54.3
Let's see if__	2	–	2	1	21.4
Let me see if__	7	2	–	–	14.2
I wanna see if__	1	1	–	2	10.1
Total	25	7	3	9	

a perception verb; rather, it functions together with *if* as a directive, drawing the interlocutors' attention to an unknown (or not yet realized) state of affairs whose status (or truth) will be revealed in the immediate future. Some typical examples are given in (55).

(55)   Adam (imperative *see* plus *if*-complement)
         See if I can push it.   4;1
         See if your car is stuck.   4;3
         See if I can do something else.   4;10
         See if the flowers would like to watch me.   4;10

Although the other matrix clauses in table 5.12 appear to be somewhat more substantial, they basically serve the same function as the simple *See if__*: they focus the interlocutors' attention on the complement clause. While some of these clauses might be considered performative (rather than formulaic), it must be emphasized that *see* does not occur in assertive matrix clauses. In fact, none of the complement-taking verbs that occur with *if*-complements is assertive: the complement-taking verbs generally appear in the present indicative active and take either a first person pronoun as subject or occur in imperative or hortative clauses. In other words, there is good evidence that children's early use of *if*-complements is restricted to the formulaic and performative uses.

Wh-complements

Wh-complements are much more frequent than *if*-complements. The data include seven complement-taking verbs that commonly occur with a *wh*-complement clause: *know* (297), *see* (121), *look* (61), *wonder* (61), *show* (16), *tell* (16), and *guess* (14) (the figures in parentheses indicate the number of tokens). Apart from *wonder* and *show,* all other complement-taking verbs also occur with S-complements. The examples in (56) and (57) illustrate the use of *see* and *look*.

(56)   Nina (first 10 utterances including *see* plus *wh*-complement)
    See where my monkey is.   2;4
    See what he doed?   2;9
    See what this is.   2;9
    I just opened that thing and see what was in there.   2;10
    See how I eat it.   2;10
    See what . . . what the babies are?   2;10
    No let me see who is that.   2;10
    Let's close the door and see what happens.   2;11
    Let's see what's in here.   3;1
    I wanna see what else is . . .   3;1

(57)   Sarah (first 10 utterances including *look* plus *wh*-complement)
    Oh . . . look what I did.   3;2
    Look . . . look . . . what's that look like.   3;6
    Look what he doing.   3;8
    Look what I made.   3;9
    Look what I made.   3;9
    Look what I found.   3;9
    Look what I have.   3;10
    See look what I made.   4;0
    Look . . . which one . . . this is . . . here.   4;4
    Look how size I have.   4;10

Like S-complements, *wh*-complements are accompanied by highly formulaic matrix clauses. *See* and *look* do not function as perception verbs in these examples; rather, they serve the same function as in sentences including S-complements: they are attention getters that draw the interlocutors' attention to the proposition expressed in the complement clause. The only difference is that *wh*-complement clauses are formally incomplete without the matrix clause, so that *see* and *look* cannot be parentheticals; instead, they function as an integral part of a lexically specific utterance frame.

The examples in (58) illustrate the use of *wonder* plus a *wh*-complement. The examples show Adam's first 10 utterances of this construction.

(58)   Adam (first 10 utterance including *wonder* plus *wh*-complement)
    I wonder what a whale fish is.   3;8
    I wonder what skinned means.   3;8
    I wonder what dat is.   3;8
    I wonder what dat noise is.   3;8
    I wonder what it is.   3;8
    Mommy . . . I wonder what dat is.   3;8
    I wonder what dey are.   3;8
    I wonder what dis is.   3;8
    I wonder where the door is.   3;8
    I wonder where the rest of it is.   3;8

All 10 examples include the same type of matrix clause consisting of the first person singular pronoun *I* and the complement-taking verb *wonder* in the present indicative active. The formulaic character of these expressions suggests that the matrix clauses are nonreferential. Specifically, *I wonder wh-__* serves to introduce an indirect question; it can be seen as a formal marker of illocutionary force. A similar analysis applies to *guess* plus *wh-*complement. Consider the sentences in (59).

(59)   Sarah and Adam (first 10 utterances including *guess* plus
        *wh-*complement)
        Guess what it is?   3;5
        Guess who we spun?   4;1
        Guess what that is?   4;5
        Guess what I can make still?   4;6
        Guess what that is?   4;6
        Guess what this is?   4;10
        Guess what it is?   4;10
        Guess what dis is?   4;11
        Guess what dis is going to be, Mommy?   5;2
        Guess how old I am?   5;2

In these examples, *guess* is the only element in an imperative matrix clause. The sentences are simple and highly formulaic. Like *I wonder wh-__*, *Guess wh-__* signals the illocutionary force of a particular speech act. Specifically, *Guess wh-__* marks the first utterance of an adjacency pair in which the speaker asks the hearer to surmise what has happened in a particular situation before revealing the answer.

The most frequent complement-taking verb of a *wh-*complement clause is *know*, which occurs in 297 utterances. The examples in (60) show the first 10 utterances that Nina produced with *know* and a *wh-*complement clause.

(60)   Nina (first 10 utterances including *know* plus *wh-*complement)
        You know what these things are called?   2;3
        Know what happened?   2;3
        Know what my making?   2;3
        Uh . . . you know what my make?   2;4
        Know what my eating . . . Mommy?   2;4
        Know what's happening?   2;4
        Know where my monkey is?   2;4
        Know what it is now?   2;5
        Know what these is?   2;5
        Know what the peas do, Mommy?   2;5

In all 10 examples, *know* serves as the complement-taking verb of a polar question, which may or may not include a second person pronoun as a subject:

(Do you) know . . .? is by far the most frequent clause type; it appears in 173 of the 297 utterances in which *know* takes a *wh*-complement clause. In most of these utterances, *(do you) know* is semantically redundant. If somebody asks, for instance, *Do you know what time it is?* the speaker is not interested in the hearer's knowledge (i.e. whether or not s/he knows the time); rather, what the speaker would like to know is the specific time at the point of the utterance. The hearer is therefore expected to provide an answer in response to the complement clause; the matrix clause is just a polite formula introducing a directive speech act.

Apart from the interrogative formula (i.e. *Do you know . . .?*), *know* occurs in two other types of matrix clauses: in *I know*, which has 38 tokens, and in *I don't/didn't know*, which occurs in 54 utterances. Although both types are short and formulaic, they cannot generally be classified as epistemic markers. In particular, when they are used contrastively they function as performative (or even assertive) matrix clauses denoting the speaker's mental state (cf. Wellman 1990; Bartsch and Wellman 1995). However, only a small proportion of the children's use of *I know* and *I don't/didn't know* is contrastive. The vast majority has a noncontrastive interpretation, which is much less substantial. Very often, the noncontrastive uses are equivocal between an interpretation as epistemic marker and performative matrix clause.

As the children grow older, they use *know* in a wider variety of constructions. Some of them can only be interpreted as assertive matrix clauses. Consider, for instance, the utterances in (61)–(64).

(61)	He doesn't know where he's driving.	[Adam 4;0]
(62)	Paul knows where it is, doesn't he?	[Adam 4;3]
(63)	This airplane doesn't know where it's going.	[Adam 4;4]
(64)	She didn't know where it was.	[Sarah 5;0]

In these examples, the subject of the matrix clause is either a third person pronoun or a lexical NP referring to a non-speech-act participant. Note also that *know* occurs in different tenses and that the matrix clauses in (61), (63), and (64) are negated. These features suggest that the complement clauses are embedded, both syntactically and semantically, in an assertive matrix clause. In other words, the utterances in (61)–(64) document the gradual development of complex sentences including *know* plus a *wh*-complement clause.

Finally, there are two complement-taking verbs, *tell* and *show,* that occur from the very beginning in a wide variety of matrix clauses with *wh*-complements.

(65)   Adam *(tell* plus *wh*-complement)
        <u>Tell me</u> where you going.   2;10
        <u>Why you told him</u> what you gonna do?   3;2
        <u>You tell me</u> what it is.   3;4
        <u>Will you tell me</u> what it is.   3;8
        <u>Tell you</u> how vegetables grow.   3;11
        <u>He's trying to tell you</u>, Paul, what're you trying to do?   3;11
        <u>Tell me</u> what all of dese are?   4;7
        <u>Mommy you tell me</u> what de directions do, ok?   4;10
        <u>Mommy, tell me</u> what de directions are.   4;10
        <u>Tell me</u> what they taste like.   4;10

(66)   Peter and Adam (*show* plus *wh*-complement)
        Yeah . . . <u>show them</u> how it works . . .   2;8
        <u>I'm gonna show you</u> where the horses feet is.   2;8
        <u>I'll show you</u> where it is.   2;8
        Oh . . . <u>let me show you</u> how I do it . . .   3;1
        <u>Show me</u> how it works.   3;4
        <u>I show you</u> what I put on wrong.   3;6
        <u>Show me</u> what color you want.   4;3
        <u>I show you</u> what I made.   4;7
        Now . . . <u>show me</u> what de directions are.   4;10
        <u>Show me</u> how I'm, gonna make a kite.   4;10

The matrix clauses in (65) and (66) are more complex and more diverse than most other matrix clauses in the data: they are declarative, interrogative, or imperative clauses, including different types of subjects, indirect objects, and verbs in different tenses. Moreover, there is one utterance in which *tell* serves as the infinitival complement of the verb *try*. The diversity of these structures suggests that the matrix clauses do not function as grammaticalized epistemic markers or discourse directives; rather, they are full-fledged (matrix) clauses making reference to an independent state of affairs. While most of them are performative matrix clauses (e.g. *Tell me where you going*), a few represent assertive uses (e.g. *He's trying to tell you, Paul, what're you trying to do*).

5.5   *Discussion*

5.5.1   *Summary*
This chapter has shown that the vast majority of children's early complement clauses are accompanied by formulaic matrix clauses. The composite structures thus contain only a single proposition expressed in the complement clause. The matrix clause does not denote an independent state of affairs; rather, it functions as an epistemic marker, attention getter, or marker of the illocutionary force.

From a formal perspective, two types of formulaic matrix clauses can be distinguished: (i) matrix clauses that function as parentheticals of S-complements; and (ii) matrix clauses that function as an integral part of a lexically specific utterance frame including *if-* or *wh-*complements. Since formulaic matrix clauses are not full-fledged clauses, the associated complement clauses are not embedded.

As the children grow older, some of the early formulaic matrix clauses become more substantial. For instance, while the earliest uses of *think* are restricted to the parenthetical formula *I think,* there are some later examples in which *think* occurs in performative and assertive matrix clauses. The performative use emerges before the assertive use and is much more common. This holds for both the class of complement-taking verbs as a whole and for individual complement-taking verbs. If the earliest use of an individual verb is formulaic (as in the case of most complement-taking verbs that appear in early child speech), it is very likely that the use of this verb is first extended to performative matrix clauses before it is used assertively. There is thus a developmental trend leading from formulaic matrix clauses via the performative use to assertive matrix clauses.

(67)   formulaic matrix clause > performative matrix clause > assertive matrix clause

However, it must be emphasized that not all complement-taking verbs pass through all three stages. Since the formulaic use is limited to the most frequent complement-taking verbs, less frequent verbs occur from the very beginning in performative and/or assertive matrix clauses. However, since the most frequent complement-taking verbs are the ones that emerge early, most early complement-taking verbs appear at first in formulaic matrix clauses. There are only four frequent complement-taking verbs in the entire corpus that never occur in formulaic matrix clauses: *say, tell, pretend*, and *show*. These four verbs appear from early on in performative and assertive matrix clauses. They are the first complement-taking verbs that take a truly embedded complement clause, i.e. a complement clause functioning as an argument of the matrix verb. However, since *say, tell, pretend,* and *show* occur in rather different constructions, it seems unlikely that young children are able to extract a complement clause schema from the data; rather, what the children of this study seem to have learned are isolated complement clause constructions that are organized around individual complement-taking verbs. In other words, what these data suggest is that a constructional schema representing the common properties of all complement clauses emerges only later when children have learned a greater

Table 5.13 *Mean proportions of the various complement-taking verbs of S-complements in the mothers' data and the mean age of their appearance in the children's data*

	Mothers' data (mean proportions)	Children's data (mean age of appearance)
think	32.8	2;7
know	21.8	2;6
see	11.5	2;8
say	8.7	2;9
tell	6.6	3;0
look	2.9	2;10
mean	2.4	3;1
guess	2.2	3;1
show	1.7	3;3
pretend	1.0	3;2
bet	0.8	3;3
wonder	0.7	3;5
hope	0.5	3;9
wish	0.4	3;5

variety of complement clause constructions (see chapter 8 for a more detailed discussion).

5.5.2   Discussion

Concluding this chapter, let us consider the factors that might motivate the described development. One crucial factor seems to be the ambient language. The mothers' data include the same type of formulaic matrix clauses as the speech of their children. Moreover, the order of acquisition seems to correlate with the amount of data that the children encounter in the ambient language. As can be seen in table 5.13, the complement-taking verbs that the mothers use most frequently are the ones that appear very early in the children's transcripts (cf. table 5a and table 5b in the appendix).

The statistical analysis reveals that the age of appearance correlates very closely with the frequency of the various complement-taking verbs in the mothers' data (Spearman's rho: $r = .559$, $p = .038$, $N = 14$). This suggests that the ambient language plays an important role in the development of finite complement clauses.

In addition, the complexity of the emerging constructions seems to influence the development. Since formulaic matrix clauses are propositionally empty, the composite structures are relatively simple: they contain a single proposition and do not involve embedding. Performative and assertive matrix clauses, on the other hand, occur in constructions that express two propositions, one of which is embedded. In other words, complex sentences including performative and assertive matrix clauses are more complex than complex sentences including formulaic matrix clauses. Thus, one might hypothesize that the complexity of performative and assertive matrix clauses contributes to their late appearance.

Finally, it is conceivable that the formulaic use of mental verbs such as *think, know*, and *remember* appears before the performative and assertive uses because the latter presuppose certain cognitive capacities that emerge only gradually during the preschool years. Specifically, the child must be able to understand that reality and mental representation do not always match and that different people might have different beliefs about the same state of affairs in order to use mental verbs in performative and assertive matrix clauses. Recent work by Bartsch and Wellmann (1995) has shown that although children as young as 3;6 years are able to make these distinctions, they are still often confused in false-belief tasks until the age of 4;0. This suggests, according to Bartsch and Wellman, that children under 4 years do not have a fully developed theory of mind (cf. Perner 1991; Astington and Jenkins 1999). If this is correct, one might hypothesize that younger children avoid the use of mental state verbs in performative and assertive matrix clauses because they lack the cognitive prerequisites for these uses. Since the formulaic use of mental verbs does not presuppose a fully developed theory of mind, it can emerge before children have the cognitive prerequisites for the performative and assertive uses. Furthermore, it might explain why the earliest use of performative and assertive matrix clauses is restricted to verbs that do not denote a cognitive stance or cognitive activity. Although all complement-taking verbs occur in the same syntactic environment, children might restrict the early use of assertive matrix clauses to verbs such as *say, tell*, and *pretend* because the assertive use of these verbs does not presuppose a theory of mind like the assertive use of mental state verbs such as *think, know*, and *guess*.[9]

9. An alternative explanation has been suggested by de Villiers (1999; see also de Villiers and de Villiers 1999). She argues that cognitive development and language acquisition are mutually dependent: while the acquisition of complex sentences including complement clauses has certain cognitive prerequisites, the syntactic development of complement clauses may support the development of the child's theory of mind. More precisely, de Villiers (1999) argues that complex sentences provide a 'representational medium' within which children can reach a better understanding of certain aspects of the mind, notably of false beliefs. Her hypothesis is based on evidence from experiments with deaf and hearing children showing that the acquisition of complement clauses improves children's performance in false-belief tasks.

In sum, the development of complex sentences seems to be determined by multiple factors. Two of them, the ambient language and the complexity of the emerging constructions, are also relevant to the development of other complex sentences. As I have argued in the previous chapter, input frequency and complexity play an important role in the development of infinitival and participial complement constructions, and as we will see in the two following chapters they are also relevant to the development of relative and conjoined clauses.

6   *Relative clauses*

Like complement clauses, relative clauses emerge from simple nonembedded sentences. The earliest relative clauses occur in presentational constructions that consist of a copular clause and a relative clause including an intransitive verb. Although these constructions are biclausal they denote only a single situation. The presentational copular clause does not serve as an independent assertion; rather, it functions to establish a referent in focus position, making it available for the predication expressed in the relative clause. The whole sentence thus contains only a single proposition, leading children frequently to conflate the two clauses: many of the early relative constructions are syntactic blends (or amalgams) in which the relative clause and the matrix clause are merged into a single syntactic unit. As children grow older, they begin to use more complex relative constructions. In contrast to the early presentational relatives, the relative constructions produced by older children denote two situations in two full-fledged clauses. Based on these data I argue that complex sentences including relative clauses develop via clause expansion: starting from presentational relatives that denote a single situation, children gradually learn the use of complex relative constructions in which two situations are expressed by two separate full clauses.

6.1   *Literature*

The acquisition of relative clauses has been studied extensively. The bulk of the literature is concerned with children's comprehension of relative clauses in experiments (cf. Brown 1971; Slobin and Welsh 1973; Smith 1974; Sheldon 1974, 1977; Tavakolian 1977, 1981a; de Villiers, Tager-Flusberg, Hakuta, and Cohen 1979; Flynn and Lust 1980; Hamburger 1980; Hakuta 1981; Goodluck and Tavakolian 1982; Hamburger and Crain 1982; Tager-Flusberg 1982; Corrêa 1982, 1995a, 1995b; Clancy, Lee, and Zoh 1986; Keenan and Hawkins 1987; Hildebrand 1987; MacWhinney and Pléh 1988; Labelle 1990, 1996; Schuele and Nicholls 2000; McKee and McDaniel 2001; Eisenberg 2002; Kidd and

Bavin 2002; Diessel and Tomasello 2004). The production of relative clauses in naturally occurring child speech has never been investigated in detail: Menyuk (1969) and Limber (1973, 1976) discuss a few aspects of children's spontaneous use of relative clauses in English; Slobin (1986) examines the emergence of relative clauses in English and Turkish, concentrating on differences in their development; and Dasinger and Toupin (1994) and Jisa and Kern (1998) analyse the discourse-pragmatic functions of relative clauses that children produced in a picture-book task. However, none of these studies provides a systematic analysis of the development of relative clauses in natural child speech. The current study presents the first comprehensive investigation of the acquisition of relative clauses based on observational data.

Two features are commonly used to characterize the structure of relative clauses: (i) the syntactic role of the matrix clause element functioning as the *head* of the relative clause, i.e. the element that is modified by the relative clause; and (ii) the syntactic role of the *gap*, i.e. the element that is *relativized* inside the relative clause. While head and gap can serve any syntactic role, the experimental literature on children's comprehension of relative clauses has concentrated on relative constructions in which head and gap function as core arguments. Specifically, the four following types of relative constructions have been examined: (i) SS-relatives, in which the matrix clause subject is modified by a relative clause including a subject gap; (ii) SO-relatives, in which the matrix clause subject is modified by a relative clause including an object gap; (iii) OS-relatives, in which the matrix clause object is modified by a relative clause including a subject gap; and (iv) OO-relatives, in which the matrix clause object is modified by a relative clause including an object gap. The following examples, adopted from Sheldon (1974:275), exemplify the four constructions (the line indicates the position of the gap):

(1)   The dog that __ jumps over the pig bumps into the lion.   SS
(2)   The lion that the horse bumps into __ jumps over the giraffe.   SO
(3)   The pig bumps into the horse that __ jumps over the giraffe.   OS
(4)   The dog stands on the horse that the giraffe jumps over __.   OO

In order to test children's comprehension of relative clauses, researchers used either an imitation task in which children had to repeat sentences including relative clauses (e.g. Smith 1974), or an act-out task in which children had to act out the meaning of such sentences using toy animals. The errors that children produced in these experiments suggest that children employ particular strategies in their interpretation of relative clauses. The following hypotheses as to how children interpret relative clauses have been proposed:

(i)   the *noninterruption hypothesis*, which asserts that children have par-
      ticular problems with relative clauses that interrupt the matrix clause
      (cf. Slobin 1973);
(ii) the *filler-gap hypothesis*, which states that children's difficulties in
      interpreting relative clauses varies with the distance between the filler
      (i.e. the head noun) and the gap (cf. O'Grady 1997);
(iii) the *NVN-schema hypothesis*, which states that children interpret rela-
      tive constructions using a Noun-Verb-Noun schema (cf. Bever 1970a);
(iv) the *parallel-function hypothesis*, which posits that children tend to
      assign the same syntactic roles to head and gap (cf. Sheldon 1974);
(v)   the *conjoined-clause hypothesis*, which states that children interpret
      early relative constructions as conjoined sentences (cf. Tavakolian
      1977).

The five hypotheses will be discussed in turn.

6.1.1   *The noninterruption hypothesis*

The noninterruption hypothesis asserts that children have greater difficulties in
processing relative clauses that interrupt the matrix clause than relative clauses
that follow (or precede) it (cf. Slobin 1973). Relative clauses that interrupt
the matrix clause are called centre-embedded relative clauses. Among the four
relative constructions in (1–4), SS- and SO-relatives are centre-embedded (cf.
examples (5a)–(5b)), whereas OS- and OO-relatives are right-branching structures (cf. examples (6a)–(6b)).

(5)   a. NP_i [— $_i$ V NP] V NP   SS   centre-embedded
       b. NP_i [NP V — $_i$] V NP   SO

(6)   a. NP V NP_i [— $_i$ V NP]   OS   right-branching
       b. NP V NP_i [NP V — $_i$]   OO

The noninterruption hypothesis is consistent with one of Slobin's (1973) operat-
ing principles, which posits that children have difficulties in interpreting grammatical structures that are interrupted by some other element. Processing a
discontinuous grammatical unit involves holding an incomplete parse in working memory while interpreting (or constructing) the intervening element. This
can easily exceed the hearer's (or speaker's) memory span, especially when the
intervening element is a complex grammatical unit such as a centre-embedded
relative clause (cf. Kuno 1973, 1974; Dryer 1980). In general, 'the greater the
separation between related parts of a sentence, the greater the tendency that the
sentence will not be adequately processed' (Slobin 1973).

The noninterruption hypothesis has been tested in a number of experimental studies with preschool children (cf. Brown 1971; Smith 1974; de Villiers et al. 1979; Corrêa 1982, 1995a, 1995b; Roth 1984; Clancy et al. 1986; Kidd and Bavin 2002). What all of these studies have found is that children tend to misinterpret centre-embedded relative clauses more often than they do relative clauses that do not interrupt the matrix clause.[1] Note that this is not a specific feature of right-branching languages like English. Like English-speaking children, children learning Korean and Japanese make more mistakes in act-out experiments with centre-embedded relative clauses than they do with relative clauses that do not interrupt the matrix clause (cf. Hakuta 1981; Clancy et al. 1986). In fact, there is some evidence that centre-embedding is even more difficult in left-branching languages like Korean and Japanese, where the relative clause precedes the head, than it is in right-branching languages like English, where the relative clause follows it (cf. Clancy et al. 1986:252).

6.1.2   The filler-gap hypothesis

The filler-gap hypothesis posits that the processing load of relative clauses is determined by the varying distance between the filler, i.e. the head of the relative clause, and the gap, i.e. the relativized element. A number of experimental studies showed that both adults and children have fewer difficulties in interpreting a subject gap than an object gap (studies examining children's comprehension of subject and object gaps include de Villiers et al. 1979, Hildebrand 1987, and Corrêa 1995a, 1995b; studies examining adults' comprehension of subject and object gaps include Hakes et al. 1976, Wanner and Maratsos 1978, and Clifton and Frazier 1989). Wanner and Maratsos (1978) explained this finding in terms of the varying distance between filler and gap. In relative clauses including a subject gap, the distance between filler and gap is minimal: the only element that occurs between them is the relativizer (cf. examples (7a)–(7b)). In relative clauses including an object gap, on the other hand, filler and gap are separated from each other by the subject and verb of the relative clause (cf. examples (8a)–(8b)).

(7)   a. NP$_i$ [*that* —$_i$ V NP] NP   SS
        b. NP V NP$_i$ [*that* —$_i$ V NP]   OS

---

1. The only study that did not fully support this hypothesis is Brown (1971). Brown used a picture-cued comprehension task in which 3–5-year-old children had to match pictures to sentences including relative clauses. While the 4-year-olds and 5-year-olds made fewer mistakes with right-branching relatives than with centre-embedded relatives, the 3-year-olds showed the reverse pattern.

(8)   a. NP$_i$ [NP V (*that*) —$_i$] V NP SO
       b. NP V NP$_i$ [(*that*) NP V —$_i$] OO

Wanner and Maratsos argued that it is difficult for the human processor to keep the filler in working memory until it encounters the gap, which provides the information necessary to integrate the filler into the relative clause. The longer the processor has to retain unintegrated information, the harder the relative clause is to parse (cf. Frazier 1987; Clifton and Frazier 1989; Gibson 1998). While Wanner and Maratsos only considered relative clauses including a subject or object gap (as in examples (9a)–(9b)), their analysis can easily be extended to other relative clauses. As can be seen in examples (9c)–(9d)), in relative clauses in which an oblique (i.e. the object of a preposition) or an indirect object is relativized, the critical region between filler and gap increases: it does not only include the subject and verb, as in relative clauses including an object gap, but also a preposition and, in the case of an indirect object gap, the direct object.

(9)   a. The boy$_i$ who —$_i$ kissed the girl.   subject gap
       b. The boy$_i$ who(m) the girl kissed —$_i$.   object gap
       c. The boy$_i$ who(m) the girl played with —$_i$.   oblique gap
       d. The boy$_i$ who(m) the girl gave the football to —$_i$. indirect object gap

Thus, if the filler-gap hypothesis is valid, relative clauses including an oblique gap and relative clauses including an indirect object gap should create greater difficulties than relative clauses including a subject gap or a direct object gap. This hypothesis is consistent with the results of several experimental studies showing that children's difficulties in interpreting relative clauses increases in oblique and indirect object relatives (cf. de Villiers et al. 1979; Hildebrand 1987; see also Diessel and Tomasello 2004 for a critique of this proposal).

   The varying distance between filler and gap correlates with the degree of embeddedness of the gap. Other things being equal, the longer the distance between filler and gap, the more deeply embedded the gap. Thus, a variant of the filler-gap hypothesis states that it is not the linear distance between filler and gap that determines the processing load of relative clauses but rather the degree of embeddedness of the gap. Specifically, it has been claimed that the processing load of relative clauses is determined by the number of nodes that must be processed in order to recognize all elements between filler and gap (cf. Hawkins 1994, 1999).

   Additional support for the filler-gap hypothesis comes from children's use of resumptive pronouns in relative clauses. A number of studies observed that young children often insert a resumptive pronoun in the place of the gap (cf. Labelle 1990, 1996; Pérez-Leroux 1995; Goodluck and Stojanovic 1997; McKee, McDaniel, and Snedeker 1998; McKee and McDaniel 2001; Diessel and Tomasello 2004). Two examples are given in (10) and (11).

(10)   Here is the girl who the boy borrowed a football from **her**.
(11)   I hurt my finger that Thomas stepped on **it**.

Interestingly, the occurrence of a resumptive pronoun seems to correlate with the degree of embeddedness (or, alternatively, the distance between filler and gap): the more deeply embedded the relativized syntactic role (or the longer the distance between filler and gap), the more likely the occurrence of a resumptive pronoun. This has been interpreted as indirect support for the filler-gap hypothesis (cf. Pérez-Leroux 1995; O'Grady 1997:180; McKee and McDaniel 2001).

While the filler-gap hypothesis might be relevant to the processing load of relative clauses in English, it does not present a universal processing strategy. As pointed out by Diessel and Tomasello (2004), in languages like German, in which the relativized syntactic role is indicated by the case feature of a fronted relative pronoun, the processor receives all the information necessary to recognize the relativized syntactic role at the beginning of the relative clause; nevertheless German-speaking children have the same difficulties in interpreting the various types of relative clauses as do English-speaking children. Since the German data cannot be explained in terms of the filler-gap hypothesis, one might wonder whether the English data really reflect the varying distance between filler and gap, or whether children's difficulties in interpreting the various relative clauses arise from a different source. Diessel and Tomasello argue that children's comprehension of relative clauses is determined by multiple factors. While the varying distance between filler and gap might play a (minor) role in English, there are other factors such as the similarity between the various types of relative clauses and simple sentences that are much more important.

6.1.3   The NVN-schema hypothesis

The NVN-schema hypothesis was first proposed by Bever (1970a). The hypothesis asserts that English-speaking children acquire a canonical sentence schema based on a prototypical transitive clause. It consists of a noun denoting an actor, a verb describing a transitive activity, and another noun denoting an undergoer. The NVN-schema can be seen as an early grammatical construction that combines a specific form, i.e. a specific order of grammaticalized categories (i.e. NP V NP), with a specific meaning: the initial NP is interpreted as the actor of

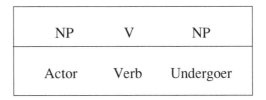

Fig. 6.1 *The NVN-schema.*

the activity expressed by the verb, which affects the second NP functioning as the patient or undergoer (cf. Townsend and Bever 2001). Figure 6.1. shows the form–function correspondences in the NVN-schema.

According to Bever, children apply the NVN-schema not only to simple transitive clauses but also to many other constructions that involve a noun–verb–noun sequence. For instance, children under the age of 5;0 tend to interpret passive sentences as active sentences based on the NVN-schema if the passive sentence is semantically reversible, i.e. if, on semantic grounds, the first NP can be interpreted as the actor of the activity described by the (passive) verb, and if the second NP (i.e. the NP that is embedded in the *by*-phrase) denotes a possible undergoer (cf. Bever 1970a; de Villiers and de Villiers 1973). It seems that word order (i.e. NP-V-NP) provides a much stronger cue for young English-speaking children than the grammatical morphemes that mark a passive construction (i.e. NP *be* V-*ed by* NP) (cf. Slobin and Bever 1982).

Like passive sentences, sentences including relative clauses can often be interpreted based on the NVN-schema. In a comprehension experiment, Bever (1970a) showed that 2- to 5-year-old children have little difficulties in comprehending relative clauses in cleft constructions if the relative clause includes a subject gap (as in example (12a)). However, if the relative clause includes an object gap (as in example (12b)), children perform randomly.

(12)   a. It was the dog that __ bit the cat.
        b. It was the cat that the dog bit __.

Bever argued that this result can be explained in terms of the NVN-schema. Since relative clauses including a subject gap involve a noun–verb–noun sequence (cf. *it was* N *that* V N), children have little difficulty in understanding this structure using the canonical sentence strategy, whereas relative clauses including an object gap are difficult to interpret because they involve a sequence of nouns and verbs that does not match the NVN-schema (cf. *it was* N *that* N V) (see Diessel and Tomasello 2004 for a detailed discussion of this proposal). A later study by de Villiers, Tager-Flusberg, Hakuta, and Cohen (1979) showed

Table 6.1 *Mean number of correct responses (out of three)* (Sheldon 1974: 276)

Age group	SS-relatives	SO-relatives	OS-relatives	OO-relatives
3;8–4;3	1.0	.18	.54	1.36
4;6–4;11	1.45	.73	.91	1.64
5;0–5;5	2.27	.64	1.17	1.55
Mean	1.58	.52	.88	1.52

that the NVN-schema might also explain children's interpretations of more complex relative constructions in which the relative clause modifies an element of a full-fledged matrix clause. Moreover, Hakuta (1981) argued that, parallel to English-speaking children, Japanese-speaking children employ an NNV-schema in their interpretation of relative clauses, based on the dominant SOV order of Japanese (see also Clancy et al. 1986).

6.1.4   The parallel-function hypothesis

The parallel-function hypothesis states that children find relative constructions in which head and gap have the same syntactic roles (i.e. SS- and OO-relatives) easier to interpret than relative constructions in which the roles are different (i.e. SO- and OS-relatives). In order to test this hypothesis, Sheldon (1974) designed a comprehension experiment in which 3- to 4-year-old children had to act out the meanings of SS-, SO-, OS-, and OO-relatives. Table 6.1 summarizes the main results of this study.

As predicted by the parallel-function hypothesis, children made fewer mistakes with relative constructions in which head and gap serve the same syntactic roles than with relative constructions in which the roles of head and gap are different: across all age groups, children's answers to SS- and OO-relatives included a significantly higher proportion of correct responses (mean scores of 1.58 and 1.52) than their answers to SO- and OS-relatives (mean scores of .64 and .88).

If we look at the developments shown in table 6.1, we find that there is much less improvement in OS- and OO-relatives than in SS- and SO-relatives. Analysing children's errors in the act-out task, Sheldon found that OS- and OO-relatives were often interpreted as if they were attached to the matrix clause subject. For instance, if the children were asked to act out a sentences such as *The dog bumps into the horse that the giraffe jumps over*, the response frequently

Table 6.2 *Children's responses to SS-relatives* (Tavakolian 1977: 46)

	12–13 correct	12–23	12–32	21–23	Other
3;0–3;6	18	2	0	1	3
4;0–4;6	16	5	0	1	2
5;0–5;6	22	0	2	0	0
Totals	56 (78%)	7 (10%)	2 (3%)	2 (3%)	5 (7%)

Table 6.3 *Children's responses to OS-relatives* (Tavakolian 1977: 50)

	12–13	12–23 correct	12–32	21–23	12–31	Other
3;0–3;6	17	1	2	1	1	2
4;0–4;6	15	4	1	0	3	1
5;0–5;6	13	9	0	1	1	0
Totals	45 (63%)	14 (19%)	3 (4%)	2 (3%)	5 (7%)	3 (4%)

involved the giraffe jumping over the dog rather than the horse; that is children interpreted the sentence as if it meant *the dog that the giraffe jumps over bumps into the horse*. Based on this finding, Sheldon argued that in addition to the parallel-function strategy, some children employ an 'extraposition rule' treating the relative clauses in OS- and OO-relatives as if they were extraposed from the position after the matrix clause subject to the end of the sentence.

6.1.5   The conjoined-clause hypothesis

Finally, the conjoined-clause hypothesis states that children interpret sentences including relative clauses as conjoined clauses (i.e. co-ordinate sentences). Using the same experimental design as Sheldon (1974), Tavakolian (1977) noticed an interesting pattern in children's performance on SS- and OS-relatives (see also Tavakolian 1981a). Table 6.2 and table 6.3 show how the children of Tavakolian's study responded. The numbers in the top row refer to the NPs of the test sentences in linear order: '1' is the first NP, '2' the second, and '3' the third (e.g. '*The sheep* [1] that knocks down *the rabbit* [2] stands on *the lion* [3]'). The number pairs indicate the act-out responses. For instance, a '12–13' response means that the child acted out two actions, one in which the first NP acts on the second ('12'), and one in which the first NP acts on the third ('13').

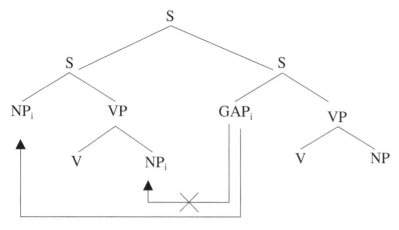

Fig. 6.2 *The conjoined clause analysis (Tavakolian 1977:8).*

As in Sheldon's study, the children of Tavakolian's study performed very well on SS-relatives, while they seemed to have great difficulties in interpreting OS-relatives: 78 per cent of the SS-relatives were acted out correctly, but only 19 per cent of the OS-relatives generated the correct response. However, if we look at the figures in table 6.2 and table 6.3 more closely, we find that the '12–13' response was by far the most frequent response pattern to both SS-relatives (where it yielded the correct response) and OS-relatives (where it yielded a false response). This suggests, according to Tavakolian, that these two structures are interpreted according to the same rules. Specifically, Tavakolian maintained that there are two rules in early child grammar that together explain the act-out responses: first, complex sentences that children cannot successfully process are interpreted as conjoined clauses (i.e. co-ordinate sentences); second, any missing noun phrase is treated as the subject of the second clause and interpreted as being coreferential with the subject of the first clause. This set of rules constitutes the core of the conjoined-clause analysis (see Tavakolian 1977:v).

Note that this analysis is based on the assumption that children ignore relative pronouns, complementizers, and other function words that may occur in between the verbs and noun phrases (cf. the NVN-schema hypothesis). Every string of the type 'NP . . . V . . . NP . . . V . . . NP' (where '. . .' indicates intervening function words) is assigned the structure in figure 6.2.

According to this analysis, children combine the string of NPs and Vs to simple nonembedded clauses, conjoin the two resulting clauses to a co-ordinate construction, and interpret the missing subject of the second clause as being coreferential with the subject of the first clause (cf. Sheldon's 'extraposition rule'). Object control is not an option for the child at this early stage of the development. This explains why the '12–13' response was the dominant response pattern to both SS- and OS-relatives.

SO- and OO-relatives were interpreted differently. In fact, the percentage of '12–13' responses was relatively low for these two structures: they account for only 31 per cent and 19 per cent, respectively. However, Tavakolian argued that the low percentage of '12–13' responses to SO- and OO-relatives does not undermine the conjoined-clause analysis because word order is different in these two structures: while SS- and OS-relatives involve the same sequence of noun phrases and verbs as two co-ordinate clauses in which the subject of the second sentence has been omitted (i.e. 'NP ... V ... NP ... V ... NP'), SO-relatives involve the string 'NP ... NP ... V ... V ... NP' and OO-relatives have the form 'NP ... V ... NP ... NP ... V'. In other words, the word order of SS- and OS-relatives is more similar to the word order of conjoined clauses than the word order of SO- and OO-relatives, which explains, according to Tavakolian (1977:65–77), why the children responded differently to the two latter types of relative clauses (i.e. why the '12–13' reponse was less frequent).

The conjoined-clause analysis has been very influential in the literature on children's acquisition of multiple-clause structures (see Lebeaux 1990; O'Grady 1997:ch. 9). In the generative literature, Lebeaux (1990) reinterpreted Tavakolian's analysis in the Principles and Parameters framework. In his account, the child is born with a parameter providing a choice between two types of relative clauses: 'adjoined relatives' that are attached to a noun phrase in the matrix clause; and 'co-relatives' that are attached to the IP-node of a neighbouring clause.[2] Adjoined relatives are subordinate constructions like the relative clauses in English; whereas co-relatives are syntactically nonembedded co-ordinate clauses, which occur, for instance, in Hindi. At the initial stage, the parameter is set to the value [+co-relative], which may be reset to the value [−co-relative] (i.e. adjoined relative) if the child encounters embedded relative clauses in the ambient language (cf. Lebeaux 1990:48–55).

While the interpretation strategies proposed by Sheldon, Tavakolian, and others may explain how children deal with relative constructions that they cannot successfully process, they do not really explain the development of relative clauses. In particular, they do not address the following questions: what are the first relative constructions that children learn? Are these constructions related

---

2. IP stands for 'inflection phrase', which, in the Principles and Parameters framework, corresponds to a simple clause.

to structures that children already master? And how does the development proceed? In this chapter I suggest answers to these and other questions based on children's spontaneous use of relative clauses. Before presenting the analysis, I briefly discuss the structure of relative clauses in adult English.

6.2   Relative clauses in adult grammar

Relative clauses are subordinate clauses that modify a referential expression in the matrix clause. The modified element is called the *head* (or *filler*) of the relative clause. The head can serve any syntactic role. For instance, it can be the subject (cf. example (13)), the object (cf. example (14)), or an oblique (cf. example (15)).

(13)   The man I met at the conference comes from India.
(14)   He saw the girl who works at the store.
(15)   We went to the restaurant that Mary recommended.

The head is coreferential with the *gap* (i.e. the missing element) inside the relative clause. Like the head, the gap can serve any syntactic role: it can be subject (cf. example (16)), the direct object (cf. example (17)), the indirect object (cf. example (18)), an oblique element (cf. example (19)), or a genitive attribute (cf. example (20)). The syntactic roles of head and gap can be freely combined yielding a wide variety of relative clause constructions (cf. below).

(16)   The man who slept.
(17)   The man I met.
(18)   The man I gave the picture to.
(19)   The man I talked to.
(20)   The man whose dog chased the cat.

On semantic grounds, relative clauses are commonly divided into restrictive and nonrestrictive relative clauses. Restrictive relative clauses function to identify the referent denoted by the head noun, whereas nonrestrictive relative clauses provide additional information about a nominal element in the matrix clause. Consider the examples in (21) and (22):

(21)   The cat was chasing the dog that had just eaten a bone.
(22)   The cat was chasing the dog, which had just eaten a bone.

Example (21) presents a restrictive relative clause that helps the hearer to identify the referent of the head noun: it was the dog that had just eaten the bone (rather than any other dog) that the cat was chasing. The nonrestrictive relative

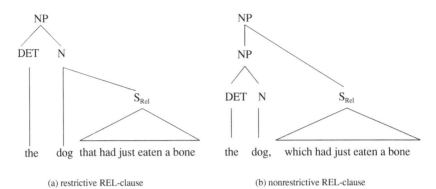

(a) restrictive REL-clause   (b) nonrestrictive REL-clause

Fig. 6.3 *External syntactic structures of restrictive and nonrestrictive relative clauses. Adopted from Lambrecht (1988).*

clause in (22), on the other hand, adds information to the nominal head without restricting the referential scope of the head noun: the dog should be identifiable for the hearer without the relative clause.

Restrictive and nonrestrictive relative clauses have some important structural properties in common: both include a relativized element that is coreferential with the head noun. However, there are also some structural differences distinguishing the two types of relative clauses: while restrictive relative clauses are intonationally bound to the matrix clause, nonrestrictive relative clauses are usually separated from the matrix clause by a break in the intonation structure. In writing, this is indicated by the occurrences of commas (cf. Quirk, Greenbaum, Leech, and Svartvik 1985:1258). Moreover, while restrictive relative clauses may include a complementizer (i.e. *that*), a relative pronoun (i.e. *who, whom, which, whose*), or just a gap in the argument structure, nonrestrictive relative clauses almost always include a relative pronoun (cf. Quirk et al. 1985:1257–1258). Finally, it has been argued that restrictive and nonrestrictive relative clauses are attached to different categories in the matrix clause. According to Langacker (1991:432), a restrictive relative clause restricts the meaning of a general type. Since types are denoted by nouns rather than by noun phrases, a restrictive relative clause is attached to a noun without the preceding determiner. A nonrestrictive relative clause, on the other hand, adds information to a referential expression. Since referential expressions are encoded by noun phrases that are grounded in the discourse by a determiner, nonrestrictive relative clauses are attached to a full NP rather than a bare noun. The tree diagrams in figure 6.3 show the different structures (the diagrams are adopted from Lambrecht 1988).

Table 6.4 *Finite and nonfinite relative clauses*

	Age range	Finite REL-clauses	Nonfinite REL-clauses
Adam	2;3–4;10	178	120
Sarah	2;3–5;1	32	36
Nina	1;11–3;4	62	71
Peter	1;9–3;2	25	44
Naomi	1;8–3;3	8	16
Total	1;9–5;1	305	287

While the syntactic and semantic features of relative clauses have been discussed extensively in the linguistic literature, their pragmatic features have been largely disregarded. Fox (1987) and Fox and Thompson (1990) are the only studies concerned with the pragmatics of relative clauses. These studies showed that relative clauses including an object gap and relative clauses including a subject gap serve different functions. Relative clauses including an object gap 'anchor' an utterance in the ongoing discourse or speech situation. For instance, in a sentence such as *Peter showed Mary the picture he made* the relative clause anchors the head noun by linking it to a previous discourse referent (i.e. *Peter*). Relative clauses including a subject gap are divided into two types: transitive and intransitive subject relatives. Transitive subject relatives (i.e. relative clauses including a subject gap and a transitive verb) serve a similar pragmatic function as object relatives: they anchor an utterance by relating it to elements of the previous discourse; but intransitive subject relatives serve a different function: 'they provide a characterization of the thing named by the head noun' (cf. *She is married to this guy who is really quiet*) (Fox 1987:859).

6.3   Data

Compared to complement clauses, relative clauses are infrequent in early child speech. Overall, the data comprise only 305 finite relative clauses. In addition, there are 287 nonfinite relative clauses, 95 participles, and 192 infinitives. This study concentrates on the development of finite relative clauses, considering infinitival and participial relatives only briefly at the end of the chapter. Table 6.4 provides an overview of the data.

Since Naomi's data are too sparse to observe any developmental changes, I excluded her relative clauses from the analysis. Without Naomi's data, there

Table 6.5 *Classification of relative constructions*

Head of REL-clause	Gap of REL-clause
SUBJ = subject	subj = subject
OBJ = object	obj = direct object
OBL = oblique	obl = oblique
PN = predicate nominal	io = indirect object
N = isolated noun (phrase)	gen = genitive

are 297 finite relative clauses in the corpus. Note that I considered only relative clauses that include an identifiable gap and modify an overt head noun. Utterances that one might analyse as relative constructions on purely semantic grounds were disregarded. Also disregarded were locational relative clauses marked by the interrogative *where* (e.g. *Sit on my place where I used to sit*; Sarah 4;6).

All relative constructions were coded for two features: (i) the syntactic role of the head noun, and (ii) the syntactic role of the gap. In contrast to previous studies, I did not distinguish only SS-, SO-, OS-, and OO-relatives but also all other relative constructions that occur in the data. Table 6.5 shows the coding scheme that was used to classify children's relative constructions.

As can be seen in this table, the head of the relative clause can be the subject, the object, an oblique, a predicate nominal, or an isolated noun (phrase). The syntactic role of the head noun is indicated in upper case. Like the head, the gap is divided into five types: subject, direct object, oblique, indirect object, and genitive. The syntactic role of the gap is indicated in lower case. Combing the various syntactic roles of head and gap yields a total of 25 distinct relative constructions. An example of each construction type is given in (23)–(47):

(23)	The person <u>who puts dem on</u> . . . has to. [Adam 3;11]	SUBJ – subj
(24)	The first thing <u>we have to do</u> (is to) put dis in. [Adam 3;11]	SUBJ – obj
(25)	The apartment <u>he lives in</u> is very loud. [not attested]	SUBJ – obl
(26)	The boy <u>he gave the ball to</u> is his friend. [not attested]	SUBJ – io
(27)	The girl <u>whose cat sits on the floor</u> is sleeping. [not attested]	SUBJ – gen
(28)	I want to see some ducks <u>that do that too</u>. [Nina 3;2]	OBJ – subj
(29)	I gon draw everything <u>I like</u>. [Adam 3;5]	OBJ – obj
(30)	You left this toy <u>I am playing with</u>. [Peter 3;1]	OBJ – obl
(31)	I know the guy <u>who she borrowed the book from</u>. [not attested]	OBJ – io
(32)	I met the woman <u>whose daughter lives next door</u>. [not attested]	OBJ – gen
(33)	I wanna go to the zoo <u>that has those animals</u>. [Nina 3;2]	OBL – subj
(34)	Change it to the very one <u>you love best</u>. [Adam 4;4]	OBL – obj

(35)	What happened to the thing <u>that I went to</u>? [Adam 4;3]	OBL – obl
(36)	I spoke to the officer <u>who Sally sent the letter to</u>. [not attested]	OBL – io
(37)	She talked to the man <u>whose dog scared the child</u>. [not attested]	OBL – gen
(38)	Here's a tiger <u>that's gonna scare him</u>. [Nina 3;1]	PN – subj
(39)	These are my duties <u>I have to do</u>. [Sarah 4;10]	PN – obj
(40)	It's the one <u>you went to last night</u>. [Peter 2;10]	PN – obl
(41)	This is the girl <u>I gave the key to</u>. [not attested]	PN – io
(42)	There is the boy <u>whose dog was barking</u>. [not attested]	PN – gen
(43)	People <u>dat can jump in dere</u>. [Adam 4;0]	N – subj
(44)	A meal <u>dat you eat</u>. [Adam 4;1]	N – obj
(45)	Those little things <u>that you play with</u>. [Adam 4;10]	N – obl
(46)	The girl <u>who I lent the bike to</u>. [not attested]	N – io
(47)	The woman <u>whose car broke</u>. [not attested]	N – gen

6.4   *Analysis*

Grammatical constructions have internal and external syntactic features. The internal features concern the structure and organization of elements that occur inside a construction, while the external features concern the syntactic properties of a construction in a larger syntactic context (cf. Fillmore and Kay 1993). In what follows I first describe the external syntax of children's early relative clauses and then consider their internal syntactic features.

6.4.1   *External syntax*

The vast majority of the children's early relative constructions contain a single proposition like simple sentences. They include a relative clause that is either attached to the predicate nominal of a copular clause or, less frequently, to an isolated head noun. Figure 6.4 shows the mean proportions of the various relative constructions in the data (cf. table 6a in the appendix).

As can be seen in this figure, almost half of the children's relative clauses are PN-relatives, i.e. they are attached to the predicate nominal of a copular clause. Most of these constructions include a declarative copular clause in which a demonstrative or third person pronoun functions as subject (cf. examples (48)–(50)), but there are also some copular questions (cf. example (51)).

(48)	This is the sugar <u>that goes in there</u>.	[Nina 3;0]
(49)	Here's a tiger <u>that's gonna scare him</u>.	[Nina 3;1]
(50)	It's something <u>that you eat</u>.	[Adam 4;0]
(51)	What is that <u>he has around his back</u>?	[Adam 3;8]

Apart from PN-relatives, N-relatives and OBJ-relatives are quite common: they account for an average of 23.8 and 21.5 per cent of all relative constructions,

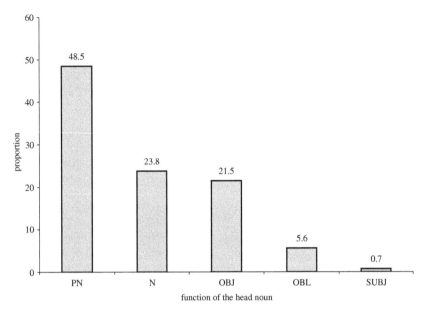

Fig. 6.4 *Mean proportions of PN-, N-, OBJ-, OBL-, and SUBJ-relatives (total).*

respectively. OBL-relatives are much less frequent; they account for an average of only 5.6 per cent of the data. Finally, SUBJ-relatives are very rare: a mean proportion of only .7 per cent of all relative constructions are SUBJ-relatives.

SUBJ-, OBJ-, and OBL-relatives occur in sentences containing two propositions expressed in two full-fledged clauses, but PN- and N-relatives include only a single proposition: since N-relatives are attached to an isolated noun (phrase), they obviouly contain only a single proposition, but PN-relatives consist of two clauses, a relative clause and a copular clause, and thus one might hypothesize that they express a relationship between two propositions. However, following Lambrecht (1988), I assume that the copular clauses of PN-relatives are 'propositionally empty' (Lambrecht 1988:326). They do not denote an independent state of affairs; rather, they function to establish a referent in focus position making it available for the predication expressed in the relative clause. The whole sentence contains a single proposition and thus can be paraphrased by a single clause (cf. examples (52)–(55))

(52)   This is the sugar <u>that goes in there.</u>   >The sugar goes in there.
(53)   Here's a tiger <u>that's gonna scare him.</u>>The tiger is gonna scare him.
(54)   It's something <u>that you eat.</u>   >You eat something.
(55)   What is that <u>he has around his back?</u> >What does he have around his back?

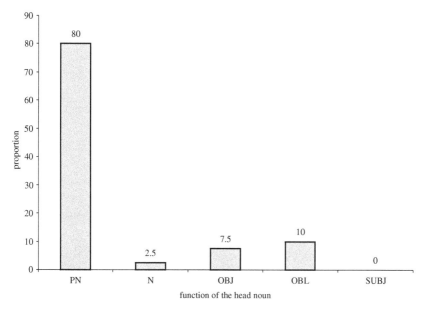

Fig. 6.5 *Mean proportions of the first 10 PN-, N-, OBJ-, OBL-, and SUBJ-relatives.*

Note that the propositional content of PN- and N-relatives is not always prag-matically presupposed (or backgrounded) as in prototypical subordinate clauses (cf. chapter 3.2). In fact, in most examples the relative clause asserts new and unfamiliar information concerning the referent established in the copular clause (cf. Lambrecht 1988:325; see also Fox and Thompson 1990:306). The informa-tion structure of sentences including PN- and N-relatives is thus very different from the information structure that one usually finds in sentences including subordinate clauses. Very often, it is similar to the information structure of simple sentences: like simple sentences, PN- and N-relatives express new and unfamiliar information in the position after the initial noun.

If we consider the children's use of PN-relatives more closely, we find that they are especially frequent in the early data. Figure 6.5 shows the mean pro-portions of the various relative clauses among the children's first ten relative constructions that occur in the transcripts of each child (cf. table 6b in the appendix).

As can be seen in this figure, an average of 80 per cent of the first ten relative clauses produced by each child is attached to the predicate nominal of a copular clause. Another 2.5 per cent modify an isolated head noun; OBJ-relatives account for 7.5 per cent of the data, OBL-relatives occur in 10 per cent of the children's early relative constructions, and SUBJ-relatives are entirely absent. If we look at the OBL-relatives more closely, we find that all of them follow an imperative matrix clause in which *look* functions as the main verb (cf. examples (56)–(58)).

(56)   Look at all the chairs that Peter's got.   [Peter 2;5]
(57)   Look at dat train . . . Ursula bought.   [Adam 2;10]
(58)   Look at dat big truck (that is) going some place.   [Adam 3;0]

The matrix clauses in (56)–(58) serve the same function as presentational copular clauses: *look* is not a perception verb in these examples; rather, it functions as an attention getter focusing the hearer on the entity expressed by the following noun phrase (similar to *look* in sentences including early complement clauses; cf. chapter 5). In other words, the imperative matrix clauses serve the same function as the copular clauses of PN-relatives. If we include these sentences in the group of PN-relatives, an average of 90 per cent of the earliest relative clauses occur in constructions containing only a single proposition.

Interestingly, in some of these constructions the relative clause follows the copular clause without a relativizer, which is standard in adult speech (if the subject is relativized). Consider the following examples, which are among the earliest relative clauses in the corpus.

(59)   That's doggy turn around.   [Nina 1;11]
(60)   This is my doggy cries.   [Nina 2;0]
(61)   That's a turtle swim.   [Nina 2;2]
(62)   Who's that fit on that train.   [Nina 2;3]
(63)   Here's a mouse go sleep.   [Nina 2;3]
(64)   That is a train go go . . . .   [Nina 2;3]
(65)   That's the roof go on that home.   [Nina 2;4]
(66)   That's the rabbit fall off.   [Nina 2;4]
(67)   What's this go in there?   [Peter 2;0]
(68)   There's a tape go around right there.   [Peter 2;0]
(69)   It's the wheels go.   [Peter 2;3]
(70)   This is the fire engine go 'whoo whoo'. [Peter 2;6]
(71)   There's somebody's gonna crash on him.   [Peter 2;9]
(72)   What is dis came out?   [Adam 3;1]
(73)   There's the green grass grow all around . . . around . . . .   [Sarah 3;6]
(74)   And that's the birdie scream.   [Sarah 4;3]

The sentences in (59)–(74) contain a copular clause and a verb phrase that one might analyse as a relative clause in which the relativizer has been omitted. Although these sentences are ungrammatical from the perspective of standard English, they *do* occur in certain nonstandard varieties of adult speech. The following attested examples are adopted from Lambrecht (1988:319).

(75)   There was a ball of fire <u>shot up through the seats in front of me</u>.
(76)   There's something <u>keeps upsetting him</u>.
(77)   There's a lot of people <u>don't know that</u>.

The sentences in (75)–(77) were produced in natural conversations by adult native speakers of English. They have the same structure as some of the early relative constructions that occur in the transcripts of the four children. Lambrecht, who analyses these sentences from a construction grammar perspective, argues that they are not ungrammatical or pragmatically ill-formed; rather, he analyses them as instances of a specific grammatical construction, which he calls the 'presentational amalgam construction' (Lambrecht 1988:335; see also Lakoff 1974). Although the occurrence of the amalgam construction is restricted to certain nonstandard varieties of adult speech, it is so widely attested that its existence cannot be disputed (cf. Quirk et al. 1985:1250; 424; Davidse 2000: 1106). Lambrecht characterizes the presentational amalgam construction as a syntactic blend in which the predicate nominal of the copular clause also serves as the syntactic subject of the clause final VP, which he considers a truncated relative clause. Based on this analysis, he classifies the amalgam construction as a subtype of the presentational relative construction in which the relative clause is clearly separated from the matrix clause.

The same analysis applies to the sentences in (59)–(74): they are syntactic amalgams that can be seen as extensions of the presentational relative construction. Since the occurrence of the syntactic amalgam is especially frequent among the earliest relative clauses (only a few later examples occur), it is reasonable to assume that the amalgam construction serves as a precursor to the presentational relative construction: three of the four children, Peter, Nina, and Sarah, used the amalgam construction several months before they used other relative clauses, and Adam began to use the amalgam construction together with presentational relatives including a relativizer.

As the children grow older, the relative constructions become increasingly more complex and diverse. While almost all of the earliest relative clauses occur in presentational constructions including a short and formulaic copular clause, the relatives of older children are frequently attached to a noun (or noun phrase) in an ordinary matrix clause. Figure 6.6 shows the development (cf. table 6c in the appendix).

As can be seen in this figure, the vast majority of the children's early relative constructions are PN-relatives, containing a single proposition. Relative constructions including two propositions are initially infrequent: up to the age of 3;0 they account for an average of only 5.2 per cent of the data. As the children grow older, the proportions change: relative constructions containing

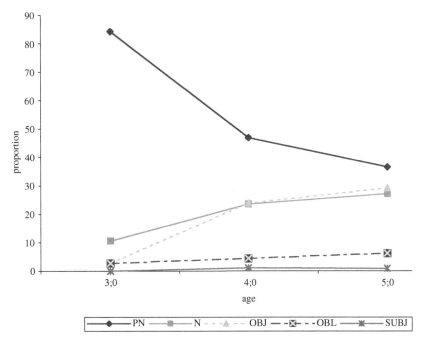

Fig. 6.6 *The development of PN-, N-, OBJ-, OBL-, and SUBJ-relatives.*

two propositions become increasingly more frequent; at age 4- to 5-years they account for an average of 36.5 per cent of the data.

The developmental changes in the matrix clause are accompanied by some interesting changes inside the relative clause; these changes will be discussed in the next section.

6.4.2   Internal syntax

The vast majority of the children's relative clauses are either marked by a *that*-relativizer or they include just a gap in the argument structure. Relative clauses that are marked by a relative pronoun are rare in early child speech. There are only 6 relative clauses in the entire corpus that include the relative pronoun *who*. All 6 examples occur in Adam's transcripts (cf. table 6.6).

Figure 6.7 shows the mean proportions of the various syntactic roles that are relativized in the children's relative clauses (cf. table 6d in the appendix):

As can be seen in this figure, the majority of the children's relative clauses are subj-relatives: an average of 57.3 per cent of the children's relative clauses include a subject gap, an average of 37 per cent include an object gap, and an average of 5.7 per cent include an oblique gap; io- and gen-relatives do not occur

Table 6.6 *That-, who-, and zero-relativizers*

	that	*who*	zero	Total
Adam	92	6	80	178
Sarah	18	–	14	32
Nina	51	–	11	62
Peter	4	–	21	25
	165	6	126	297

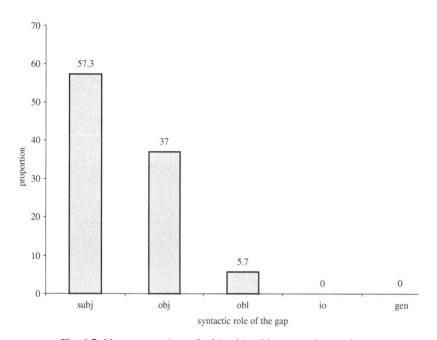

Fig. 6.7 *Mean proportions of subj-, obj-, obl-, io-, and gen-relatives.*

in the data. Note that the oblique relatives always include a stranded preposition (e.g. *those little things that you play **with***; Adam 4;10); 'pied-piping' (i.e. the combined fronting of the preposition and relativizer; e.g. *those little things **with** **which** you play*) does not occur in the data.

Among the earliest relative clauses, the proportion of subj-relatives is even higher than in the entire database: a mean proportion of 72.5 per cent of the first 10 relative clauses are subj-relatives; many of them occur in syntactic amalgams (see above). The other 27.5 per cent are obj-relatives. Obl-relatives

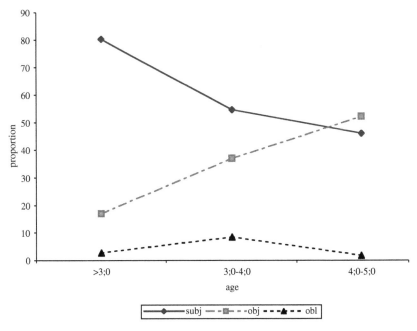

Fig. 6.8 *The development of subj-, obj-, and obl-relatives.*

are not among earliest relative clauses (cf. table 6e in the appendix). Figure 6.8 shows the changing proportions of the children's subj-, obj-, and obl-relatives between the ages of 3;0 and 5;0 (cf. table 6f in the appendix).

As can be seen from this figure, up to the age of 3;0 the children use primarily subj-relatives, while obj-relatives and especially obl-relatives are infrequent. As the children grow older, the proportions change: the relative frequency of subj-relatives decreases, while the proportions of obj-relatives increases. In fact, at age 4;0 to 5;0, obj-relatives are more common than subj-relatives. Obl-relatives are infrequent throughout the entire time period of the study.

If we look at the subj-relatives more closely, we find that most of them include an intransitive verb. As can be seen in table 6.7, a mean proportion of 72.7 per cent of the children's subj-relatives include an intransitive verb and an average of only 27.3 per cent include a transitive verb. In obj-relatives, the verb of the relative clause is transitive by definition: an object gap can occur only if the verb of the relative clause takes both a subject and direct object. However, even if we include obj-relatives, the vast majority of the children's relative clauses contain an intransitive verb.

Table 6.7 *Transitive and intransitive subj-relatives*

	Peter	Nina	Sarah	Adam	Total	Mean
Total						
intransitive	14	26	13	50	103	72.7
transitive	4	9	7	18	38	27.3
First 10						
intransitive	9	10	9	9	37	92.5
transitive	1	0	1	1	3	7.5

Transitive relative clauses are especially infrequent among the earliest relative constructions. The proportion of transitive relative clauses increases only gradually with age. The increase is primarily due to the growing proportion of obj-relatives, but the proportion of transitive subj-relatives increases too. As can be seen in table 6.7, while an average of 27.3 per cent of *all* subj-relatives include a transitive verb, only 7.5 per cent of the *earliest* (i.e. the first 10) subj-relatives are transitive. In other words, the earliest subj-relatives include a much larger proportion of transitive verbs than the subj-relatives in the entire corpus. This suggests that the proportion of transitive subj-relatives increases during language acquisition.

6.4.3 Infinitival and participial relative constructions
Having described the development of finite relative constructions, let us consider the children's use of infinitival and participial relative clauses. Participial relative clauses occur in the same type of construction as finite relative clauses. The vast majority of children's early participial relatives are attached to the predicate nominal of a presentational copular clause. Some typical examples are given in (78)–(81).

(78)	That's the horse <u>sleeping in a cradle, their bed</u>.	[Peter 2;8]
(79)	Who is that <u>standing on the bed</u>?	[Nina 3;3]
(80)	Here's the other cars <u>coming . . . in the car rally</u>.	[Adam 4;1]
(81)	Dere's was a kitty <u>walking by</u>.	[Sarah 4;3]

Note that all of the relative clauses in these examples include a present participle. Relative clauses including a past participle are relatively rare in early child speech; their occurrence is restricted to a few highly routinized forms (e.g. *a doggie named Skipper*).

Apart from the copular *be*, *look at* is quite frequent in the matrix clauses of participial relatives (cf. (82)–(83)).

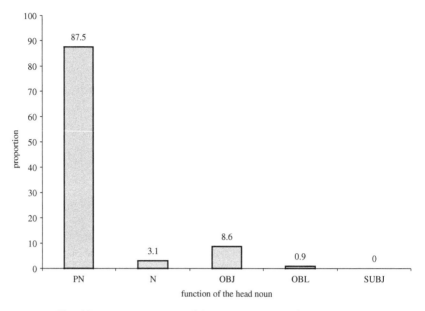

Fig. 6.9 *Mean proportions of the syntactic heads of participial relatives.*

(82)   Look at that girl <u>standing up</u>.   [Sarah 3;6]
(83)   Look at the doggy <u>standing on the shelf</u>.   [Nina 3;0]

The matrix clauses in (82) and (83) serve the same function as presentational copular clauses. They establish a referent in focus position, making it available for the predication expressed in the relative clause. If we include these constructions in the group of PN-relatives, there are only a few participial relative clauses that do not occur in presentational constructions. Figure 6.9 shows the mean proportions of the various participial relative clauses in the data (cf. table 6g in the appendix).

As can be seen in this figure, an average of 87.5 per cent of all participial relatives modify the predicate nominal of a copular clause. Apart from the large number of PN-relatives, there are a few N-, OBJ-, and OBL-relatives; SUBJ-relatives do not occur.

Note that in participial relative clauses the subject is the only element that can be gapped or relativized; i.e. all participial relative clauses are subj-relatives; there is no variation in the internal syntax of participial relative clauses in English.

The infinitival relatives are different from both finite and participial relative clauses. Most of them define the meaning of a pronominal or generic head noun. Some typical examples are given in (84)–(92).

(84)	I want *something* to drink.	[Nina 2;10]
(85)	I want *somewhere* to sit.	[Adam 4;0]
(86)	He wants *somebody* to take him.	[Peter 3;19]
(87)	He doesn't like *nothing* to eat.	[Nina 2;9]
(88)	Here's *another one* for you to keep.	[Nina 3;3]
(89)	She don't get *no one* to play with.	[Sarah 4;10]
(90)	I don't have no *place* to put dis.	[Adam 4;3]
(91)	I'm the right *person* to do that.	[Peter 3;1]
(92)	That's a wonder *thing* to play with.	[Peter 2;4]

The infinitival relative clauses in (84)–(89) are attached to an (indefinite) pronoun while those in (90)–(92) modify a generic head noun. In both constructions, the head of the relative clause is semantically empty or underspecified. It functions to provide an anchor for the infinitive. The whole construction serves to define a nominal, similar to a headless relative clause. Relative clauses of this type do not really denote an independent situation; rather, they function as quasi-nominal expressions denoting an object, person, or place. Thus, like other early complex sentences, sentences including infinitival relative clauses contain only a single proposition in which a reduced relative clause serves the same function as a nominal expression.

6.5   Discussion

6.5.1   Summary

This chapter has shown that the development of sentences including relative clauses originates from simple lexically specific constructions. The earliest relative clauses modify the predicate nominal of a copular clause. They usually include an intransitive verb and a relativized subject. The whole construction comprises four elements: a pronominal subject (i.e. *that, this, there, here, it*); the copular *be*; and two open slots for the predicate nominal and the relative clause (cf. (93)).

(93)   PRO be [—$_{NP}$ —$_{REL}$] $_{NP}$

Two types of this construction can be distinguished: (i) PN-relatives in which the relative clause is syntactically separated from the matrix clause; and (ii) PN-amalgams in which the relative clause is conflated with the matrix clause. Since the occurrence of the amalgam construction is especially frequent among the earliest relative clauses, it can be seen as a precursor of regular PN-relatives. Both relative constructions designate a single situation; however, since the amalgam construction does not include two separate full clauses, it is syntactically more tightly organized than are regular PN-relatives.

As children grow older, they begin to use more complex relative constructions in which a relative clause including an intransitive *or* transitive verb is attached to a noun of a full-fledged matrix clause. Such relative constructions contain two propositions expressed in two clauses. The whole development can be seen as a process of clause expansion: starting from the amalgam construction, which expresses a single proposition in a structure that is not truly biclausal, children gradually learn the use of complex relative constructions in which two propositions are expressed in two separate full clauses.

6.5.2   *Comprehension vs. production*

The vast majority of the children's relative clauses occur in right-branching structures; centre-embedded relative clauses are rare in early child speech. Overall, there are only five centre-embedded relative clauses in the entire data; all five examples occur in Adam's transcripts. Note that the infrequent use of centre-embedded relative clauses does not necessarily support the non-interruption hypothesis (cf. section 6.2). As pointed out by Limber (1976), centre-embedded relative clauses might be rare in spontaneous child speech because of pragmatic reasons: centre-embedded relative clauses modify the matrix clause subject, which is usually the topic of the clause. Since the topic is familiar to the interlocutors it is often expressed by a (third person) pronoun, which does not occur with a relative clause. Thus, while it is conceivable that centre-embedded relative clauses cause comprehension problems because they interrupt the matrix clause, the infrequent occurrence of centre-embeddd relative clauses might have other, notably pragmatic, reasons.

In general, the observational data analysed in this chapter do not immediately bear on most of the issues raised in comprehension studies. Comprehension and production involve different linguistic capacities. In fact, most comprehension studies have argued that children's early comprehension of relative clauses is based on interpretation strategies such as the conjoined clause analysis or the NVN-schema analysis that are completely irrelevant to the production of relative clauses. While these strategies might explain how children deal with relative constructions they have not yet mastered, they say very little about the acquisition process.

Interestingly, although the children of most comprehension experiments were significantly older than the children of the current study, they had great difficulty in understanding relative clauses. Does that mean that production precedes comprehension? No, it doesn't, because children's early relative constructions are very different from those that have been used in most experiments. The test sentences children had to act out in comprehesion studies typically consisted of two transitive clauses (including three lexical NPs), as in the following example from Goodluck and Tavakolian (1982:3):

(94)   The lion kisses the duck that hits the pig.

The relative constructions of early child speech are much simpler: they consist of an intransitive relative clause that is attached to the predicate nominal of a copular clause or an isolated noun (phrase). More complex relative constructions emerge only later. The acquisition process proceeds in an incremental fashion: rather than learning some general rules that can immediately generate all kinds of relative clauses, children begin with some isolated relative constructions that are restricted in their form, meaning, and use. While these early relative constructions may look like relative clauses in adult language, they mark only the beginning of the developmental process whereby children acquire a network of interrelated relative constructions. The particular relative constructions that have been used in most experiments emerge very late in the acquisition process. This explains why children performed so poorly in most experiments. I suspect that if the experiments had involved relative constructions similar to the ones we have seen in this chapter, children's performance would have been much better (cf. Diessel and Tomasello 2004). In other words, children's comprehension of relative clauses does not lag behind production; rather, it seems that children had so much difficulty in most comprehension studies because they were often confronted with relative constructions that are very different from the ones of early child speech. If we recognize that the acquisition of relative clauses is a gradual process and that children do not immediately master the full range of relative constructions once the first relative clauses appear, the apparent discrepancy between comprehension and production disappears.

6.5.3   Discussion

Finally let us ask what motivates the described development. In particular, let us ask why PN-relatives are the earliest and most frequent relative constructions in the data. Is this a specific feature of English or is the early and frequent use of presentational relatives also characteristic of other languages?

   While I am not aware of any observational study that would bear on this issue, there has been one recent investigation by Jisa and Kern (1998) that analyses the use of different relative constructions produced by French-speaking children in a picture-book task (cf. Berman and Slobin 1994). Although the children examined by Jisa and Kern were older than the children of the current study (their youngest children were between 5;0 and 5;11), they also made extensive use of PN-relatives. It is thus conceivable that the development of relative clauses described here for English is also characteristic of the acquisition of relative clauses in other languages. In the remainder of this chapter I will consider five factors that might explain the early and frequent use of presentational relative constructions in English.

First, the earliest relative clauses are built on lexically specific constructions that are deeply entrenched at the time when children begin to use relative clauses. The matrix clauses of presentational relatives are copular clauses that consist of three components: (i) a pronominal subject, (ii) the copula *be*, and (iii) a predicate nominal, which is basically an open slot that can be filled by any nominal expression. Since presentational copular clauses emerge very early (cf. Braine 1976; Lieven, Pine, and Baldwin 1997), it can be argued that children's presentational relatives are formed by a very simple procedure, whereby a prefabricated copular clause (i.e. a clause of the type *That's __, There's __, What's __*) is combined with a second component, either a verb phrase, as in the amalgam construction, or a full relative clause, as in later examples.

Second, both parents and children use presentational relatives for specific communicative functions that are characteristic of parent–child speech: children tend to talk about elements in their environment; and adult speakers usually do the same when they talk to young children. Since presentational relatives are commonly used to focus the hearer's attention on elements in the surrounding situation, which are then further characterized in the relative clause, they are pragmatically very useful in parent–child speech.

Third, the propositional content of PN-relatives is usually asserted rather than pragmatically presupposed as in restrictive relative clauses. The information structure of the whole construction is thus very similar to the information structure of simple sentences, which should make it relatively easy for children to learn this type of relative clause. If the content of the relative clause were pragmatically presupposed, as in prototypical subordinate clauses, children probably would have more difficulties in learning these constructions because pragmatically presupposed information is often ignored by younger children (cf. Bever 1970b).

In addition to these three factors, the input frequency and the complexity of the emerging constructions seem to have an effect on the development. Like preschool children, adults make frequent use of PN-relatives in child-directed speech. Table 6.8 shows how frequently the various relative constructions occur in the mothers' data.

Table 6.8 *The mothers' relative clauses (external syntax)*

	PN	N	OBJ	OBL	SUBJ	Total
Adam's mother	73	20	55	2	2	152
Sarah's mother	66	35	38	4	2	145
Nina's mother	87	12	93	8	3	203
Peter's mother	11	5	5	2	0	23
Total	237	72	191	16	7	523
Mean	46.1	16.2	32.5	4.2	1.1	

The mothers used the same types of relative clauses as their children: almost half of their relative clauses are PN-relatives (mean proportion of 46.1 per cent); OBJ- and N-relatives are also quite common, but OBL-relatives and especially SUBJ-relatives are rare. The statistical analysis shows that the frequency of the various relative constructions in the children's data correlates very closely with the frequency of the corresponding relative clauses in their mothers' speech (Pearson: $r = .94$; $N = 5$; $p = .02$). This suggests that the ambient language plays an important role in the acquisition process.

Interestingly, there are no examples of the amalgam construction in the mothers' data. It is therefore unlikely that the children's common use of this construction is based on direct imitation of adult speech. Rather, it appears that children 'create' the amalgam construction in an attempt to match the syntactic structure of PN-relatives with their meaning: since PN-relatives contain a single proposition, children tend to merge the two clauses of this construction into a single syntactic unit. The emergence of the amalgam construction is thus semantically motivated; it seems that both children *and* adults 'invent' this construction independently of each other but for the same semantic reasons.

Moreover, while the mothers' relative clauses have the same external syntactic features as the relative clauses of their children, their internal syntactic features are different. Consider the numbers in table 6.9.

As can be seen in this table, an average of 57.9 per cent of the mothers' relative clauses includes an object gap and only an average of 34.3 per cent includes a subject gap. In the children's data the proportions are reversed: an average of 57.3 per cent of the children's relative clauses includes a subject gap and only an average of 37 per cent includes an object gap (cf. figure 6.7). In other words, although obj-relatives are the most frequent relatives in the mothers'

Table 6.9 *The mothers' relative clauses (internal syntax)*

	subj	obj	obl	io	gen	Total
Adam's mother	70	72	10	0	0	152
Sarah's mother	43	89	13	0	0	145
Nina's mother	63	125	15	0	0	203
Peter's mother	7	14	2	0	0	23
Total	183	300	40	0	0	523
Mean	34.3	57.9	7.9	0.0	0.0	

data, subj-relatives emerge before obj-relative clauses in the children's speech. How do we account for this finding?

I suggest that subj-relatives are dominant in early child speech because they are similar to simple sentences when they occur in presentational constructions. If a subj-relative clause is attached to the predicate nominal of a copular clause or to an isolated noun phrase, the composite structure involves the same sequence of nouns and verbs as simple sentences: the first referent of the construction is expressed by the head of the relative clause functioning as the actor or agent of the activity expressed by the verb, which might be followed by a second noun (phrase) denoting the undergoer. In other words, subj-relatives that are added to the predicate nominal of a copular clause or to an isolated noun phrase instantiate the NV(N)-schema of simple sentences (cf. Bever 1970a, de Villiers, Tager-Flusberg, Hakuta, and Cohen 1979; Slobin and Bever 1982; Townsend and Bever 2001). Obj-relatives do not instantiate the same schema: they express the undergoer before the actor and verb. Thus, one might hypothesize that children find subj-relatives easier than obj-relatives (if they are attached to a predicate nominal or an isolated noun phrase) because they involve the same sequence of actor, verb, and undergoer as simple sentences (cf. Bever 1970a).

Strong support for this hypothesis comes from an experimental study by Diessel and Tomasello (2004). Using presentational relative constructions similar to the ones that children produce in natural speech, they asked 4-year-old children to repeat various types of relative clauses. While the children had little difficulties in repeating subj-relatives, they made frequent mistakes with obj-, obl-, and io-relatives. Specifically, they often converted these relatives to subj-relatives by changing the word order from NNV (i.e. undergoer–actor–verb) to NVN (i.e. actor–verb–undergoer). This suggests that the NVN-schema has a significant effect on the acquisition of English relative clauses.

Finally, I suspect that the complexity of the emerging constructions plays an important role in the acquisition process. The earliest relative constructions children learn express a single proposition, as do simple sentences. Complex sentences including two or more propositions emerge only later. The late appearance of these constructions might be due to their complexity: in order to produce SUBJ-, OBJ-, and OBL-relatives the child must be able to hold two propositions in working memory while constructing the utterance.

Moreover, one might hypothesize that children's early relative clauses tend to be intransitive because transitive relative clauses are more complex. As Goodluck and Tavakolian (1982) and Hamburger and Crain (1982) have argued, children find intransitive relatives much easier than transitive relatives because transitive clauses include an extra argument. However, while the extra argument might increase the processing load, I suspect that the dominance of intransitive subj-relatives in early child speech is primarily motivated by pragmatic factors. As Fox and Thompson (1990) have shown, while transitive subj-relatives anchor the complex sentence in the ongoing discourse, intransitive subj-relatives function to characterize the head noun. Since 3-year-old children do not use complex discourse structures, they have little reason to employ transitive subj-relative clauses; however, characterizing a discourse referent appears to be a very common task, and thus one might hypothesize that children use intransitive relatives more frequently than transitive relatives because intransitive relatives are pragmatically more useful.

That complexity is an important factor in the acquisition of relative clauses has also been suggested in a connectionist study by Elman (1993). Using a simple recurrent network (cf. Elman 1990), Elman simulated the development of relative clauses in children. The simulation showed that the network was able to learn relative clauses only if training started with a limited viewing window that essentially excluded all complex sentences from processing, or, alternatively, if the network was initially only trained on simple sentences before complex sentences were included in the input data. Interestingly, the simulation failed when training started from the very beginning with an unlimited viewing window and the full data. Based on these results, Elman suggested that the development of complex sentences (and other complex syntactic structures) proceeds in an incremental fashion: before children are able to learn complex sentences they must have acquired simple nonembedded sentences.

To summarize, this chapter has shown that relative clauses emerge in presentational constructions in which an intransitive subj-relative is attached to the predicate nominal of a lexically specific copular clause. Five factors have been considered that seem to motivate the early appearance of PN-relatives and N-relatives: (i) the formulaic character of the matrix clause, (ii) the information structure of the sentence, (iii) the pragmatic function of presentational relatives, (iv) the ambient language, and (v) the complexity of the emerging constructions.

7 *Adverbial and co-ordinate clauses*

In traditional grammar, adverbial and co-ordinate clauses are categorically distinguished: adverbial clauses are classified as subordinate clauses and co-ordinate clauses are considered nonembedded sentences. For English, as well as for many other languages, this analysis is problematic, because there are no sufficient criteria to establish a clear-out division between adverbial and co-ordinate clauses. Rather, adverbial subordination and clausal co-ordination form a continuum of related constructions. In what follows, I refer to the continuum of adverbial and co-ordinate clauses as *conjoined clauses*.

Like complement and relative clauses, conjoined clauses evolve from simple nonembedded sentences, but the development takes a different pathway: while complement and relative clauses evolve via clause expansion, conjoined clauses develop through a process of clause integration. The development originates from two independent utterances that are pragmatically combined in the ongoing discourse. Starting from such discourse structures, children gradually learn the use of complex sentences in which two or more clauses are integrated in a specific grammatical unit.

7.1   Literature

The literature on the acquisition of conjoined clauses includes both observational and experimental studies (observational studies: Clark 1970, 1973; Clancy, Jacobson, and Silva 1976; Bates 1976; Hood, Lahey, Lifter, and Bloom 1978; Lust and Mervis 1980; Hood and Bloom 1979; Bloom, Lahey, Hood, Lifter, and Fliess 1980; Eisenberg 1980; Braunwald 1985; Reilly 1986; Silva 1991; Rothweiler 1993; Kyratzis and Ervin-Tripp 1999; experimental studies: Piaget 1948; Katz and Brent 1968; Clark and Clark 1968; Clark 1971; Ferreiro and Sinclair 1971; Amidon and Carey 1972; Johnson 1975; Corrigan 1975; Johansson and Sjöln 1975; Amidon 1976; Kuhn and Phelps 1976; Homzie and Gravitt 1977; French and Brown 1977; Coker 1978; Kavanaugh 1979; Emerson 1979, 1980; Townsend, Ottaviano, and Bever 1979; Townsend and

Ravelo 1980; Feagans 1980; Tibbits 1980; Johnson and Chapman 1980; Bebout, Segalowitz, and White 1980; Braine and Rumain 1981; Wing and Scholnick 1981; Carni and French 1984; Kail and Weissenborn 1984; Irwin and Pulver 1984; Peterson and McCabe 1985, 1987, 1988; Peterson 1986; French and Nelson 1985; French 1986, 1988). Interestingly, the two types of studies yielded very different results. While the experimental studies suggested that even 6-, 7-, and 8-year-old children do not fully comprehend certain semantic types of conjoined clauses, the observational studies found that children as young as 3 years make appropriate use of a wide variety of adverbial and co-ordinate clauses. The discrepancy between comprehension and production studies led to a debate over the advantages and disadvantages of different methods. Some researchers argued that the spontaneous use of conjoined clauses does not really indicate children's linguistic knowledge because children might produce adult-like conjoined clauses without having full grammatical competence (cf. Clark 1983:811). Other researchers argued that the results of experimental comprehension studies can be misleading because many experiments involve a 'cognitive overload' for younger children (cf. French and Nelson 1985:91). Specifically, these researchers claimed that children have difficulties in comprehension experiments because the test sentences often denote an arbitrary relationship between two novel situations, which might confuse the child for conceptual rather than linguistic reasons. In accordance with this hypothesis, a number of experimental studies have shown that children as young as 3 years are able to comprehend conjoined clauses if they denote relationships between familiar situations (cf. French and Brown 1977; Kavanaugh 1979; Peterson and McCabe 1985; Carni and French 1984; French and Nelson 1985; French 1986, 1988).

One of the issues that has been investigated in several observational studies is the developmental order in which the various conjoined clauses appear (cf. Clark 1970, 1973; Clancy, Jacobsen, and Silva 1976; Bloom, Lahey, Hood, Lifter, and Fliess 1980; Eisenberg 1980; Braunwald 1985). What all of these studies found is that children begin to combine simple sentences before they produce adverbial or co-ordinate clauses. Two simple sentences that are juxtaposed can express the same semantic relationships as conjoined clauses, but linguistically they are not combined to complex sentences: they do not include a conjunction or any other linguistic device that indicates the link between the semantically associated clauses. Complex sentences including an adverbial or co-ordinate conjunction emerge only later. This has been taken as evidence for the hypothesis that the child's cognitive development precedes the linguistic development of conjoined clauses: children seem to learn temporal, causal, and conditional relationships before they are able to indicate these relationships by temporal, causal, and conditional conjunctions (cf. Bloom et al. 1980; Eisenberg 1980).

The first conjunction that all researchers found in spontaneous child speech is *and,* followed by *because, so, but,* and *when.* Conditional *if*-clauses, co-ordinate *or*-clauses, and temporal clauses marked by *while, since, after,* and *before* tend to appear later. Other types of adverbial clauses such as *although*-clauses did not occur in any of the corpora that have been examined (cf. Clark 1970, 1973; Clancy, Jacobsen, and Silva 1976; Bloom, et al. 1980; Eisenberg 1980; Lust and Mervis 1980; McCabe, Evely, Abramovitch, Corter, and Pepler 1983; Braunwald 1985; Peterson and McCabe 1985).

One of the factors that seems to play an important role in the acquisition of conjoined clauses is the temporal or logical ordering of the events they describe. This was first suggested by Piaget (1948), who showed that children under 7 years have difficulty in interpreting the order of cause and effect in causal sentences. Specifically, he reported that children often name an effect rather than a cause or reason when asked to complete a sentence such as *He fell from his bicycle because . . .* [CHILD: *he broke his arm*]. Similar results were obtained in a number of more recent studies testing children's comprehension of causal sentences in various experiments (cf. Corrigan 1975; Emerson 1979, 1980; Bebout, Segalowitz, and White 1980; McCabe and Peterson 1985). What all of these studies found is that children tend to interpret a sentence such as 'X because Y' as if it meant 'X so that Y' (or 'X and then Y'). In other words, children invert the order of cause and effect in their interpretation of causal *because*-clauses.[1]

The same type of mistake occurred in experimental studies testing children's comprehension of temporal clauses (cf. Clark 1971; Ferreiro and Sinclair 1971; Johnson 1975; Feagans 1980). For instance, Clark (1971) reported that preschool children often interpret a sentence such as *He went home after he had played with Sally* as if it meant 'He went home and then he played with Sally'. In other words, children do not seem to recognize that the *after*-clause is temporally prior to the matrix clause and interpret the sentence iconically, such that the order of the combined clauses mirrors the order of the events they describe. Clark referred to this strategy as the 'order-of-mention principle', which, in her view, is one of the major factors involved in the acquisition of conjoined clauses.

---

1. Note that Kuhn and Phelps (1976), Homzie and Gravitt (1977), and Johnson and Chapman (1980) did not find any support for this hypothesis.

Note that the order-of-mention principle does not necessarily lead to a false interpretation. For instance, if *after* is replaced by *before*, children should interpret the sentence correctly because unlike *after*, *before* indicates that the situation in the matrix clause occurs prior to the one in the adverbial clause. In other words, if children employ an order-of-mention strategy, they will have more difficulty in interpreting *after*-clauses than in interpreting *before*-clauses, because *after*-clauses violate the order-of-mention principle if they follow the matrix clause (as conjoined clauses usually do in early child speech; see below). This hypothesis was confirmed in experimental studies by Clark (1971), Ferreiro and Sinclair (1971), and Johnson (1975).

Having argued that children's early interpretations of conjoined clauses crucially depend on the order-of-mention principle, Clark proposed that the acquisition of conjunctions can be described in terms of semantic features. Specifically, she argued that the development of *after* and *before* involves three semantic components: [+/−time]; [+/−simultaneous]; and [+/−prior]. According to her analysis, these features are acquired in a specific order. The first semantic feature that children learn is [+ time]; that is, they realize that *after* and *before* indicate a temporal relationship, which distinguishes them from nontemporal conjunctions such as *because*. Second, children learn that the two situations related by *after* and *before* occur in sequence; that is, they realize that both conjunctions express the feature [−simultaneous], which sets them apart from other temporal conjunctions such as *while*. Finally, children learn that *after* and *before* differ with regard to the temporal orderings they denote. Specifically, they realize that the order-of-mention strategy does not determine the order of events expressed in matrix and adverbial clauses; rather, *after* and *before* encode the temporal ordering directly by the feature [+/−prior].

Clark's semantic feature analysis had a significant impact on the literature on children's acquisition of conjoined clauses. Following her analysis of *after* and *before*, other studies described the development of temporal, causal, and conditional conjunctions in terms of distinctive features that children acquire in a specific order (cf. Coker 1978; Feagans 1980; Emerson 1979, 1980).

While the previous literature has concentrated on semantic issues, notably on the semantic features of conjunctions, the current study describes the development of conjoined clauses primarily from a grammatical point of view.

7.2   *Adverbial and co-ordinate clauses in adult grammar*

Co-ordinate clauses are nonembedded sentences whereas adverbial clauses are commonly analysed as subordinate clauses (e.g. Quirk, Greenbaum, Leech, and Svartvik 1985:987–991). The division between co-ordinate and adverbial clauses corresponds to the division between co-ordinate and adverbial conjunctions. *And, but*, and *or* are co-ordinate conjunctions. *And* expresses a wide variety of semantic relationships that may also be expressed by other conjunctions; *or* indicates a disjunction (or choice); and *but* marks an adversative relationship (or contrast). In addition to *and, but*, and *or, for* and *so* are sometimes considered co-ordinate conjunctions; however, as Quirk et al. (1985:920–926) point out, *for* and *so* have a number of features that distinguish them from ordinary co-ordinate conjunctions. For instance, while *and, but*, and *or* may combine both clauses and noun phrases, *for* and *so* only combine clauses.

Co-ordinate conjunctions must be distinguished from connectives such as *thus, then, however,* and *therefore,* which are sometimes called conjunctive adverbs. Like co-ordinate conjunctions, conjunctive adverbs indicate a link between nonembedded clauses, but they differ in their distribution: while the occurrence of co-ordinate conjunctions is restricted to the position at the beginning of a conjoined clause, conjunctive adverbs may occur in various positions. As can be seen in examples (1a–c), they can occur at the beginning, in the middle, and at the end of a conjoined clause. Conjunctive adverbs are extremely rare in early child speech and will not be examined in this study.

(1) a. We slept all night long; **however**, we were still tired when we got up.
     b. We slept all night long; we were still tired, **however**, when we got up.
     c. We slept all night long; we were still tired when we got up, **however**.

Adverbial conjunctions are commonly divided into various semantic classes: conditional conjunctions (e.g. *if, unless*), temporal conjunctions (e.g. *after, before*), causal conjunctions (e.g. *because, since*), concessive conjunctions (e.g. *although, whereas*), and various others (Quirk et al. 1985:1077–1120). From a morphological perspective, subordinate conjunctions can be divided into simple and complex forms. Simple subordinate conjunctions are monomorphemic words (e.g. *when*), while complex subordinate conjunctions are either phrasal (e.g. *on condition that*) or morphologically complex (e.g. *inasmuch*). Complex subordinate conjunctions are primarily used in written genres and do not occur in early child speech.

The division between adverbial and co-ordinate clauses is based on a number of features concerning both their form and function. To begin with, there are two pragmatic criteria that are commonly used to distinguish adverbial from co-ordinate clauses.

(i)   While adverbial clauses provide background information, co-ordinate clauses typically present foreground information (cf. Tomlin 1985; Thompson 1985; Matthiessen and Thompson 1988).

(ii) While co-ordinate clauses are independent speech acts, adverbial clauses lack illocutionary force (cf. Haiman and Thompson 1984; Lehmann 1988; Cristofaro 2003).

In addition to the pragmatic criteria, there are a number of syntactic tests (or operations) that are commonly used to demonstrate that adverbial clauses are grammatically distinguished from co-ordinate constructions (cf. Haspelmath 1995; Diessel 2001):

(iii) While (preposed) adverbial clauses may include a cataphoric pronoun that is controlled by a coreferential noun in the following matrix clause, co-ordinate clauses do *not* allow for 'backwards pronominalization' (cf. Reinhart 1983).

a.	When he$_i$ came to Leipzig, Peter$_i$ met Mary.	[adverbial]
b.	*He$_i$ came to Leipzig, and Peter$_i$ met Mary.	[co-ordinate]

(iv) While it is possible to extract a question word from a clause that is modified by an adverbial clause, a question word cannot be extracted from a clause that is accompanied by a co-ordinate clause (cf. Ross 1986).

a.	What did you tell her __ when you left?	[adverbial]
b.	*What did you tell her __ and you left.	[co-ordinate]

(v)   While adverbial clauses may precede, follow, or interrupt the matrix clause, co-ordinate clauses always follow the associated clause (cf. Haspelmath 1995).

a.	Peter admitted that Mary was right [before he left]	[adverbial]
b.	[Before he left] Peter admitted that Mary was right.	[adverbial]
c.	Peter admitted, [before he left], that Mary was right.	[adverbial]
d.	Peter admitted that Mary was right [and (then he) left].	[co-ordinate]
e.	*[And he left] Peter admitted that Mary was right.	[co-ordinate]
f.	*Peter admitted, [and he left], that Mary was right.	[co-ordinate]

(vi) While adverbial clauses cannot occur with a tag question, a tag question can be added to a co-ordinate clause (cf. Cristofaro 2003).

a.	*She went to bed when she was tired, wasn't she?	[adverbial]
b.	She went to bed, but she wasn't tired, was she?	[co-ordinate]

(vii)   While co-ordinate clauses allow for the deletion of the verb in the
        second conjunct (which is sometimes called 'gapping'; cf. Ross 1970),
        this is not permissible in adverbial clauses (cf. Diessel 2001).

      a. *Bill played the guitar when John __ the piano.   [adverbial]
      b. Bill played the guitar and John __ the piano.   [co-ordinate]

Note that none of the criteria in (i)–(vii) applies to the whole class of adverbial and/or co-ordinate clauses; rather, they define specific subsets of conjoined clauses that are marked by adverbial and/or co-ordinate conjunctions.
For instance, while adverbial clauses are usually backgrounded (or pragmatically presupposed), they may also function to assert new information as in
example (2), where the matrix clause provides a thematic ground for unfamiliar
information encoded in the *when*-clause.

(2)   A: When did you come back?
         B: We came back **when** it started to rain last night.

Similarly, while adverbial clauses usually lack illocutionary force, there are
constructions in which the matrix clause and the adverbial clause function as
two independent speech acts. Consider, for instance, example (3), in which the
adverbial clause functions to explain the content of the associated matrix clause.
The complex sentence comprises two speech acts: a proposal (or suggestion)
expressed in the matrix clause; and an explanation expressed in the *because*-
clause.

(3)   I suggest that we turn around and take the highway, **because** if we stay on
         this road we won't be in Leipzig before midnight.

Like the pragmatic criteria, the syntactic criteria do not apply to all adverbial
and/or co-ordinate clauses. For instance, while initial adverbial clauses may
include a cataphoric pronoun, final adverbial clauses do not allow for backwards pronominalization, and while most adverbial clauses may precede the
semantically associated clause, result clauses always follow it (cf. Quirk et al.
1985:1109).

   In general, the criteria that are commonly used to define adverbial and/or
co-ordinate clauses fall short of dividing the group of conjoined clauses into
two discrete classes; rather, they describe divisions between various subtypes
of conjoined clauses. I therefore suggest abandoning the categorial distinction
between adverbial subordination and clausal co-ordination, which one might
see as the two poles of a continuum (cf. Lehmann 1988; Diessel 2001). In my

Table 7.1 *Conjoined clauses*

	Age range	Clauses commonly classified as co-ordinate clauses	Clauses commonly classified as adverbial clauses	Total
Adam	2;3–4;10	989	470	1,459
Sarah	2;3–5;1	664	334	998
Nina	1;11–3;4	884	472	1,356
Peter	1;9–3;2	529	159	688
Naomi	1;8–3;3	298	119	417
Total	1;8–5;1	3,364	1,554	4,918

view, English has a wide variety of conjoined clauses that differ in their degree of syntactic integration. The degree of integration is determined by several factors: the semantic link between the conjoined clauses, their pragmatic functions, their ordering, and intonation. In what follows, I describe the acquisition of conjoined clauses based on these features.

7.3   Data

There are 4,918 finite conjoined clauses in the transcripts. In addition, the corpus includes 69 nonfinite adverbial clauses. Most of them are infinitival purpose clauses; there are only a few instances of participial adverbial clauses in the corpus. Since the data on nonfinite adverbial clauses are too sparse to analyse their development, this chapter concentrates on finite adverbial clauses.

The data of finite adverbial clauses include all complex sentences that are marked by a co-ordinate or subordinate conjunction. Multiple-clause utterances that are linked by a conjunctive adverb and multiple-clause utterances that comprise juxtaposed clauses were disregarded. Table 7.1 shows the total number of finite conjoined clauses that occur in the transcripts of each child.

All 4,918 conjoined clauses were coded for three features:

   (i) the semantic link between the conjoined clause and the semantically associated clause (i.e. temporal, causal, conditional);
  (ii) the position of the conjoined clause vis-à-vis the semantically associated clause (i.e. initial vs. final);
 (iii) the occurrence of intonation boundaries, as indicated by a comma or a full stop between the conjoined clause and the semantically associated clause.

Table 7.2 *Frequency of the children's individual conjoined clauses/conjunctions*

	Naomi	Peter	Nina	Sarah	Adam	Total	Mean
and	254	480	719	464	706	2623	55.7
because	92	125	383	173	176	949	19.6
so	20	27	84	56	199	386	6.8
but	24	18	81	137	68	328	6.6
when	11	22	65	94	125	317	5.7
if	10	9	9	57	112	197	3.6
or	0	4	0	7	16	27	0.5
after	1	0	4	6	15	26	0.4
while	1	1	6	1	14	23	0.4
until	3	1	5	0	11	20	0.4
before	1	1	0	3	11	16	0.3
since	0	0	0	0	6	6	0.1
Total	417	688	1,356	998	1,459	4,918	

Overall the data include only twelve different conjunctions: *and, but, because, so, or, when, if, after, before, while, until,* and *since*. As can be seen in table 7.2, *and* is by far the most frequent conjunction; it occurs in more than half of all conjoined clauses. Note that I considered the use of *and* only in full clauses; phrasal co-ordinations (e.g. *Peter and Mary*) were disregarded (see Ardery 1980 and Goodluck and Mervis 1980 for an analysis of the relationship between phrasal and sentential co-ordination in sponatenous child speech). Apart from *and*, the children make frequent use of *because, so, but, when,* and *if*. All other conjunctions occur infrequently, and, with the exception of *while*, are only used by some of the children. Note that English has a variety of other conjunctions that do not occur in the transcripts. There are, for instance, no concessive clauses marked by *although* or *whereas*, and many temporal and conditional conjunctions are also entirely absent (e.g. *once, as soon as, whenever, unless*). Thus, the children use only a small subset of conjunctions that are available in English to indicate a link between two conjoined clauses.

   The vast majority of the children's conjoined clauses follow the semantically associated clause: overall, there are only 169 initial conjoined clauses in the data. They are introduced by five conjunctions: *when, if, after, since,* and *while*. All other conjunctions occur exclusively in final conjoined clauses, although some of them could in principle also occur in initial conjoined clauses (e.g. *because, before*).

In what follows, I examine the development of conjoined clauses following the order in which they appear in the transcripts. The investigation is divided into two sections: section 7.4.1 describes the development of early conjoined clauses marked by *and, because, so,* and *but*; and section 7.4.2 investigates the children's use of later conjoined clauses marked by *if, when,* and various temporal conjunctions.

7.4   Analysis

7.4.1   Early conjoined clauses

The earliest multiple-clause utterances that the five children produce consist of juxtaposed clauses, i.e. clauses in which the link between two semantically associated clauses is not overtly expressed by a conjunction (cf. examples (4)–(6)) (cf. Bloom et al. 1980; Eisenberg 1980):

(4)	Diapers on. Fix it.	[Naomi 1;9]
(5)	There's the lion. Here kitty.	[Nina 2;0]
(6)	Hit ball. Get it.	[Adam 2;3]

The first conjunction that appears in the transcripts of all five children is *and,* which emerges around the second birthday (cf. Bloom et al. 1980). Like adults, children use *and* to express a wide variety of semantic relationships. The sentences in (7)–(11) show that *and* occurs in temporal, conditional, consecutive, contrastive, and additive clauses. The examples are taken from Adam's transcripts; similar examples occur in the data of the four other children.

(7)	Move over to here **and** then come over here. . . . (temporal)	[Adam 4;4]
(8)	You push it **and** it goes up. (conditional)	[Adam 3;6]
(9)	I shot you **and** then you may die. (consecutive)	[Adam 3;11]
(10)	This is Paul's **and** dis is yours. (contrastive)	[Adam 3;5]
(11)	We have two **and** I have eight. (additive)	[Adam 3;7]

Interestingly, more than 80 per cent of the children's *and*-clauses are linked to a clause that is terminated by a full stop. In the CHILDES format, a full stop indicates the end of an utterance (MacWhinney 1995:60). An utterance is a communicative unit marked by a specific intonation contour and/or pauses. Thus, the vast majority of the children's *and*-clauses are intonationally separated from the previous utterance; they are linked to a clause that functions as an independent intonation unit. Moreover, many *and*-clauses are associated with an utterance across speaker turns, i.e. they are linked to a clause that is produced by a different speaker. Some typical examples are given in (12)–(16).

(12)   CHILD: Nina has dolly sleeping.
       ADULT: The doll is sleeping too?
       CHILD: **And** the man's sleeping on the big bed.   [Nina 2;2]

(13)   ADULT: That's yours?
       ADULT: Ok.
       CHILD: **And** this is mine.   [Peter 2;5]

(14)   CHILD: Piggy went to market.
       ADULT: Yes.
       CHILD: **And** piggy had none.   [Naomi 2;7]

(15)   CHILD: I gon to put his finger through here.
       CHILD: **And** I gon to listen to his heart.   [Adam 3;4]

(16)   ADULT: Flipper's on TV yeah.
       CHILD: **And** Shaggy's not on TV.   [Sarah 3;8]

Although the child's utterances are introduced by *and,* they do not function as co-ordinate clauses; rather, I maintain that these examples show two independent sentences that are pragmatically combined in the ongoing discourse. This is not only suggested by the intonation but also by certain grammatical features that distinguish intonationally unbound *and*-clauses from co-ordinate *and*-constructions. For instance, as can be seen in (17), co-ordinate constructions including *and* allow for certain types of ellipses that are not permissible in intonationally unbound *and*-clauses.

(17)   a. Peter likes __, **and** Mary hates, your pancakes.
       b. *Peter likes __. **And** Mary hates your pancakes.

I suggest therefore distinguishing sentences in which *and* serves as a co-ordinate conjunction from sentences in which *and* functions as a discourse connective. Co-ordinate *and*-clauses are part of a biclausal constructions in which two clauses are integrated in a specific grammatical unit, whereas pragmatically combined *and*-clauses are grammatically independent.

Children make common use of both pragmatically combined *and*-clauses and co-ordinate *and*-clauses. However, since the earliest *and*-clauses are almost exclusively linked to an independent utterance, it seems reasonable to assume that children learn the use of pragmatically combined *and*-clauses before they begin to produce co-ordinate *and*-constructions.

Note that the pragmatic use of *and*-clauses is not a specific trait of child language. There are also many *and*-clauses in the mothers' data that are intonationally unbound (i.e. separated by a period from the previous utterance). In

Table 7.3 *Intonationally bound and intonationally unbound* and-*clauses*

Age		Naomi	Peter	Nina	Sarah	Adam	Total	Mean
> 3;0	bound	9	102	42	0	2	155	15.8
	unbound	154	331	257	0	8	750	84.2
3;0–4;0	bound	21	21	58	16	65	181	21.7
	unbound	70	26	362	131	346	935	78.3
4;0–5;0	bound				79	97	176	29.5
	unbound				238	188	426	70.5
Total		254	480	719	464	706	2,623	

fact, it seems that the pragmatic use of certain types of conjoined clauses is a common feature of spoken adult English (cf. van Dijk 1979, 1981).

As the children grow older, the proportion of co-ordinate *and*-clauses increases. Table 7.3 shows that up to the age of 3;0 an average of only 15.8 per cent of the children's *and*-clauses are linked to a clause within the same utterance; between the ages of 3;0 and 4;0 an average of 21.7 per cent of all *and*-clauses are intonationally bound; and between the ages of 4;0 and 5;0 an average of 29.5 per cent of all *and*-clauses are intonationally associated with the preceding clause.

Following *and,* two causal conjunctions emerge, *because* and *so.* The vast majority of the children's *because*- and *so*-clauses refer to psychological causes or reasons. More precisely, they denote the child's own motifs or intentions (cf. Hood and Bloom 1979; McCabe and Peterson 1985; Bloom and Capatides 1987); however, there are also some causal clauses that express physical or logical causality. Two examples are given in (18) and (19).

(18)   CHILD: I can't get them out **because** my hand is too big.   [Adam 3;3]

(19)   ADULT: Why should they come from Africa?   [Adam 3;2]
        CHILD: **Because** they live in Africa.

Like *and, because* and *so* are primarily used to indicate a link between two independent utterances. Overall a mean proportion of 75.1 per cent of the children's *because*-clauses and a mean proportion of 71.3 per cent of their *so*-clauses are associated with a clause that is terminated by a full stop (cf. table 7a in the appendix).

Interestingly, *because* is initially almost always used in response to a causal question. In particular, the occurrence of *because* after *Why?* is very common (cf. Eisenberg 1980). The following examples show the first 10 *because*-clauses

that occur in Peter's transcripts; all of them are produced in response to a causal
why-question.[2]

(17)   ADULT: Did you run over my blocks?   [Peter 2;5]
        CHILD: Mmhm.
        ADULT: Why?
        CHILD: **Because** it's a fire engine.

(18)   CHILD: No you can't get a napkin.   [Peter 2;7]
        ADULT: Hmhm.
        CHILD: No!
        ADULT: Why?
        CHILD: **Cause** it's Mommy's, . . . Mommy's cleaning.

(19)   CHILD: No, don't touch this camera.   [Peter 2;7]
        ADULT: Why?
        CHILD: **Cause** it's broken.

(20)   CHILD: The microphone.   [Peter 2;7]
        CHILD: Don't touch it!
        ADULT: Why?
        CHILD: **Cause** it's . . . I wanna put this right there.

(21)   CHILD: Over here right over here, . . . don't put it there. [Peter 2;8]
        ADULT: Why not?
        CHILD: **Cause** it's my horse.

(22)   ADULT: On the truck?   [Peter 2;8]
        CHILD: Yeah
        ADULT: Why?
        CHILD: **Cause** . . . you need to?

(23)   ADULT: Is that one better?   [Peter 2;8]
        CHILD: Yeah.
        ADULT: Why?
        CHILD: **Cause** . . . other one is too small.

(24)   CHILD: You can't have this!   [Peter 2;8]
        ADULT: Why?
        CHILD: **Cause** . . . I'm using it.

(25)   ADULT: Why did you put them in the car?   [Peter 2;8]
        CHILD: **Cause** Jenny's gonna get the crayons.

(26)   CHILD: Daddy taked it off.   [Peter 2;8]
        ADULT: Hmhm, . . . why did he do that?
        CHILD: **Cause** it was going and it was going up.

2. Note that some of the children occasionally responded to a *why*-question with an isolated
   because: MOTHER: *Why are you holding your spoon like that, Nomi?* CHILD: *Because.*).
   Such isolated uses of *because* have not been included in the corpus.

Table 7.4 Because-*clauses that occur in response to a causal question*

	Naomi	Peter	Nina	Sarah	Adam	Total	Mean
Why? How come? What for? – Because	14	15	10	13	12	64	86.6
Other uses of *because*	1	0	5	2	3	11	13.3
Total	15	15	15	15	15	75	

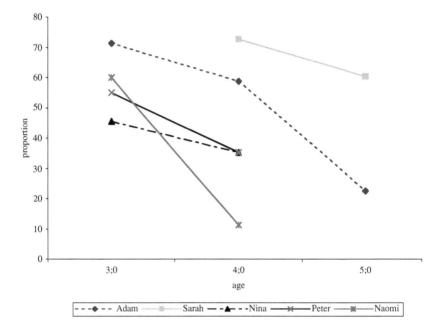

Fig. 7.1 *The proportions of children's* because-*clauses that occur in response to a causal question.*

Similar *because*-clauses occur in Adam's, Sarah's, and Naomi's data; only Nina uses *because* in a variety of discourse contexts. However, the use of *because* after *why* is also dominant in Nina's early data. As can be seen in table 7.4, a mean proportion of 86.6 per cent of the children's first 15 *because*-clauses occur in response to a causal question such as *Why . . .?, How come . . .?*, or *What . . . for?*

As the children grow older, the use of *because* is gradually extended to other discourse contexts. As can be seen in figure 7.1, the proportion of *because*-clauses that are produced in response to a causal question decreases steadily between the ages of 3;0 and 5;0 (cf. table 7b in the appendix).

Note that the children's early use of *because* violates the order-of-mention principle. All 949 *because*-clauses included in the corpus follow the semantically associated clause, despite the fact that a *because*-clause refers to an event that is temporally and/or logically prior to the event encoded in the semantically associated clause. This suggests that the order-of-mention principle does not affect the acquisition of causal *because*-clauses (although it seems to have an effect on temporal clauses; cf. Clark 1970, 1971, 1973; Kuhn and Phelps 1976; Johnson and Chapman 1980).

Like *because, so* indicates a causal relationship, but while the children's early *because*-clauses occur in response to a *why*-question, their early use of *so*-clauses is self-initiated. Some typical examples are given in (27)–(31):

(27)   ADULT: Hey, what happened?   [Nina 2;9]
       CHILD: It opened.
       CHILD: **So** the horsie could get out.

(28)   ADULT: What are you doing to the radio?   [Nina 2;9]
       CHILD: Putting it on.
       CHILD: **So** you can watch it.

(29)   ADULT: What is that?   [Nina 2;9]
       CHILD: That's a little duckling.
       CHILD: **So** we put him in the forest.

(30)   ADULT: Are you leaning it against the box?   [Nina 2;10]
       CHILD: Yes.
       ADULT: I see.
       CHILD: **So** it could stand up.

(31)   ADULT: How many blankets are you putting on Snoopy?   [Nina 2;11]
       CHILD: Two.
       CHILD: **So** he could sleep.

As can be seen in these examples, the *so*-clauses continue the child's own speech. The *because*-clauses, on the other hand, are initially always used in response to a causal question. The two conjunctions are tied to different discourse patterns: *so* functions to indicate a consequence of the child's previous utterance, whereas *because* is used to explain (or to justify) a state of affairs that is challenged by a *why*-question (cf. Donaldson 1986:62).

Like *and, because*, and *so, but* is frequently used to indicate a link between two independent utterances. An average of 77.9 per cent of the children's *but*-clauses are associated with a clause that is terminated by a full stop (cf. table 7a in the appendix). Moreover, the majority of the children's *but*-clauses are linked

Table 7.5 But-*clauses across and within speaker turns*

	Naomi	Peter	Nina	Sarah	Adam	Total	Mean
Across	14	9	61	56	32	172	54.3
Within	3	7	12	62	28	112	30.5
Unclear	7	2	8	19	8	44	15.2
Total	24	18	81	137	68	328	

to an adult speaker's utterance (cf. Eisenberg 1980:76). As can be seen in table 7.5, an average of 54.3 per cent of all *but*-clauses are associated with an utterance across speaker turns. Some typical examples are given in (32)–(36).

(32)   ADULT: It is called the skin of the peanut.   [Naomi 2;11]
       CHILD: **But** this isn't the skin.

(33)   ADULT: No, it's not raining today Pete.   [Peter 2;6]
       CHILD: **But** . . . it's raining here.

(34)   ADULT: I think it's time to put your dolly to bed.   [Nina 2;11]
       CHILD: **But** the Snoopy is asleep.

(35)   ADULT: You go find them.   [Sarah 3;0]
       CHILD: **But** you find them . . . you could find them . . . too.

(36)   ADULT: David doesn't shave yet.   [Adam 3;8]
       CHILD: Uhuh. **But** I shave.

The use of *but* across speaker turns is especially frequent in the early data. A mean proportion of 80 per cent of the children's first 15 *but*-clauses is linked to an utterance that is produced by an adult speaker. The frequent use of *but* across speaker turns suggests that *but* does not function as an ordinary co-ordinate conjunction: rather than indicating a specific semantic link between two conjoined clauses, the children use *but* to mark an objection to an adult speaker's prior utterance. Like *because, but* is initially tied to a conversational routine that involves two utterances produced by different speakers.

All four conjunctions occur in clauses that at first are linked to an independent utterance. As the children grow older, the proportions of intonationally bound *and-, but-, because-*, and *so*-clauses increase. Figure 7.2 shows the development (cf. table 7d in the appendix).

As can be seen in this figure, up to the age of 3;0 an average of only 15.3 per cent of the children's early conjoined clauses are intonationally bound to a previous clause, i.e. they are integrated in a biclausal construction. As the children grow older, the proportion of bound conjoined clauses increases:

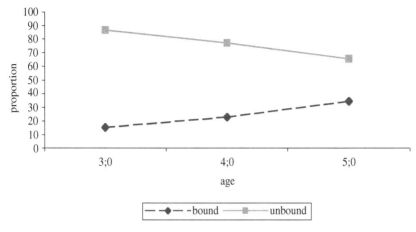

Fig. 7.2 *The development of bound and unbound early conjoined clauses (i.e.* and-, but-, because-, *and* so-*clauses).*

between the ages of 3;0 and 4;0, an average of 22.9 per cent of the children's *and-, but-, because-,* and *so*-clauses are linked to a clause within the same utterance, and between the ages of 4;0 and 5;0 the proportion of intonationally bound clauses reaches an average of 34.3 per cent.

To summarize the discussion thus far, we have seen that the earliest conjoined clauses are simple nonembedded utterances that are pragmatically combined with the preceding sentence. They are intonationally unbound and often linked to an utterance across speaker turns. Moreover, we have seen that some of the early conjoined clauses occur in specific conversational routines. This is perhaps most obvious in the case of *because,* which some children initially always use in response to a causal *why*-question.

7.4.2   Later conjoined clauses

Following *and, but, because,* and *so,* several temporal and conditional conjunctions emerge: *when, if, while, until, after,* and *before.* With the exception of *when,* these conjunctions are rare before the age of 3;0. They appear in constructions that are very different from children's early conjoined clauses. Three features distinguish the temporal and conditional clauses from children's early conjoined clauses marked by *and, but, because,* and *so.*

(i)   First, while the children's early conjoined clauses tend to be (intonationally) unbound, the temporal and conditional clauses are usually bound to the semantically associated clause.

(ii)   Second, while the children's early conjoined clauses assert new and unfamiliar information, the temporal and conditional clauses are often pragmatically presupposed and/or backgrounded.

(iii) Third, while the children's early conjoined clauses always follow the associated utterance, the temporal and conditional clauses also precede the semantically associated clause.

The three features suggest that children's later conjoined clauses marked by temporal and conditional conjunctions are more tightly bound to the associated clause than the early conjoined clauses marked by *and, but, because,* and *so.* However, not all of the children's temporal and conditional clauses carry the three features that are characteristic of later conjoined clauses. For instance, there are several *when*-clauses that the children use as independent speech acts in response to a temporal question. An example is given in (37).

(37)   ADULT: When did you do that?   [Nina 3;0]
         CHILD: **When** I was bigger.

Such isolated *when*-clauses are among the earliest *when*-clauses in the data. Like children's early *because*-clauses, these *when*-clauses assert new and unfamiliar information in response to a question. However, isolated *when*-clauses are rare. Like other temporal and conditional conjunctions, *when* appears primarily in utterances consisting of multiple clauses. As can be seen in figure 7.3, while an average of 78.2 per cent of the early conjoined clauses (i.e. clauses marked by *and, but, because,* and *so*) are intonationally unbound, only 17.5 per cent of the later conjoined clauses (i.e. temporal and conditional clauses) are linked to a clause across an utterance boundary. In other words, while most of the children's early conjoined clauses are pragmatically combined with an independent utterance, the great majority of their later conjoined clauses are integrated in biclausal constructions (cf. table 7d in the appendix).

Conjoined clauses that are linked to an independent utterance tend to assert new and unfamiliar information, whereas conjoined clauses that are intonationally bound are often pragmatically presupposed (i.e. they provide familiar information). Clauses that are pragmatically presupposed function to support the hearer's interpretation of the semantically associated clause. Consider for instance examples (38)–(40).

(38)   ADULT: Did you sleep in the same room with Elizabeth?   [Nina 3;3]
         CHILD: Yes.
         CHILD: And we both sleep on the floor **when** we take naps.

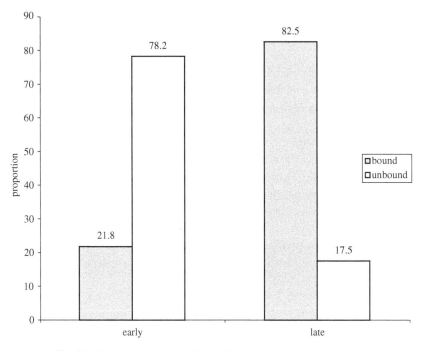

Fig. 7.3 *Mean proportions of the children's early and late conjoined clauses that are intonationally bound/unbound to the semantically associated clause.*

(39) CHILD: The Mommy would eat the cake.   [Nina 3;0]
      CHILD: The doggy's sharing it.
      CHILD: He bite the tongue **while** he was eating.

(40) CHILD: I put all the dollies in, see?   [Naomi 3;4]
      CHILD: It's getting crowded **after** I put all the dollies in.

In all three examples, the conjoined clause provides familiar information from the previous discourse. It relates the associated matrix clause to elements that are already in the hearer's knowledge store. Note, however, that conjoined clauses are not always pragmatically presupposed if they are linked to a clause within the same utterance (cf. chapter 3.2). Consider for instance examples (41) and (42).

(41) ADULT: You go on a black train?   [Peter 2;9]
      CHILD: Yep.
      ADULT: When
      CHILD: It was . . . **when** Daddy goes on it.

(42)   ADULT: How did she break it?   [Nina 3;3]
        CHILD: She broke it **when** she was playing with
               her mother's stuff.

In both examples, the conjoined clause asserts new and unfamiliar information
that is grounded by a thematic matrix clause. Thus, in these examples it is the
matrix clause, rather than the conjoined clause, that relates the complex sentence
to elements that are already in the hearer's knowledge store. However, in the vast
majority of the children's complex sentences, it is the conjoined clause, rather
than the matrix clause, that provides the necessary grounding. In particular, if
the conjoined clause precedes the matrix clause, the conjoined clause functions
to ground (or situate) the utterance in the ongoing discourse. As argued by Chafe
(1984), Thompson and Longacre (1985), Givón (1990), Ford (1993), and many
others, adverbial clauses that precede the semantically associated clause are
commonly used to organize the information flow in discourse. They provide an
orientation in terms of which subsequent clauses are to be understood. Consider,
for instance, examples (43)–(45).

(43)   ADULT: Wait until it dries off.   [Sarah 2;9]
        CHILD That?
        CHILD **After** it dries off . . . then you can make the bottom.
(44)   CHILD: It's got a flat tire.   [Adam 3;2]
        ADULT: Yeah.
        CHILD: **When** it's got a flat tire . . . it's need to go to the . . . to the station.
(45)   ADULT: He can take some.   [Adam 4;10]
        CHILD: **If** he takes all of them I'm gonna beat him up.

In all three examples, the adverbial clause provides a thematic ground (or an orientation) for the associated matrix clause; it functions as a 'scene-setting topic'
that lays the foundation for the interpretation of subsequent clauses (Lambrecht
1994:125).

   The vast majority of the children's conjoined clauses follow the matrix clause;
initial conjoined clauses are infrequent and emerge relatively late in the transcripts of the five children (cf. Clark 1970, 1973). As can be seen in table 7.6,
the data of the three younger children, Naomi, Peter, and Nina, whose transcripts end a few months after the third birthday, include only very few initial
conjoined clauses. The majority of the children's initial conjoined clauses occur
in the transcripts of the two older children, Sarah and Adam.

   Most initial conjoined clauses are marked by *if* or *when*. *When* appears initially only in final conjoined clauses, which emerge at a mean age of 2;9. The
first initial *when*-clauses appear five months later at a mean age of 3;2. In
contrast to *when, if* occurs from the very beginning in both initial and final

Table 7.6 *Mean proportions of the children's initial and final conjoined clauses*

	Naomi	Peter	Nina	Sarah	Adam	Total	Mean
Initial	3	11	10	45	100	169	2.9
Final	411	677	1,338	930	1,337	4,693	96.1
Unclear	3	0	8	23	22	56	1.0
Total	417	688	1,356	998	1,459	4,918	

conjoined clause, but *if* emerges several months after *when* at around the same time that *when* first appears in initial conjoined clauses. Apart from *when* and *if,* there are only three other conjunctions, *after, while,* and *since,* that some of the children use in initial conjoined clauses; but all three conjunctions have only a few tokens and appear primarily in final conjoined clauses. *If* and *when* are the only conjunctions that all five children use in a significant number of initial conjoined clauses. The proportions of initial *if-* and *when*-clauses increase steadily. At first both conjunctions are primarily used in final conjoined clauses, but as the children grow older they produce a continuously growing proportion of initial *if-* and *when*-clauses. Figure 7.4 shows the developmental changes in the positioning of children's *when*-clauses (cf. table 7e in the appendix).

As can be seen in this figure, up to the age of 3;0, an average of only 6.5 per cent of the children's *when*-clauses precede the associated matrix clause, but with time the proportion of initial *when*-clauses increases: between 3;0 and 4;0, an average of 31.3 per cent of the *when*-clauses precede the associated clause, and between 4;0 and 5;0, an average of 42.1 per cent of the children's *when*-clauses occur sentence-initially. While there are not enough data to plot the changing proportions of initial and final *if*-clauses, they seem to undergo a similar development (cf. table 7f in the appendix).

7.5 *Discussion*

7.5.1 *Summary*
This chapter has shown that the development of conjoined clauses involves a number of interrelated constructions. The constructions are marked by a small number of subordinate and co-ordinate conjunctions. Each conjunction is associated with a construction that undergoes a particular development. Some of the children's conjoined clauses function as independent sentences that are pragmatically combined with a previous utterance, whereas others are integrated

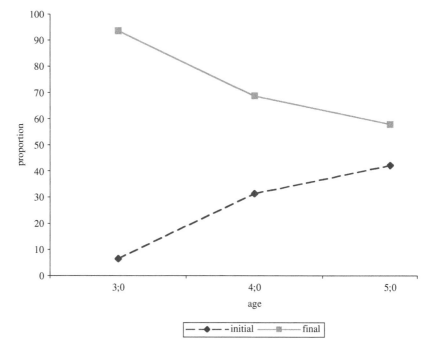

Fig. 7.4 *The development of initial and final* when-*clauses.*

in specific biclausal constructions. Conjoined clauses functioning as independent sentences emerge prior to conjoined clauses that are integrated in biclausal constructions. Figure 7.5 summarizes the described development.

As can be seen in this figure, the earliest multiple-clause utterances consist of two juxtaposed sentences. While juxtaposed sentences are semantically related, the semantic link is not overtly expressed by a conjunction. The first conjunctions children use function to combine two independent utterances. The combined utterances are often produced by different speakers and tied to particular discourse routines. For instance, children's early *because*-clauses are commonly used to support a previous utterance that has been challenged by a *why*-question. Although the early conjoined clauses are linked by a conjunction, they are grammatically independent; they function as two separate sentences that are pragmatically combined in the ongoing discourse. Following such pragmatically combined sentences, co-ordinate clauses and final adverbial clauses emerge. They are part of a biclausal construction: co-ordinate clauses occur in symmetrical constructions consisting of two clauses that assert new and unfamiliar information; adverbial clauses, on the other hand, occur in asymmetrical

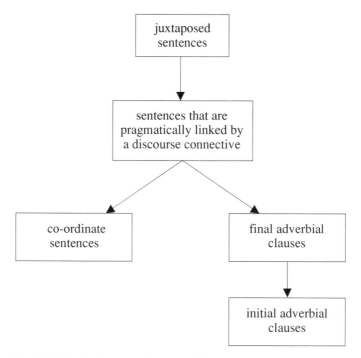

Fig. 7.5 *The development of conjoined clauses.*

constructions in which one of the two clauses asserts new and unfamiliar information whose interpretation is supported by the associated clause. Finally, children begin to use adverbial clauses that precede the matrix clause. Initial adverbial clauses serve particular discourse-pragmatic functions: they lay the foundation for the interpretation of subsequent clauses enhancing discourse coherence.

The development of conjoined clauses contrasts sharply with the development of other complex sentence constructions. While complement and relative clauses evolve via clause expansion, the development of conjoined clauses can be seen as a process of clause integration. Starting from multiple-clause structures that consist of juxtaposed clauses, children gradually learn the use of complex sentences in which two or more clauses are integrated in tightly organized grammatical constructions.

7.5.2 *Discussion*
Like the acquisition of complement and relative clauses, the acquisition of conjoined clauses is crucially affected by the ambient language. Table 7.7 shows

Table 7.7 *Mean proportions of the mothers' conjoined clauses and the mean age of their appearance in the children's data*

	Mothers' data (mean proportions)	Children's data (mean age of appearance)
and	33.5	2;2
because	13.1	2;5
so	8.7	2;7
but	10.3	2;8
when	13.7	2;10
if	10.8	3;0
while	1.5	3;2
before	2.2	3;2
after	1.7	3;4
until	1.2	3;4
since	0.2	3;11
others	3.1	

the mean proportions of the most frequent conjoined clauses in the mothers' data and the mean age of their appearance in the children's speech (cf. Table 7g and Table 7h in the appendix).

The age of appearance correlates with the frequency of the various conjoined clauses in the mothers' data: the more frequent a specific conjoined clause appears in the mothers' data, the earlier it emerges in the children's speech (Spearman: $r = .868$; $p = .001$; $N = 11$). This suggests that the ambient language plays an important role in the acquisition process. However, the correlation between frequency and age of appearance has some exceptions; notably *when*- and *if*-clauses appear after *so*- and *but*-clauses despite the fact that they are more frequent in the mothers' speech (note that *when*-clauses are even slightly more frequent than *because*-clauses). In contrast to all other conjoined clauses, *when*- and *if*-clauses commonly precede the associated clause, suggesting that this is the reason why they appear relatively late in the children's data. There are two factors that may lead to the late appearance of initial conjoined clauses.

First, initial conjoined clauses are more difficult to plan and to produce than final conjoined clauses (cf. Diessel forthcoming). If the conjoined clause precedes the associated clause, the conjunction creates the link between the related clauses at the beginning of the whole utterance. The speaker has to keep both clauses in working memory while producing the composite structure. If, on the other hand, the conjoined clause follows the associated clause, the complex sentence can be planned and constructed successively, i.e. one clause at a time, because the link between the two clauses is only created after the first clause has been produced. Thus, while initial conjoined clauses are planned as part of a biclausal unit, final conjoined clauses may be planned post dictum, i.e. after the semantically associated clause has been produced. This suggests that complex sentences including initial conjoined clauses carry a heavier processing load than complex sentences including final conjoined clauses.

Second, initial conjoined clauses serve discourse pragmatic functions that are not really needed in early child speech (cf. Clark 1970, 1973). As has been pointed out above, initial conjoined clauses provide an orientation for the interpretation of subsequent clauses enhancing discourse coherence. Since young children tend to talk about simple events in the surrounding speech situation, there usually is little need for linguistic means functioning to enhance discourse coherence. In other words, children under the age of 3;0 may not employ initial conjoined clauses because the occurrence of initial conjoined clauses is tied to complex discourse structures that evolve only gradually during the preschool years.[3]

In sum, there are several factors influencing the development of conjoined clauses: the frequency of the various types of conjoined clauses in the ambient language, the differential processing complexity of initial and final conjoined clauses, and the particular discourse-pragmatic functions of initial conjoined clauses.

---

3. In addition, there may be particular semantic reasons for the late appearance of conditional clauses (i.e. *if*-clauses). Specifically, one might hypothesize that children find conditional clauses especially difficult to learn because they have a hypothetical meaning. However, Bowerman (1986) points out that children use sentences with hypothetical meanings long before they begin to use conditional clauses.

8   Conclusion

The bulk of the literature on the acquisition of complex sentences has been concerned with children's comprehension of multiple-clause structures in experiments. Almost all of these studies found that children have great difficulties in understanding complex sentences until well into the school years. For instance, Chomsky (1969) reported that 5- to 9-year-olds often misinterpret certain types of nonfinite complement clauses, and Sheldon (1974) and Tavakolian (1977) observed that relative clauses create tremendous difficulties at least until the early school years. Similarly, Piaget (1948) reported that children as old as 7 years tend to confuse cause and effect in causal clauses, and Clark (1971) found that 3- to 5-year-olds have difficulties comprehending temporal clauses marked by *after* and *before*. Many of these studies have argued that children's comprehension of complex sentences involves an interpretation strategy, such as the conjoined clause analysis or the order-of-mention principle, which seems to suggest that children learn very little about complex sentences during the preschool years.

Although young children have great difficulties in comprehending complex sentences in experiments, they use them at a very early age. As we have seen throughout this book, children begin to produce a wide variety of complex sentences during the preschool years. The earliest complex sentences emerge around the second birthday. They include the complement-taking verb *wanna* and a bare infinitive. Shortly thereafter, children begin to combine clauses by *and*. In the following months various other constructions emerge: sentences including infinitival and participial complements that are selected by modal-like verbs; sentences including finite complement clauses that are accompanied by formulaic matrix clauses; sentences including causal and adversative clauses marked by *because*, *but*, and *so*; and sentences including relative clauses that modify the predicate nominal of a copular clause or an isolated noun phrase. By the age of 3;0, children make common use of a wide variety of complex sentences, but these multiple-clause structures are less complex and more concrete than complex sentences in adult speech: they are organized around concrete lexical expressions, and although they consist of two clauses, they only contain a single proposition and do not involve embedding. More abstract representations of complex sentences expressing two propositions in two full-fledged clauses evolve only gradually during the preschool years. This explains why children have such tremendous difficulties comprehending complex sentences in experiments, despite the fact that they begin to use them at an early age. If we acknowledge that the acquisition process proceeds in a piecemeal bottom-up fashion, and that the development of complex sentences originates from simple item-based constructions, the discrepancy between children's performance in comprehension experiments and their use of complex sentence in spontaneous speech disappears.

This final chapter summarizes the main results of the previous analyses and considers the factors determining the acquisition process. The empirical findings can be summarized in two major points.

- First, the development of complex sentences originates from simple nonembedded sentences.
- Second, children's early complex sentences are lexically specific constructions that are associated with concrete expressions.

The remainder of this chapter discusses the two points in turn.

8.1   *From simple sentences to multiple-clause constructions*

The development of complex sentences from simple nonembedded sentences comprises two different pathways: (i) complex sentences including complement and relative clauses develop from simple sentences via clause expansion; and (ii) complex sentences including adverbial and co-ordinate clauses evolve by integrating two independent sentences into a single grammatical unit.

The earliest multiple-clause structures that English-speaking children learn include the complement-taking verbs *wanna* and *hafta* and a bare infinitive that one might analyse as a nonfinite complement clause. Although the complement-taking verbs behave grammatically like ordinary matrix verbs, semantically they function like modals: rather than denoting an independent state of affairs, they indicate the child's desire or obligation to perform the activity denoted by the nonfinite verb. The whole utterance describes a single situation and thus does not involve embedding. Other early infinitival and participial complements occur with aspectual verbs such as *start* and *stop*, which specify the temporal (or aspectual) structure of the nonfinite verb. Like the early quasi-modals, the aspectual verbs do not denote an independent situation; rather, they elaborate the meaning of the activity denoted by the nonfinite verb. As children grow older, these constructions become increasingly more complex and diverse. Many of the complement-taking verbs that children learn later describe activities that are semantically more independent of the nonfinite verb than the early quasi-modals and aspectual verbs. Moreover, while children's early nonfinite complement clauses are bare infinitives that are controlled by the matrix clause subject, later nonfinite complement clauses are usually marked by a subordinating morpheme and are often controlled by an object NP.

The earliest finite complement clauses occur in sentences including a short and formulaic matrix clause such as *I think* or *I know* and a complement clause that is either unmarked or introduced by a *wh*-adverb or *wh*-pronoun. Although these structures comprise two finite clauses, they function like simple sentences. The matrix clauses are nonreferential: rather than denoting an independent state of affairs, they serve as epistemic markers, attention getters, or markers of the illocutionary force. From a formal point of view, two types of construction can be distinguished: constructions in which the matrix clause functions as a parenthetical of an S-complement clause; and constructions in which the matrix clause functions as an integral part of a lexically specific utterance frame including a *wh-* or *if*-complement clause. As children grow older, some of the early matrix clauses become semantically more substantial and new complement-taking verbs emerge that denote a mental state or verbal activity. In contrast to children's early complement clause constructions, these sentences are truly biclausal: they designate two related situations expressed by a referential matrix clause and a complement clause functioning as an argument of the complement-taking verb. However, since the occurrence of these sentences remains limited to a few complement-taking verbs, it seems to be unlikely that these sentences instantiate a constructional schema; rather, they are isolated constructions that children learn in combination with particular complement-taking verbs.

The first relative clauses occur in presentational constructions that consist of a copular clause including a pronominal subject and a relative clause containing an intransitive verb. Although these constructions are biclausal, they designate only a single state of affairs. The presentational copular clause does not serve as an independent assertion; rather, it functions to establish a referent in focus position such that it becomes available for the predication expressed in the relative clause. Thus, the whole sentence contains only a single proposition leading young children to conflate the two clauses: many of the early relative constructions are syntactic blends (or amalgams) in which the relative clause and the matrix clause are merged into a single syntactic unit. As children grow older, they begin to use more complex relative constructions in which an intransitive *or* transitive relative clause is attached to a noun (phrase) in a non-copular clause. In contrast to the early presentational relatives, these structures contain two propositions expressed in two full-fledged clauses.

Like complement and relative clauses, conjoined clauses develop from simple nonembedded sentences, but the path of evolution is different: while complement and relative clauses evolve via clause expansion, adverbial and co-ordinate clauses evolve by integrating two separate sentences into a specific biclausal unit. The earliest adverbial and co-ordinate clauses are independent sentences that are pragmatically linked to a previous utterance. Although these structures may include a connective, they comprise two sentences that are grammatically independent. Starting from such discourse structures, children gradually learn the use of complex sentences in which two clauses are integrated in a specific grammatical construction. The first constructions of this type include either two co-ordinate clauses or a matrix clause and a final adverbial clause. Complex sentences including initial adverbial clauses emerge only later, and their occurrence is at first restricted to particular conjunctions.

What the developments of *all* complex sentences have in common is that they proceed in an incremental fashion: starting from sentences that contain a single proposition and do not involve embedding, children gradually learn various types of complex sentences in which two propositions are expressed by two clauses.

As we have seen throughout this book, there are various factors that seem to affect the acquisition process: the ambient language, the complexity of the emerging constructions, the pragmatic functions of particular subordinate clauses, and the child's general cognitive development.

One of the factors that seems to be involved in the development of *all* complex sentences is the frequency of a particular construction in the ambient language. Other things being equal, constructions that children frequently encounter in the input tend to appear before constructions that they hear infrequently. Frequency has an important effect on the storage and organization of grammatical knowledge: constructions that are frequent in the ambient language are soon well entrenched in the child's mental grammar, which in turn facilitates the activation of these constructions in spontaneous language use. This seems to explain why multiple-clause structures that children frequently encounter in the ambient language tend to emerge at an early age.

However, children do not just memorize the linguistic structures they hear; they also analyse and organize the input data. Other things being equal, complex sentences are more difficult to analyse and organize than are simple sentences. In fact, it has been argued that complex sentences are initially too complex for young children to be processed successfully: children are able to learn complex sentences only after they have learned simple sentences (cf. Elman 1993; Newport 1990). This might explain why children's early complex sentences are relatively simple and why the acquisition process proceeds in an incremental fashion.

Since the earliest multiple-clause structures are both simple and frequent, the two factors, i.e. frequency and complexity, are difficult to disentangle. However, that complexity is an important factor independent of frequency is suggested by the 'delay' in the acquisition of some especially complex structures.

There are several constructions that should have emerged earlier if the emergence of complex sentences were solely determined by input frequency. For instance, constructions including the complement-taking verb *know* and a *wh*-infinitive emerge after constructions including the complement-taking verbs *got, hard, need, stop,* and *start* and a *to*-infinitive, although *know* plus *wh*-infinitive occurs more frequently in the input data. I suggest that the late occurrence of *know* plus *wh*-infinite can be explained in terms of the complexity of this construction: in contrast to children's early infinitival complements, *know* plus *wh*-infinitive includes a cognition-utterance verb, rather than a modality verb, and an infinitive that is marked by two subordinating morphemes, namely the infinitive marker *to* and a *wh*-adverb/pronoun.

Other constructions that emerge with some 'delay' in the children's data include adverbial clauses marked by *if* and *when*. Although *if* and *when* are more frequent in the ambient language than *but* and *so*, they appear later in the children's speech. In contrast to *but* and *so,* which are exclusively used in final conjoined clauses, *if* and *when* tend to appear in initial conjoined clauses. Since initial conjoined clauses are more difficult to plan and to produce than are final conjoined clauses, it seems reasonable to assume that *if* and *when* appear after *but* and *so* because they tend to occur in more complex structures.

In general, all of the constructions that emerge with some delay in the children's data are especially complex sentences that are difficult to plan and to produce. It is therefore a plausible hypothesis that the incremental development of complex sentences is partially motivated by the complexity of the emerging structures.

Additional support for this hypothesis comes from the fact that complex sentences including nonfinite subordinate clauses are initially more frequent than complex sentences including two finite clauses. As can be seen in figure 8.1, up to the age of 3;0 the majority of the children's multiple-clause structures includes a nonfinite subordinate clause, but after the third birthday the proportions change and complex sentences including two finite clauses are more frequent (cf. table 8a in the appendix).

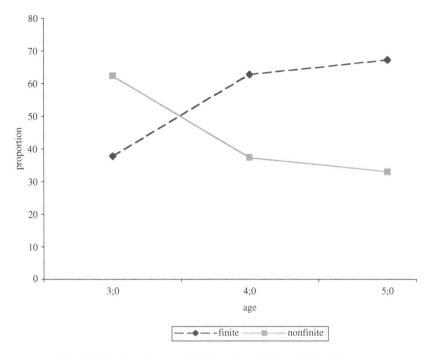

Fig. 8.1 *The development of finite and nonfinite multiple-clause structures.*

Since nonfinite subordinate clauses are shorter and semantically more tightly bound to the matrix clause than are finite subordinate clauses (or co-ordinate clauses), one might hypothesize that the development shown in figure 8.1 is motivated by the complexity of the emerging constructions: complex sentences including nonfinite subordinate clauses are initially more frequent than complex sentences including two finite clauses because the latter are more complex.

In addition to frequency and complexity, the pragmatic functions of complex sentences can have a significant effect on their development. For instance, as argued in chapter 6, one of the reasons why children start to use relative clauses in presentational constructions might be that these constructions are especially useful in parent–child speech. Children (and parents) tend to talk about elements that are present in the speech situation. Since presentational relatives function to focus the hearer's attention on elements in the surrounding situation, they are pragmatically especially well suited for parent–child speech, which might be part of the reason why the earliest relative clauses occur in presentational constructions.

Other complex sentences seem to emerge late because their pragmatic functions are not really useful in early child speech. For instance, as argued in chapter 7, initial adverbial clauses function to lay the foundation for the interpretation of subsequent clauses making discourse more coherent. Since young children usually do not produce long strings of utterances, there is little need for linguistic means that function to enhance discourse coherence. Thus, another reason why initial adverbial clauses tend to emerge late might be that these structures are not particularly useful in early child speech.

Finally, it has been suggested that the first finite complement clauses appear with formulaic matrix clauses such as *I think __, Do you know __?*, or *Remember__?* because performative and assertive matrix clauses presuppose a theory of mind that develops only gradually during the preschool years. In other words, children might avoid the use of mental verbs in performative and assertive matrix clauses because they lack the cognitive prerequisites for these uses. Since formulaic matrix clauses including mental verbs are not affected by the child's developing theory of mind, it can emerge before the child has acquired the cognitive prerequisites for the two other uses.

In sum, it seems that the development of complex sentences is determined by multiple factors that affect the acquisition process in different ways. Two of these factors, frequency and complexity, appear to be involved in the acquisition of *all* complex sentences, but pragmatic and cognitive factors are also important. If and to what extent the various factors determine the described developments need to be further investigated in experiments.

8.2   *From lexically specific constructions to constructional schemas*

As we have seen throughout this book, children's early complex sentences are tied to concrete lexical items: they are lexically specific constructions that are organized around a formulaic matrix clause, a particular conjunction, or some other lexical expressions providing a frame for the rest of the utterance.

The earliest complement clauses occur with a small number of complement-taking verbs. Very often, these verbs are part of a holophrastic matrix clause consisting of a first or second person pronoun and the complement-taking verb. For instance, the earliest infinitival complements occur with the formulaic *I want* (or *I wanna*), which also appears with nominal complements in simple transitive clauses. Likewise, the earliest finite complement clauses occur with formulaic matrix clauses such as *I think* or *Do you know wh-*, which function as epistemic markers or markers of illocutionary force. In both constructions the matrix clause provides a lexically specific frame for the rest of the utterance (cf. examples (1)–(2)).

(1)   I wanna ____ INF
(2)   Do you know wh- ____ S

Similarly, children's early relative clauses appear in constructions that are organized around concrete expressions: they are attached to the predicate nominal
of a presentational copular clause consisting of a pronominal subject, the copular *be*, and a noun (phrase). The pronominal subject is drawn from a small set
of demonstratives, interrogatives, and third person pronouns followed by the
copular in the present tense, which is usually cliticized to the preceding pronoun. The pronominal subject and the copula constitute the constant part of a
lexically specific utterance frame that includes an open slot for a noun (phrase)
modified by a relative clause (cf. example (3)).

(3)   That's [____ NP ____ REL] NP

Finally, children's early conjoined clauses are organized around a small number
of conjunctions such as *and, but, because*, and *so*. Since some of these conjunctions are tied to specific discourse patterns, their use is initially more restricted
than in adult language. For instance, some of the children use *because* at first
only in response to a causal *why*-question. This suggests that *because* is initially
part of a specific discourse routine (cf. example (4)).

(4)   A: ____ S
         B: Why?
         A: Because ____ S

As children grow older, the use of *because* becomes more variable: it is extended
to other discourse contexts and other grammatical constructions.

   In general, children's early complex sentences are organized around concrete
lexical expressions. More abstract representations of complex sentences emerge
only later, when children have acquired enough lexically specific constructions
to generalize across them. What children eventually learn is a network of interrelated constructions. The network includes constructions at different levels of
abstraction, ranging from concrete utterances (or parts of concrete utterances) to
highly abstract schemas. The constructions are related to each other by specific
links. Two types of links are commonly distinguished: (i) instantiation links,
which indicate a relationship between a schematic construction and a more
concrete construction that elaborates the former through specific information;
and (ii) extension links, which also indicate a relationship between a schematic
construction and a more concrete construction, but in this case there is some
conflict in value: although the more concrete construction shares some important features with the more abstract construction it is not simply an instance

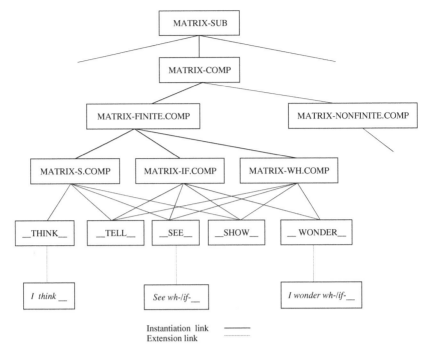

Fig. 8.2 *Network of finite complement clause constructions.*

of the latter because some of its features are not compatible with the constructional schema (cf. Langacker 2000; see also Flickinger, Pollard, and Wasow 1985; Lakoff 1987; Goldberg 1995). Consider, for instance, the network in figure 8.2, which represents the various complement clause constructions and their connections based on the analysis in chapter 5.

The vertical dimension of the network indicates the degree of abstractness or schematicity: constructions near the top of the network are more schematic than constructions at the bottom. In fact, the lowest level of the network shows constructions that include concrete lexical items. These items represent formulaic matrix clauses, stored as prefabricated chunks, that combine with specific types of complement clauses. They can be seen as (diachronic) extensions (rather than instantiations) of performative and assertive matrix clauses. The two latter comprise constructions of various degrees of abstractness. At the lowest level (i.e. above the formulaic expressions), the matrix clauses are lexically specific; they are organized around individual complement-taking verbs, but in contrast to the formulaic matrix clauses the lexically specific constructions are instantiations of more schematic constructions including abstract grammatical categories.

What the children included in this study had learned at the end of the time period I examined are isolated constructions at the bottom of the network. Most of these constructions are organized around formulaic matrix clauses. The performative and assertive uses are initially restricted to *say, tell, pretend,* and *show,* which are later supplemented by other complement-taking verbs that gradually become more substantial (e.g. *think, know, see*). Since the emergence of a constructional schema presupposes a significant number of types, it is unlikely that preschool children are able to extract a complement-clause schema from the data. In other words, I suspect that the constructional schemas in the upper part of the network emerge only later when children have learned a greater variety of complement-taking verbs in assertive and performative matrix clauses.

As Braine (1976), Tomasello (1992, 2000b, 2003), and many others have argued, children's early utterances are lexically specific constructions: they centre on individual verbs or other relational terms that are part of these constructions (see examples in chapter 1.2). Like children's early simple sentences, their early complex sentences are lexically specific; they are organized around a formulaic matrix clause, a specific conjunction, or some other lexical expression providing a frame for the rest of the utterance. Let me repeat, however, that the existence of lexically specific constructions is not a particular trait of child language; there are also many lexically specific constructions in adult grammar (cf. chapter 2). However, what children initially lack are constructional schemas, which in adult grammar exist side by side with lexically specific constructions. In contrast to the grammatical constructions of adult speakers, children's early constructions are *always* associated with some concrete forms.

Such lexically specific constructions play an important role in language acquisition: they provide the link between lexical learning and grammatical development. The development of grammatical patterns is based on analogy. Analogical reasoning has been studied in great detail by Gentner and other psychologists (e.g. Gentner 1983; Gentner and Median 1998). Analogy is a cognitive process, which crucially involves the recognition of similarity. Gentner distinguishes two basic types of similarity: (i) object similarity, which involves shared attributes (e.g. the same colour); and (ii) structural or relational similarity, which involves shared structures or relations (e.g. the shoulder of a person and the shoulder of a road). Interestingly, while adult speakers tend to focus on structural similarities, children find object similarities much easier to understand. It seems that the ability to recognize structural similarities emerges only gradually during the preschool years (cf. Gentner 1989; Rattermann and Gentner 1998). Gentner argues that the 'developmental shift' from object similarity to structural similarity is related to the child's growing knowledge: structural similarities can be recognized only within a rich database, which emerges only gradually in the child.

Gentner's research concentrates on nonlinguistic phenomena, but the developmental shift from object similarity to structural similarity can also be observed in the domain of grammar. Children's early one-word utterances and holophrases are acquired by rote learning: children recognize a string of speech sounds as an instance of a particular (utterance) type based on its phonetic substance, which can be seen as an object attribute of the construction. In other words, the acquisition of one-word utterances and holophrases involves children's ability to recognize object similarities (i.e. phonetic similarities). As children grow older, their early one-word utterances and holophrases are gradually extended to multiple word utterances that centre on specific terms. The emergence of such lexically specific constructions involves both the recognition of object similarities and the recognition of structural similarities: object similarity is involved in the recognition of the constant part; and structural similarity is involved in the recognition of the relationship between the constant part and the associated slot. As children acquire a gradually growing number of such lexically specific constructions, they obtain the ability to generalize across them, giving rise to grammatical schemas that are exclusively defined by structural or relational properties. In other words, the emergence of constructional schemas is based on the ability to recognize structural or relational similarities across lexically specific constructions in a gradually growing database.

Thus, the acquisition of grammar seems to involve the same developmental shift from object similarity to structural similarity that Gentner observed in other cognitive domains. Lexically specific constructions play an important role in this process: they combine concrete object attributes (i.e. phonetic substance) with structural relations (i.e. the association of the constant part with a slot), which helps the child to bridge the gap between rote learning (i.e. the recognition of object similarities) and grammatical development (i.e. the recognition of abstract structures and relations).

8.3   Conclusion

To conclude, this study has shown that the acquisition of complex sentences involves two important dimensions. First, children's complex sentences become increasingly more complex. The earliest multiple-clause structures are either simple sentences that denote a single situation and do not involve embedding or they comprise two independent utterances that are pragmatically combined in the ongoing discourse. Starting from such simple nonembedded structures, children gradually learn the use of complex sentences in which two related situations are expressed by two full-fledged clauses.

Second, children's complex sentences become increasingly more abstract. The earliest multiple-clause structures are lexically specific constructions that are associated with concrete lexical expressions. Starting from such item-based constructions, children gradually acquire a network of interrelated constructions in which the concrete constructions of early child speech are linked to abstract constructional schemas.

Appendix

Table 1a *Mean proportions of complex sentences in the children's transcripts*

Age	Type	Naomi	Peter	Nina	Sarah	Adam	Total
> 2;0	All utterances	4,712	4,889	2,088			11,689
	Complex Ss	37	2	5			44
	Proportion of complex Ss	0.8	0.0	0.2			0.33
2;0–3;0	All utterances	7,964	23,291	23,967	11,433	16,319	82,974
	Complex Ss	404	1,447	1,117	158	369	3495
	Proportion of complex Ss	5.1	6.2	4.7	1.4	2.3	3.94
3;0–4;0	All utterances	1,983	2,087	6,175	11,979	18,728	40,952
	Complex Ss	364	294	1,423	693	1,948	4,722
	Proportion of complex Ss	18.4	14.1	23.0	5.8	10.4	14.34

Table 4a *Mean proportions of the children's bare infinitives, to-infinitives, wh-infinitives, and participles*

	Naomi	Peter	Nina	·Sarah	Adam	Total	Mean
Bare INF	266	644	614	710	1,052	3,286	77.8
To-INF	21	46	152	156	510	885	15.5
WH-INF	6	9	8	74	108	205	3.6
PTC	12	10	28	6	100	156	3.0
Total	305	709	802	946	1,770	4,532	

Table 4b *Mean proportions of the children's complement-taking verbs in
NP-V-VP constructions*

	Naomi	Peter	Nina	Sarah	Adam	Mean
wanna	220	452	404	492	649	64.8
hafta	35	45	129	94	228	13.8
gotta	0	113	5	77	34	6.1
know	2	1	5	66	85	3.3
try	8	7	17	29	66	3.1
like	3	4	35	14	75	2.9
need	4	0	12	1	35	1.2
finish	0	0	11	0	33	0.9
stop	2	1	3	0	28	0.7
hard	2	6	2	8	7	0.7
start	3	2	1	8	5	0.6
forget	0	3	6	1	8	0.4
ready	0	2	0	0	13	0.3
learn	2	0	2	4	2	0.3
love	0	0	0	4	5	0.2
begin	0	2	0	1	1	0.1
wonder	0	0	0	0	3	0.1
help	0	3	0	1	1	0.1
say	0	0	0	4	1	0.1
mean	0	0	0	1	1	0.1
hear	0	0	0	1	0	0.1
pretend	0	0	1	0	1	0.1
promise	0	0	0	0	1	0.1
seem	0	0	0	0	1	0.1
glad	1	0	0	0	1	0.1
happy	0	1	0	0	0	0.1
Total	282	642	633	806	1,284	

Table 4c *Mean age of appearance: complement-taking verbs of the children's NP-V-VP constructions*[a]

	Naomi	Peter	Nina	Sarah	Adam	Months	Year
wanna	1;10	2;0	1;11	2;3	2;3	24;6	2;1
hafta	2;2	2;0	2;2	2;9	2;4	27;4	2;3
gotta	(3;5)	2;0	2;3	2;7	2;3	30;0	2;6
know	3;5	3;1	2;10	4;1	3;1	39;6	3;4
try	2;4	2;1	2;1	3;2	2;10	30;0	2;6
like	2;3	1;11	2;3	3;5	2;3	29;0	2;5
need	1;10	(3;5)	3;1	4;0	2;11	36;6	3;1
finish	(3;5)	(3;5)	2;9	(3;5)	2;10	38;0	3;2
stop	1;10	2;6	3;0	(5;0)	2;6	35;6	3;0
hard	2;0	2;3	2;3	4;0	3;4	33;2	2;9
start	3;5	2;3	2;9	3;8	4;6	39;8	3;4
forget	(3;5)	2;5	2;9	5;0	3;5	40;8	3;5
ready	(3;5)	2;10	(3;5)	(5;0)	3;5	43;2	3;7
learn	(3;5)	(3;5)	(3;5)	4;3	2;11	41;8	3;6
love	(3;5)	(3;5)	(3;5)	3;8	4;1	43;3	3;7
begin	(3;5)	2;6	(3;5)	3;8	3;6	39;6	3;4
wonder	(3;5)	(3;5)	(3;5)	3;8	(5;0)	45;4	3;9
help	(3;5)	2;0	(3;5)	3;1	3;2	36;2	3;0
say	(3;5)	(3;5)	(3;5)	(5;0)	4;10	48;2	4;0
mean	(3;5)	(3;5)	(3;5)	4;7	3;6	42;0	3;6
hear	(3;5)	(3;5)	(3;5)	4;6	(5;0)	45;4	3;9
pretend	(3;5)	(3;5)	2;11	(5;0)	3;7	44;0	3;8
promise	(3;5)	(3;5)	(3;5)	(5;0)	4;10	48;2	4;0
seem	(3;5)	(3;5)	(3;5)	(5;0)	3;7	45;2	3;9
glad	2;5	(3;5)	(3;5)	(5;0)	4;4	44;6	3;9
happy	(3;5)	2;3	(3;5)	(5;0)	(5;0)	45;8	3;10

[a] If a complement-taking verb does not occur in the transcripts of a particular child, the verb has been assigned a default value for the age of appearance, which is 3;5 for the three younger children, Naomi, Peter, and Nina, and 5;0 for the two older children, Sarah and Adam. The default age is indicated in parentheses.

Table 4d *Mean proportions of the children's complement-taking verbs in NP-V-NP-VP constructions*

	Naomi	Peter	Nina	Sarah	Adam	Mean
want	6	15	70	76	298	40.8
make	3	19	56	21	41	19.5
see	7	11	12	15	48	14.8
show	2	8	1	1	17	5.1
watch	0	3	6	10	30	4.3
put	2	2	9	0	0	3.4
help	0	4	6	4	5	2.7
hear	1	0	0	3	17	2.0
got	0	4	3	1	4	1.9
like	1	0	2	0	4	1.3
have	0	1	2	1	7	1.0
need	1	0	1	0	0	1.0
teach	0	0	0	6	3	1.0
tell	0	0	1	3	10	0.9
stop	0	0	0	1	1	0.2
ask	0	0	0	0	1	0.1
learn	0	0	0	1	0	0.1
start	0	0	0	1	0	0.1
Total	23	67	169	144	486	

Table 4e *Mean age of appearance: complement-taking verbs of the children's NP-V-NP-VP constructions*

	Naomi	Peter	Nina	Sarah	Adam	Months	Year
want	2;11	2;3	2;3	2;10	2;6	30.6	2;7
make	2;3	2;5	2;4	2;10	3;0	30.8	2;7
see	2;0	2;6	2;1	3;3	2;4	29;2	2;5
show	3;5	2;8	3;2	4;9	3;6	42;0	3;6
watch	(3;5)	2;4	2;5	2;11	2;9	33.2	2;9
put	2;11	2;7	2;3	(5;0)	(5;0)	42.6	3;8
help	(3;5)	2;0	2;1	2;11	2;6	31.0	2;7
hear	3;4	(3;5)	(3;5)	3;6	3;3	40.6	3;5
got	(3;5)	2;8	2;3	2;10	2;6	32.8	2;9
like	2;3	(3;5)	2;11	(5;0)	2;3	38.0	3;2
have	(3;5)	2;10	2;2	4;1	2;6	36.0	3;0
need	2;8	(3;5)	3;1	(5;0)	(5;0)	46.0	3;10
tell	(3;5)	(3;5)	2;10	3;10	3;7	41.0	3;5
teach	(3;5)	(3;5)	(3;5)	3;4	3;8	41.4	3;5
ask	(3;5)	(3;5)	(3;5)	(5;0)	4;10	48;2	4;0
learn	(3;5)	(3;5)	(3;5)	4;3	(5;0)	46;8	3;11
stop	(3;5)	(3;5)	(3;5)	4;10	(5;0)	48;2	4;0
start	(3;5)	(3;5)	(3;5)	3;8	(5;0)	45;4	3;9

Table 4f *Mean proportions of the mothers' complement-taking verbs in NP-V-VP constructions*

	Naomi's mother	Peter's mother	Nina's mother	Sarah's mother	Adam's mother	Total	Mean
want	128	116	787	244	157	1,432	43.0
have	62	33	348	245	215	903	26.1
like	40	11	293	66	93	503	12.7
try	18	10	37	55	36	156	5.5
know	4	8	22	47	20	101	3.3
got	5	4	8	78	1	96	2.9
be hard	12	5	39	2	4	62	2.2
need	5	2	16	0	35	58	2.0
start	5	1	1	24	10	41	1.4
stop	3	1	6	17	10	37	1.2
Total	282	191	1,557	778	581	3,389	

Table 4g *Mean proportions of the mothers' complement-taking verbs in NP-V-NP-VP constructions*

	Naomi's mother	Peter's mother	Nina's mother	Sarah's mother	Adam's mother	Total	Mean
want	50	50	254	79	66	499	50.0
make	25	6	115	22	25	193	16.8
see	5	4	20	20	21	70	7.7
help	1	7	39	9	10	66	5.9
tell	10	3	8	18	4	43	5.4
hear	2	3	4	21	12	42	5.1
like	4	1	4	7	5	21	2.6
have	3	1	8	7	4	23	2.4
show	1	0	6	3	6	16	1.6
watch	3	0	2	2	2	9	1.1
got	1	3	1	2	0	7	1.2
Total	105	78	461	190	155	989	

Table 5a *Mean proportions of the children's complement-taking verbs of finite complement clauses*

	Naomi	Peter	Nina	Sarah	Adam	Total	Mean
think	103	74	857	398	615	2,047	32.8
know	93	47	269	749	194	1,352	21.8
see	54	28	304	209	98	693	11.5
say	79	9	88	158	121	455	8.7
tell	28	9	116	198	92	443	6.6
look	23	3	112	26	20	184	2.9
mean	15	4	53	36	33	141	2.4
guess	5	3	58	32	52	150	2.2
show	10	2	38	35	21	106	1.7
pretend	2	3	60	0	6	71	1.0
bet	2	0	44	27	0	73	0.8
wonder	3	0	36	11	5	55	0.7
hope	2	2	6	6	4	20	0.5
wish	1	2	3	17	0	23	0.4
others	13	27	120	34	99	293	6.1
Total	433	213	2,164	1,936	1,360	6,106	

Table 5b *Mean age of appearance: children's complement-taking verbs of finite complement clauses*

	Naomi	Peter	Nina	Sarah	Adam	Months	Years
think	2;11	2;0	2;2	3;1	2;11	31.4	2;7
know	2;6	2;3	2;3	3;2	2;6	30.4	2;6
see	2;3	2;3	2;1	2;9	2;4	28.0	2;4
say	2;6	2;3	(3;5)	3;0	2;8	33.2	2;9
tell	2;11	2;5	2;10	4;2	2;10	36.4	3;0
look	2;11	2;2	2;3	3;8	2;5	31.8	2;8
mean	(3;5)	2;5	2;10	3;6	3;5	37.4	3;1
guess	2;11	2;3	(3;5)	3;5	3;5	37.0	3;1
show	2;11	2;8	(3;5)	4;1	3;4	39.4	3;3
pretend	3;5	2;5	2;3	4;5	3;4	38.0	3;2
bet	(3;5)	2;9	2;5	3;4	4;4	39.0	3;3
wonder	(3;5)	2;10	2;3	(5;0)	3;8	41.2	3;5
hope	(3;5)	(3;5)	(3;5)	(5;0)	3;6	45.0	3;9
wish	(3;5)	(3;5)	(3;5)	3;6	3;5	41.2	3;5

Table 6a *Mean proportions of the children's PN-, N-, OBJ-, OBL-, and SUBJ-relatives (total)*

	Peter	Nina	Sarah	Adam	Total	Mean
PN	14	31	12	90	147	48.5
N	8	11	10	25	54	23.8
OBJ	2	16	8	48	74	21.5
OBL	1	4	2	10	17	5.6
SUBJ	0	0	0	5	5	0.7
Total	25	62	32	178	297	

Table 6b *Mean proportions of the children's PN-, N-, OBJ-, OBL-, and SUBJ-relatives (first 10)*

	Peter	Nina	Sarah	Adam	Total	Mean
PN	8	10	8	6	32	80.0
N	0	0	0	1	1	2.5
OBJ	1	0	2	1	4	10.0
OBL	1	0	0	2	3	7.5
SUBJ	0	0	0	0	0	0.0
Total	10	10	10	10	40	

Table 6c *Development of the children's PN-, N-, OBJ-, OBL-, and SUBJ-relatives*

Age	Type	Peter	Nina	Sarah	Adam	Mean
> 3;0	PN	13	11	0	0	84.2
	N	4	0	0	0	10.6
	OBJ	1	0	0	0	2.7
	OBL	1	0	0	0	2.7
	SUBJ	0	0	0	0	0.0
3;0–4;0	PN	1	20	5	38	46.9
	N	3	12	1	4	23.6
	OBJ	2	14	1	13	23.9
	OBL	0	5	0	5	4.4
	SUBJ	0	0	0	3	1.2
4;0–5;0	PN			7	52	36.6
	N			9	21	27.2
	OBJ			7	35	29.2
	OBL			2	5	6.2
	SUBJ			0	2	0.9

Table 6d *Mean proportions of the children's subj-, obj-, obl-, io-, and gen-relatives (total)*

	Peter	Nina	Sarah	Adam	Total	Mean
subj	18	35	20	68	141	57.3
obj	5	20	12	104	141	37.0
obl	2	7	0	6	15	5.7
io	0	0	0	0	0	0
gen	0	0	0	0	0	0
Total	25	62	32	178	297	100

Table 6e *Mean proportions of the children's subj-, obj-, obl-, io-, and gen-relatives (first 10)*

	Peter	Nina	Sarah	Adam	Total	Mean
subj	9	8	7	5	29	72.5
obj	1	2	3	5	11	27.5
obl	0	0	0	0	0	0.0
io	0	0	0	0	0	0.0
gen	0	0	0	0	0	0.0
Total	10	10	10	10	40	

Table 6f *Development of the children's subj-, obj-, obl-, io-, and gen-relatives*

Age	Type	Peter	Nina	Sarah	Adam	Mean
>3;0	subj	15	9	0	0	80.4
	obj	3	2	0	0	17.0
	obl	1	0	0	0	2.7
	io	0	0	0	0	0.0
	gen	0	0	0	0	0.0
3;0–4;0	subj	15	9	5	29	54.6
	obj	3	2	1	32	37.0
	obl	1	0	0	2	8.4
	io	0	0	0	0	0.0
	gen	0	0	0	0	0.0
4;0–5;0	subj			15	37	46.1
	obj			10	74	52.2
	obl			0	4	1.8
	io			0	0	0.0
	gen			0	0	0.0

Table 6g *Mean proportions of the children's PN-, N-, OBJ-, OBL-, and SUBJ-participial relatives (total)*

	Peter	Nina	Sarah	Adam	Total	Mean
SUBJ	0	0	0	0	0	0.0
OBJ	1	1	2	5	9	8.6
OBL	0	0	1	0	1	0.9
PN	16	16	24	26	82	87.5
N	0	1	1	1	3	3.1
Total	17	18	28	32	95	

Table 7a *Children's early bound and unbound conjoined-clauses (total)*

		Naomi	Peter	Nina	Sarah	Adam	Total	Mean
and	bound	30	123	100	95	164	512	19.0
	unbound	224	357	619	369	542	2,111	81.0
	Total	254	480	719	464	706	2,623	
because	bound	23	36	78	27	61	225	24.9
	unbound	69	89	305	146	115	724	75.1
	Total	92	125	383	173	176	949	
so	bound	3	3	39	11	102	158	28.7
	unbound	17	24	45	45	97	228	71.3
	Total	20	27	84	56	199	386	
but	bound	3	7	1	49	15	75	22.1
	unbound	21	11	80	88	53	253	77.9
	Total	24	18	81	137	68	328	

Table 7b *Development of the children's* because-*clauses that occur in response to a causal question*

Age	Type	Naomi	Peter	Nina	Sarah	Adam
>3;0	*why? because*	18	50	50	1	5
	Other	12	41	60	0	2
	Total	30	91	110	1	7
3;0–4;0	*why? because*	7	10	96	24	47
	Other	55	24	177	9	33
	Total	62	34	273	33	80
4;0–5;0	*why? because*				84	20
	Other				55	69
	Total				139	89

Table 7c *Development of the children's early conjoined clauses: bound vs. unbound*[a]

Age	Type	Naomi		Peter		Nina		Sarah		Adam	
		+b	−b	+b	−b	+b	+b	−b	−b	+b	−b
>3;0	*and*	9	154	102	331	42	257	0	0	2	8
	because	2	28	23	68	19	107	0	0	0	7
	so	0	6	0	14	14	21	0	0	0	0
	but	2	4	5	7	0	24	0	0	0	0
	MEAN	11.4	88.6	22.6	77.4	17.3	82.7	0.0	0.0	10.0	90.0
3;0–4;0	*and*	21	70	21	26	58	362	16	129	65	346
	because	21	41	13	21	59	198	2	32	18	63
	so	3	11	3	10	25	24	3	17	52	63
	but	1	17	2	4	1	56	3	12	2	20
	MEAN	21.0	79.0	34.8	65.2	22.4	77.6	13.0	87.0	23.1	76.9
4;0–5;0	*and*							81	238	97	188
	because							25	114	43	45
	so							8	28	50	34
	but							46	76	13	33
	MEAN							25.8	74.4	42.7	57.3

[a] +b = intonationally bound, −b = intonationally unbound.

Table 7d *Children's bound and unbound conjoined clauses: early conjoined clauses (i.e.* and-, but, because-, *and* so-*clauses) vs. later conjoined clauses (i.e.* if-, when-, *and various other temporal clauses)*

	Naomi	Peter	Nina	Sarah	Adam	Total	Mean
Early CONJ-cl. (i.e. and, but, because, so)							
Bound	59	169	218	184	342	972	21.8
Unbound	331	481	1,049	648	807	3,316	78.2
Total	390	650	1,267	832	1,149	4,288	
Late CONJ-cl. (i.e. if, when, before, while, until, since)							
Bound	23	30	65	128	254	500	82.5
Unbound	4	4	24	33	40	105	17.5
Total	27	34	89	161	294	605	

Table 7e *Development of the children's initial and final when-clauses*[a]

Age	Type	Naomi	Peter	Nina	Sarah	Adam	Mean
>3;0	Initial	0	1	2	0	0	6.5
	Final	6	11	16	0	0	93.5
	Total	6	12	18	0	0	
3;0–4;0	Initial	2	6	4	2	13	31.3
	Final	3	2	37	17	48	68.7
	Total	5	8	41	19	61	
4;0–5;0	Initial				22	31	42.1
	Final				44	30	57.9
	Total				66	61	

[a] In 19 utterances the ordering of matrix clause and *when*-clause is unclear.

Table 7f *Development of the children's initial and final if-clauses*[a]

Age	Type	Naomi	Peter	Nina	Sarah	Adam	Mean
>3;0	Initial	0	0	1	0	0	16.7
	Final	2	0	2	0	0	83.3
	Total	2	0	3	0	0	
3;0–4;0	Initial	1	4	1	2	9	34.9
	Final	4	3	3	7	9	65.1
	Total	5	7	4	9	18	
4;0–5;0	Initial				19	40	53.2
	Final				16	37	46.9
	Total				35	77	

[a] In 37 utterances the ordering of matrix clause and *if*-clause is unclear.

Table 7g *Mean proportions of the mothers' conjoined clauses*

	Naomi's mother	Peter's mother	Nina's mother	Sarah's mother	Adam's mother	Total	Mean
and	121	60	1,094	596	392	2,263	33.5
because	45	39	242	214	191	731	13.1
so	35	19	249	135	112	550	8.7
but	71	15	197	164	144	591	10.3
when	75	30	199	272	179	755	13.7
if	53	28	101	173	198	553	10.8
or	14	12	53	36	30	145	3.0
after	14	6	12	21	10	63	1.7
while	12	3	22	11	27	75	1.5
until	10	2	16	17	15	60	1.2
before	8	10	51	32	11	112	2.2
since	0	1	0	5	3	9	0.2
Total	458	225	2,236	1,676	1,312	5,907	

Table 7h *Appearance of the children's conjoined clauses*

	Naomi	Peter	Nina	Sarah	Adam	Months	Year
and	2;0	1;11	1;11	2;6	2;7	26.2	2;2
because	2;1	2;5	2;2	2;8	2;8	28.8	2;5
so	2;8	2;5	2;5	2;11	2;8	31.4	2;7
but	2;7	2;8	2;5	3;0	2;9	32;2	2;8
when	2;11	2;7	2;4	3;2	3;0	33.6	2;10
if	2;11	2;7	2;9	3;6	3;1	35.6	3;0
while	3;3	2;9	2;10	3;8	3;2	37.6	3;2
before	2;11	2;8	(3;5)	3;6	3;5	38.2	3;2
after	3;4	(3;5)	2;9	3;10	3;5	40.2	3;4
until	2;5	2;8	2;8	(5;0)	4;1	40.4	3;4
since	(3;5)	(3;5)	(3;5)	(5;0)	4;3	46.8	3;11

Table 8a *Mean proportions of the children's finite and nonfinite complex sentences*

Age	Type	Naomi	Peter	Nina	Sarah	Adam	Mean
>3;0	Finite	234	763	649	8	72	37.7
	Nonfinite	208	686	468	150	297	62.3
	Total	442	1,449	1,117	158	369	
3;0–4;0	Finite	239	209	980	350	1,034	62.7
	Nonfinite	121	74	430	343	906	37.3
	Total	360	283	1,410	693	1,940	
4;0–5;0	Finite				2,243	1,323	67.1
	Nonfinite				496	733	32.9
	Total				2,739	2,056	

References

Abott-Smith, Kirsten, Elena V. M. Lieven, and Michael Tomasello. 2001. What preschool children do and do not do with ungrammatical word orders, *Cognitive Development* 16:679–692.

Amidon, Arlene and Peter Carey. 1972. Why five-year-olds cannot understand *before* and *after*, *Journal of Verbal Learning and Verbal Behavior* 11:417–423.

Amidon, Arlene. 1976. Children's understanding of sentences with contingent relations: why are temporal and conditional connectives so difficult, *Journal of Experimental Psychology* 22:423–437.

Ardery, Gail. 1980. On coordination in child language, *Journal of Child Language* 7:305–320.

Astington, Janet Wilde and Jennifer M. Jenkins. 1999. A longitudinal study of the relationship between language and theory-of-mind development, *Developmental Psychology* 35:1311–1320.

Austin, L. John. 1962. *How to Do Things with Words*, 2nd edn. Cambridge, Mass.: Harvard University Press.

Barlow, Michael and Susanne Kemmer (eds.). 2000. *Usage-based Models of Language*, Stanford: CSLI Publications.

Bartsch, Karen and Henry M. Wellman. 1995. *Children Talk about the Mind*, New York: Oxford University Press.

Bates, Elizabeth. 1976. *Language in Context*, New York: Academic Press.

Bates, Elizabeth and Brian MacWhinney. 1987. Competition, variation, and language learning, in Brian MacWhinney (ed.), *Mechanisms of Language Acquisition*, 157–193, Hillsdale, NJ: Laurence Erlbaum.

1989. Functionalism and the competition model, in Brian MacWhinney and Elizabeth Bates (eds.), *The Cross-linguistic Study of Sentence Processing*, 3–73, Cambridge: Cambridge University Press.

Bebout, L. J., S. J. Segalowitz, and G. J. White. 1980. Children's comprehension of causal constructions with *because* and *so*, *Child Development* 51:656–568.

Behrens, Heike. 2002. Learning multiple regularities: evidence from overgeneralization errors in the German plural, *Boston University Conference on Language Development* 26:72–83.

Bencini, Guilia M. L. and Adele E. Goldberg. 2000. The contribution of argument structure constructions to sentence meaning, *Journal of Memory and Language* 43:640–651.

Berman, Ruth A. and Dan I. Slobin (eds.). 1994. *Relating Events in Narrative: A Crosslinguistic Developmental Study*, Hillsdale, NY: Lawrence Erlbaum.

Bever, Thomas G. 1970a. The cognitive basis for linguistic structures, in J. R. Hayes (ed.), *Cognition and Development of Language*, 279–352, New York: Wiley.

1970b. The comprehension of sentences with temporal relations, in G. B. Flores d'Arcais and W. J. M. Levelt (eds.), *Advances in Psycholinguistics*, 285–291, Amsterdam: North-Holland.

Bloom, Lois P. 1973. *One Word at a Time. The Use of Single Word Utterances*, The Hague: Mouton.

1991. *Language Development from Two to Three*, Cambridge: Cambridge University Press.

Bloom, Lois, Margaret Lahey, Lois Hood, Karin Lifter, and Kathleen Fliess. 1980. Complex sentences: acquisition of syntactic connectives and the semantic relations they encode, *Journal of Child Language* 7:235–6 [reprinted in Bloom 1991, 261–289].

Bloom, Lois, Jo Tackeff, and Margaret Lahey. 1984. Learning 'to' in complement constructions, *Journal of Child Language* 11:101–120 [reprinted in Bloom 1991, 290–309].

Bloom, Lois and Joanne Bitetti Capatides. 1987. Sources of meaning in the acquisition of complex syntax: the sample case of causality, *Journal of Experimental Child Psychology* 43:112–128 [reprinted in Bloom 1991, 375–393].

Bloom, Lois, Matthew Rispoli, Barbara Gartner, and Jeremie Hafitz. 1989. Acquisition of complementation, *Journal of Child Language* 16:101–120 [reprinted in Bloom 1991, 310–332].

Boas, Hans. 2003. *A Constructional Approach to Resultatives*, Stanford: CSLI Publications.

Bock, J. Kathryn. 1977. The effect of a pragmatic presupposition on syntactic structure in question answering, *Journal of Verbal Learning and Verbal Behavior* 16:723–734.

Borer, Hagit and Kenneth Wexler. 1987. The maturation of syntax, in Thomas Roeper and Edwin Williams (eds.) *Parameter Setting*, 123–172, Dordrecht: Reidel.

Bowerman, Melissa. 1976. *Early Syntactic Development: A Cross-linguistic Study with Special Reference to Finnish*, Cambridge: Cambridge University Press.

1979. The acquisition of complex sentences, in Paul Fletcher and Michael Garman (eds.), *Language Acquisition: Studies in First Language Development*, 285–305, Cambridge: Cambridge University Press.

1986. First steps in acquiring conditionals, in Elizabeth Closs Traugott, Alice ter Meulen, Judy Snitzer Reilly, and Charles A. Ferguson (eds.), *On Conditionals*, 285–307, Cambridge: Cambridge University Press.

Braine, Martin D. S. 1976, Children's first word combinations, *Monographs of the Society for Research in Child Development* 41.

Braine, Martin D. S. and Barbara Rumain. 1981. Development and comprehension of *or*: evidence for a sequence of competencies, *Journal of Experimental Child Psychology* 31:46–70.

Braunwald, Susan R. 1985. The development of connectives, *Journal of Pragmatics* 9:513–525.

Brent, Michael R. and Timothy A. Cartwright. 1996. Distributional regularity and phono-
tactic constraints are useful for segmentation, *Cognition* 61:93–125.

Bresnan, Joan and Judith Aissen. 2002. Optimality and functionality: objections and
refutations, *Natural Language and Linguistic Theory* 20:81–95.

Brooks, Patricia J. and Michael Tomasello. 1999. Young children learn to produce
passives with nonce verbs, *Developmental Psychology* 35:29–44.

Brown, H. Douglas. 1971. Children's comprehension of relativized English sentences,
Child Development 42:1923–1936.

Brown, Roger. 1973. *A First Language*, Cambridge, Mass.: Harvard University Press.

Bruner, Jerome. 1983. *Child's Talk: Learning to Use Language*, New York: W. W.
Norton.

Bybee, Joan. 1985. *Morphology*, Amsterdam: John Benjamins.

   1995. Regular morphology and the lexicon, *Language and Cognitive Processes*
   10:425–455.

   1998. The emergent lexicon, *Chicago Linguistic Society* 42:1–435.

   2000. The phonology of the lexicon: evidence from lexical diffusion, in Barlow and
   Kemmer (eds.), 65–85.

   2001. *Phonology and Language Use*, Cambridge: Cambridge University Press.

Bybee, Joan and Dan Slobin. 1982. Rules and schemas in the development and use of
the English past tense, *Language* 58:265–289.

Bybee, Joan, Revere Perkins, and William Pagliuca. 1994. *The Evolution of Grammar.
Tense, Aspect, and Modality in the Languages of the World*, Chicago: The University
of Chicago Press.

Bybee, Joan and Sandra Thompson. 1997. Three frequency effects in syntax, *Berkeley
Linguistics Society* 23:378–388.

Bybee, Joan and Joanne Scheibman. 1999. The effect of usage on degrees of
constituency: the reduction of *don't* in English, *Linguistics* 37:575–596.

Bybee, Joan and Paul Hopper (eds.) 2001. *Frequency and the Emergence of Linguistic
Structure*, Amsterdam: John Benjamins.

Cairns, Helen Smith, Dana McDaniel, Jennifer Ryan Hsu, and Michelle Rapp. 1994.
A longitudinal study of principles of control and pronominal reference in child
English, *Language* 70:260–288.

Cambon, Jacqueline and Hermine Sinclair. 1974. Relations between syntax and semantics: are they 'easy to see'?, *British Journal of Psychology* 65:133–140.

Carni, Ellen and Lucia A. French. 1984. The acquisition of *before* and *after* reconsidered:
what develops?, *Journal of Experimental Child Psychology* 37:394–403.

Cartwright, Timothy A. and Michael Brent. 1997. Syntactic categorization in early
language acquisition: formalizing the role of distributional analysis, *Cognition*
63:121–170.

Chafe, Wallace L. 1984. How people use adverbial clauses, *Berkeley Linguistics Society*
10:437–449.

Chipman, Harold H. and Josselyne Gerard. 1987. Some evidence for and against a
'proximity strategy' in the acquisition of subject control sentences, in Lust (ed.),
Vol. II, 61–87.

Chomsky, Carol S. 1969. *The Acquisition of Syntax in Children from 5 to 10*, Cambridge,
Mass.: MIT Press.

Chomsky, Noam. 1965. *Aspects of the Theory of Syntax*, Cambridge, Mass.: MIT Press.

1972. *Studies on Semantics in Generative Grammar*, The Hague: Princeton.

1981. *Lectures on Government and Binding*, Dordrecht: Foris.

1986. *Barriers*, Cambridge, Mass.: MIT Press.

1995. *The Minimalist Program*, Cambridge, Mass: MIT Press.

1999. On the nature, use, and acquisition of language, in William C. Ritchie and Tej K. Bhatia (eds.), *Handbook of Child Language Acquisition*, 33–54, Cambridge: Cambridge University Press (repr. from *Sophie Linguistica*, Special Issue 11, 1987).

2000. *New Horizons in the Study of Language and Mind*, Cambridge: Cambridge University Press.

Clahsen, Harald. 1999. Lexical entries and rules of language: a multidisciplinary study of German inflection, *Behavioral and Brain Sciences* 22:991–1060.

Clahsen, Harald, Monika Rothweiler, Andreas Woest, and Gary F. Marcus. 1992. Regular and irregular inflection in the acquisition of German noun plurals, *Cognition* 45:225–255.

Clancy, Patricia, Terry Jacobsen, and Marilyn Silva. 1976. The acquisition of conjunction: a crosslinguistic study, *Stanford Papers and Reports on Child Language* 12:71–80.

Clancy, Patricia, Hyeonjin Lee, and Myeong-Han Zoh. 1986. Processing strategies in the acquisition of relative clauses: universal principles and language-specific realizations, *Cognition* 24:225–262.

Clark, Eve V. 1970. How young children describe events in time, in G. B. Flores D'Arcais and W. J. M. Levelt (eds.), *Advances in Psycholinguistics*, 275–284, Amsterdam: North-Holland.

1971. On the acquisition of the meaning of *before* and *after*, *Journal of Verbal Learning and Verbal Behavior* 10:266–275.

1973. How children describe time and order, in Ferguson and Slobin (eds.), 585–606.

1983. Meaning and concepts, in P. Mussen (ed.), *Handbook of Child Psychology*, Vol. III, 787–840, New York: Wiley.

2003. *First Language Acquisition*, Cambridge: Cambridge University Press.

Clark, Herbert H. and Eve V. Clark. 1968. Semantic distinctions and memory for complex sentences, *Quarterly Journal of Experimental Psychology* 20:129–138.

Clifton, Charles and Lyn Frazier. 1989. Comprehending sentences with long-distance dependencies, in Greg N. Carslon and Michael K. Tannenhaus (eds.), *Linguistic Structure in Language Processing*, 273–317, Dordrecht: Kluwer.

Coker, Pamela L. 1978. Syntactic and semantic factors in the acquisition of *before* and *after*, *Journal of Child Language* 5:261–277.

Corrêa, Letícia M. Sicuro. 1982. Strategies in the acquisition of relative clauses, in J. Aitchison and N. Harvey (eds.), *Working Papers of the London Psycholinguistic Research Group* 4:37–49.

1995a. An alternative assessment of children's comprehension of relative clauses, *Journal of Psycholinguistic Research* 24:183–203.

1995b. The relative difficulty of children's comprehension of relative clauses: a procedural account, in K. Nelson and Z. Réger (eds.), *Children's Language*, Vol. VIII, 225–243, Hillsdale, NJ: Lawrence Erlbaum.

Corrigan, Roberta. 1975. A scalogram analysis of the development of the use and comprehension of *because* in children, *Child Development* 46:195–201.

Crain, Stephen. 1991. Language acquisition in the absence of experience, *Behavioral and Brain Sciences* 14:597–650.

Crain, Stephen, Cecile McKee, and Maria Emiliani. 1990. Visiting relatives in Italy, in Frazier and de Villiers (eds.), 335–356.

Crain, Stephen and Paul Pietroski. 2001. Nature, nurture and universal grammar. *Linguistics and Philosophy* 24:139–186.

Cristofaro, Sonia. 2003. *Subordination Strategies. A Typological Study*, Oxford: Oxford University Press.

Croft, William. 1995. Autonomy and functionalist linguistics, *Language* 71:490–532.

    2001. *Radical Construction Grammar*, Oxford: Oxford University Press.

    2003. *Typology and Universals*, 2nd edn. Cambridge: Cambridge University Press.

Croft, William and Alan Cruse. 2003. *Cognitive Linguistics*, Cambridge: Cambridge University Press.

Cromer, Richard. 1974. Child and adult learning of surface structure clues to deep structure using a picture card technique, *Journal of Psycholinguistic Research* 3:1–14.

Culicover, Peter W. 1998. *Syntactic Nuts. Hard Cases, Syntactic Theory, and Language Acquisition*, Oxford: Oxford University Press.

Custer, W. L. 1996. A comparison of young children's understanding of contradictory representations in pretense, memory, and belief, *Child Development* 67:678–688.

Dabrowska, Eva. 2000. From formula to schema: the acquisition of English questions, *Cognitive Linguistics* 11:83–102.

Dasinger, Lisa and Cecile Toupin. 1994. The development of relative clause functions in narratives, in Berman and Slobin (eds.), 457–514.

Davidse, Kristin. 2000. A constructional approach to clefts, *Linguistics* 38:1101–1131.

de Villiers, Jill G. 1999. Language and theory of mind: what are the developmental relationships, in S. Baron-Cohen, H. Tager-Flusberg, and D. Cohen (eds.), *Understanding Other Minds: Perspectives from Autism and Developmental Cognitive Neuroscience*, 2nd edn. 83–123, Oxford: Oxford University Press.

de Villiers, Jill G. and Peter A. de Villiers. 1973. Development of the use of word order in comprehension, *Journal of Psycholinguistic Research* 2:331–341.

    1999. Linguistic determinism and understanding of false beliefs, in P. Mitchell and K. Riggs (eds.), *Children's Reasoning and the Mind*, 189–226, Hove: Psychology Press.

de Villiers, Jill G., Helen B. Tager-Flusberg, Kenji Hakuta, and Michael Cohen. 1979. Children's comprehension of relative clauses, *Journal of Psycholinguistic Research* 8:499–518.

de Villiers, Jill G., Thomas Roeper, and Anne Vainikka. 1990. The acquisition of long-distance rules, in Frazier and de Villiers (eds.), 257–297.

Diessel, Holger. 1996. Processing factors of pre- and postposed adverbial clauses, *Berkeley Linguistics Society* 22:71–82.

    1997a. The diachronic reanalysis of demonstratives in crosslinguistic perspective, *Chicago Linguistic Society* 33:83–98.

1997b. Verb-first constructions in German, in Marjolijn Verspoor, Lee Kee Dong, and Eve Sweetser (eds.), *Lexical and Syntactical Constructions and the Construction of Meaning*, 51–68, Amsterdam: John Benjamins.

1999a. The morphosyntax of demonstratives in synchrony and diachrony, *Linguistic Typology* 3:1–49.

1999b. *Demonstratives. Form, Function, and Grammaticalization*, Amsterdam: John Benjamins.

2001. The ordering distribution of main and adverbial clauses: a typological study, *Language* 77:343–365.

2003a. The relationship between demonstratives and interrogatives, *Studies in Language* 27:581–602.

2003b. *Verb-first Constructions in English*, Leipzig: Max Planck Institute for Evolutionary Anthropology.

forthcoming. Competing motivations for the ordering of main and adverbial clauses, *Linguistics*.

Diessel, Holger and Michael Tomasello. 1999. Why complement clauses do not include a *that*-complementizer in early child language, *Berkeley Linguistics Society* 25: 86–97.

2000. The development of relative clauses in English, *Cognitive Linguistics* 11:131–151.

2001. The acquisition of finite complement clauses in English: a corpus-based analysis, *Cognitive Linguistics* 12:1–45.

2004. *A New Look at the Acquisition of Relative Clauses in English and German*, Leipzig: Max Planck Institute for Evolutionary Anthropology.

Dixon, R. M. W. 1982. *Where Have all the Adjectives Gone*, Berlin: Mouton.

Donaldson, Morag L. 1986. *Children's Explanations: A Psycholinguistic Study*, Cambridge: Cambridge University Press.

Dryer, Matthew. 1980. The positional tendencies of sentential noun phrases in universal grammar, *The Canadian Journal of Linguistics* 25:123–195.

1992. The Greenbergian word order correlations, *Language* 68:81–138.

1997a. Why statistical universals are better than absolute universals, *Chicago Linguistic Society* 33:123–145.

1997b. Are grammatical relations universal?, in Joan Bybee, John Haiman, and Sandra A. Thompson (eds.), *Essays on Language Function and Language Type. Dedicated to Talmy Givón*, 115–143, Amsterdam: John Benjamins.

DuBois, John A. 1985. Competing motivations, in John Haiman (ed.), *Iconicity in Syntax*, 343–366, Amsterdam: John Benjamins.

1987. The discourse basis of ergativity, *Language* 64:805–855.

Eisenberg, Ann R. 1980. A syntactic, semantic, and pragmatic analysis of conjunction, *Stanford Papers and Reports on Child Language Development* 19:129–138.

Eisenberg, Sarita L. 2002. Interpretation of relative clauses by young children: another look, *Journal of Child Language* 29:177–188.

Eisenberg, Sarita L. and Helen S. Cairns. 1994. The development of infinitives from three to five, *Journal of Child Language* 21:713–731.

Elman, Jeffrey L. 1990. Finding structure in time, *Cognitive Science* 14:179–211.

1993. Learning and development in neural networks: the importance to start small, *Cognition* 48:71–99.

Elman, Jeffrey L., Elizabeth A. Bates, Mark H. Johnson, Annette Karmiloff-Smith, Domencio Parisi, and Kim Plunkett. 1996. *Rethinking Innateness. A Connectionist Perspective on Development*, Cambridge, Mass.: MIT Press.

Emerson, Harriet F. 1979. Children's comprehension of *because* in reversible and non-reversible sentences, *Journal of Child Language* 6:279–300.

1980. Children's judgements of correct and reversed sentences with *if*, *Journal of Child Language* 7:137–155.

Erman, Britt and Beatrice Warren. 1999. The idiom principle and the open choice principle, *Text* 20:29–62.

Fabian-Kraus, Veronica and Paul Ammon. 1980. Assessing linguistic competence: when are children hard to understand?, *Journal of Child Language* 7:401–412.

Feagans, Lynne. 1980. Children's understanding of some temporal terms denoting order, duration, and simultaneity, *Journal of Psycholinguistic Research* 9:41–57.

Ferguson, Charles A. and Dan I. Slobin (eds.). 1973. *Studies of Child Language Development*, 175–208, New York: Holt, Rinehart and Winston.

Ferreiro, Emilia and Hermina Sinclair. 1971. Temporal relations in language, *International Journal of Psychology* 6:39–47.

Fillmore, Charles J. 1988. Mechanisms of Construction Grammar, *Berkeley Linguistic Society* 14:35–55.

Fillmore, Charles J. and Paul Kay. 1993. *Construction Grammar*, Berkeley: University of California.

Fillmore, Charles J, Paul Kay, and Catherine O'Connor. 1988. Regularity and idiomaticity in grammatical constructions: the case of *let alone*, *Language* 64:501–538.

Flickinger, Daniel, Carl Pollard, and Thomas Wasow. 1985. Structure sharing in lexical representations, *Association of Computational Linguistics* 23:262–267.

Flynn, Suzanne and Barbara Lust. 1980. Acquisition of relative clauses. Developmental changes of their heads, in Harbert, W. Herschensohn (eds.), *Cornell Working Papers in Linguistics* 1, 33–45, Ithaca: Cornell University.

Foley, William A. and Robert D. Van Valin. 1984. *Functional Syntax and Universal Grammar*, Cambridge: Cambridge University Press.

Ford, Cecilia E. 1993. *Grammar in Interaction: Adverbial Clauses in American English Conversations*, Cambridge: Cambridge University Press.

Fox, Barbara A. 1987. The noun phrase accessibility hierarchy reinterpreted: subject primacy or the absolutive hypothesis, *Language* 63:856–870.

Fox, Barbara A. and Sandra A. Thompson. 1990. A discourse explanation of the grammar of relative clauses in English conversation, *Language* 66:297–316.

Frazier, Lyn. 1985. Syntactic complexity, in David R. Dowty, Lauri Karttunen, and Arnold Zwicky (eds.), *Natural Language Parsing: Psychological, Computational, and Theoretical Perspectives*, 129–189, Cambridge: Cambridge University Press.

1987. Syntactic processing: evidence from Dutch, *Natural Language and Linguistic Theory* 5:519–559.

Frazier, Lyn and Keith Rayner. 1988. Parameterizing the language processing system: left versus right-branching within and across languages, in John Hawkins (ed.),

Explaining Linguistic Universals, 247–279, Cambridge: Cambridge University Press.

Frazier, Lyn and Jill de Villiers (eds.). 1990. *Language Processing and Language Acquisition*, Boston: Kluwer.

French, Lucia A. 1986. Acquiring and using words to express logical relationships, in S. Kuczaj and M. Barrett (eds.) 1986, *The Development of Word Meaning*, 303–338, New York: Springer-Verlag.

    1988. The development of children's understanding of *because* and *so*, *Journal of Experimental Child Psychology* 45:262–279.

French, Lucia A. and Ann L. Brown. 1977. Comprehension of *before* and *after* in logical and arbitrary sequences, *Journal of Child Language* 4:247–256.

French Lucia A. and Katherine Nelson. 1985. *Young Children's Knowledge of Relational Terms: Some ifs, ands, and buts*, New York: Springer-Verlag.

Gawlitzek-Maiwald, Ira. 1997. *Der monolinguale und bilinguale Erwerb von Infinitivkonstruktionen: Ein Vergleich von Deutsch und Englisch.* Tübingen: Niemeyer.

Gentner, Dedre. 1983. Structure-mapping: a theoretical framework for analogy, *Cognitive Science* 7:155–170.

    1989. The mechanisms of analogical learning, in S. Vosniadou and A. Ortony (eds.), *Similarity and Analogical Reasoning*, 199–241, New York: Cambridge University Press.

Gentner, Dedre and José Median. 1998. Similarity and the development of rules, *Cognition* 65:263–262.

Gerhardt, Julie. 1991. The meaning and use of the modals *hafta, needta* and *wanna* in children's speech, *Journal of Pragmatics* 16:531–590.

Gibson, Edward. 1998. Linguistic complexity: locality of syntactic dependencies, *Cognition* 68:1–76.

Givón, Talmy. 1979. *On Understanding Grammar*, New York: Academic Press.

    1980. The binding hierarchy and the typology of complements, *Studies in Language* 4:333–377.

    1984. *Syntax: A Functional-typological Introduction*, Vol. I, Amsterdam: John Benjamins.

    1990. *Syntax: A Functional-typological Introduction*, Vol. II, Amsterdam: John Benjamins.

    1995. *Functionalism and Grammar*, Amsterdam: John Benjamins.

Goldberg, Adele E. 1995. *A Construction Grammar Approach to Argument Structure*, Chicago: The University of Chicago Press.

Goodluck, Helen. 1981. Children's grammar of complement-subject interpretation, in Tavakolian (ed.), 139–166.

    1987. Children's interpretation of pronouns and null NP's, in Lust (ed.), Vol. II, 247–269.

    2001. The nominal analysis of children's interpretation of adjunct pro clauses, *Language* 77:494–509.

Goodluck, Helen and Cynthia A. Mervis. 1980. Development of coordination in the natural speech of young children, *Journal of Child Language* 7:279–304.

Goodluck, Helen and Susan Tavakolian. 1982. Competence and processing in children's grammar of relative clauses, *Cognition* 11:1–27.

Goodluck, Helen and Dawn Behne. 1992. Development in control and extraction, in Jürgen Weissenborn, Helen Goodluck, and Thomas Roeper (eds.), *Theoretical Issues in Language Acquisition*, 151–171, Hillsdale, NJ: Lawrence Erlbaum.

Goodluck, Helen and Danijela Stojanovic. 1997. The structure and acquisition of relative clauses in Serbo-Croation, *Language Acquisition* 5:285–315.

Gregory, Michelle, William D. Raymond, Alan Bell, Eric Fosler-Lussier, and Daniel Jurfsky. 1999. The effects of collocational strength and contextual predictability in lexical production, *Chicago Linguistic Society* 35:151–166.

Gries, Stefan T. 2003. *Multifactorial Analysis in Corpus Linguistics: A Study of Particle Placement*, London: Continuum.

Haiman, John. 1983. Iconic and economic motivation, *Language* 59:781–819.

1985. *Natural Syntax: Iconicity and Erosion*, Cambridge: Cambridge University Press.

1994. Ritualization and the development of language, in William Pagliuca (ed.), *Perspectives on Grammaticalization*, 3–28, Amsterdam: John Benjamins.

1998. *Talk is Cheap: Sarcasm, Alienation, and the Evolution of Language*, New York: Oxford University Press.

Haiman, John and Sandra A. Thompson. 1984. 'Subordination' in universal grammar, *Berkeley Linguistics Society* 10:510–523.

(eds.). 1988. *Clause Combining in Grammar and Discourse*, Amsterdam: John Benjamins.

Hakes, David T., Judith S. Evans, and Linda L. Brannon. 1976. Understanding sentences with relative clauses, *Memory and Cognition* 4:283–290.

Hakuta, Kenji. 1981. Grammatical description versus configurational arrangement in language acquisition: the case of relative clauses in Japanese, *Cognition* 9:197–236.

Halliday, Michael A. K. 1985. *An Introduction to Functional Grammar*, Baltimore: University Park Press.

Hamburger, Henry. 1980. A deletion ahead of its time, *Cognition* 8:389–416.

Hamburger, Henry and Stephen Crain. 1982. Relative acquisition, in Stan Kuczaj (ed.), *Language Development*, Vol. I, *Syntax and Semantics*, 245–274, Hillsdale, NJ: Lawrence Erlbaum.

Hare, Mary, Jeff L. Elman, and Kim G. Daugherty. 1995. Default generalization in connectionist networks, *Language and Cognitive Processes* 10:601–630.

Hare, Mary and Adele E. Goldberg. 2000. Structural priming: purely syntactic?, *Proceedings of the Twenty-first Annual Meeting of the Cognitive Science Society*, 208–211, Mahwah: Lawrence Erlbaum.

Haspelmath, Martin. 1995. The converb as a cross-linguistic valid category, in Martin Haspelmath and Ekkehard König (eds.), *Structure and Meaning of Adverbial Verb Forms – Adverbials, Participials, Gerunds*, 1–55, Berlin: Mouton de Gruyter.

Hawkins, John A. 1990. A parsing theory of word order universals, *Linguistic Inquiry* 21:223–261.

1994. *A Performance Theory of Order and Constituency*, Cambridge: Cambridge University Press.

1998. Some issues in performance theory of word order, in Anna Siewierska (ed.), *Constituent Order in the Languages of Europe*, 729–780, Berlin: Mouton de Gruyter.

1999. Processing complexity and filler-gap dependencies across grammars, *Language* 75:244–285.

Heine, Bernd, Ulrike Claudi, and Friederike Hünnemeyer. 1991. *Grammaticalization, a Conceptual Framework*, Chicago: Chicago University Press.

Hildebrand, Joyce. 1987. The acquisition of preposition stranding, *Canadian Journal of Linguistics* 32:65–85.

Höhle, Barbara and Jürgen Weissenborn. 1999. The origins of syntactic knowledge: recognition of determiners in one-year-old German children, *Boston University Conference on Language Development* 24:418–429.

Homzie, M. J. and Carol B. Gravitt. 1977. Children's reproductions: effects of event order and implied vs. directly stated causation, *Journal of Child Language* 4:237–246.

Hood, Lois, Margaret Lahey, Karin Lifter, and Lois Bloom. 1978. Observational, descriptive methodology in studying child language: preliminary results on the development of complex sentences, in G. P. Sackett (ed.), *Observing Behavior*, Vol. I, *Theory and Application in Mental Retardation*, 239–263, Baltimore: University Park Press.

Hood, Lois and Lois Bloom. 1979. What, when, and how about why: a longitudinal study of early expressions of causality, *Monographs of the Society for Research in Child Development* 44.

Hooper, Joan B. 1975. On assertive predicates, in John Kimball (ed.), *Syntax and Semantics* 4:91–124, New York: Academic Press.

Hooper, Joan B. and Sandra A. Thompson. 1973. On the applicability of root transformations, *Linguistic Inquiry* 4:465–497.

Hopper, Paul J. 1979. Aspect and foregrounding in discourse, in Talmy Givón (ed.), *Syntax and Semantics* 12:213–241, New York: Academic Press.

1987. Emergent Grammar, *Berkeley Linguistics Society* 13:139–157.

Hopper, Paul J. and Sandra A. Thompson. 1980. Transitivity in grammar and discourse, *Language* 56:251–299.

1984. The discourse basis for lexical categories in universal grammar, *Language* 60:703–772.

Hopper, Paul and Elizabeth Closs Traugott. 1993. *Grammaticalization*, Cambridge: Cambridge University Press.

Hsu, Jennifer Ryan, Helen Smith Cairns, and Robert Fiengo. 1985. The development of grammars underlying children's interpretation of complex sentences, *Cognition* 20:25–48.

Hsu, Jennifer Ryan, Helen Smith Cairns, Sarita Eisenberg, and Gloria Schlisselberg. 1989. Control and coreference in early child language, *Journal of Child Language* 16:599–622.

Hudson, Richard A. 1990. *Word Grammar*, Oxford: Blackwell.

Hyams, Nina. 1986. *Language Acquisition and Theory of Parameters*, Dordrecht: Reidel.

Irwin, Judith W. and Cynthia J. Pulver. 1984. Effects of explicitness, clause order, and reversibility on children's comprehension of causal relationships, *Journal of Educational Psychology* 76:399–407.

Israel, Michael, Christopher Johnson, and Patrica J. Brooks. 2000. From states to events: the acquisition of English passive participles, *Cognitive Linguistics* 11:103–129.

Jackendoff, Ray. 1975. Morphological and semantic regularities in the lexicon, *Language* 51:639–671.

1990. *Semantic Structures*, Cambridge: Cambridge University Press.

1997. Twistin' the night away, *Language* 73:534–559.

Jisa, Harriet and Sophie Kern. 1998. Relative clauses in French children's narrative texts, *Journal of Child Language* 25:623–652.

Johnson, Helen L. 1975. The meaning of *before* and *after* for preschool children, *Journal of Experimental Child Psychology* 19:88–99.

Johnson, Helen L. and Robin S. Chapman. 1980. Children's judgment and recall of causal connectives – a developmental study of *because, so,* and *and, Journal of Psycholinguistic Research* 9:243–260.

Johnson, Christopher. 1999. Metaphor vs. conflation in the acquisition of polysemy: the case of *see*, in Masako K. Hiraga, Chris Sinha, and Sherman Wilcox (eds.), *Cultural, Typological, and Psychological Perspectives in Cognitive Linguistics*, 155–169, Amsterdam: John Benjamins.

Johansson, Bo S. and Barbro Sjöln. 1975. Preschool children's understanding of the coordinators *and* and *or, Journal of Experimental Child Psychology* 19:233–240.

Jurafsky, Daniel, Alan Bell, Michelle Gregory, and William D. Raymond. 2001. Probabilistic relations between words: evidence from reduction in lexical production, in Bybee and Hopper (eds.), 229–253.

Jusczyk, Peter W. 1997. *The Discovery of Spoken Language*, Cambridge, Mass.: MIT Press.

Kail, Michèl and Jürgen Weissenborn. 1984. A developmental cross-linguistic study of adversative connectives: French 'mais' and German 'aber/sondern', *Journal of Child Language* 11:143–158.

Kaschak, Michael P. and Arthur M. Glenberg. 2000. Constructing meaning: the role of affordances and grammatical constructions in sentence comprehension, *Journal of Memory and Language* 43:508–529.

Katz, Evelyn Walker and Sandor B. Brent. 1968. Understanding connectives, *Journal of Verbal Learning and Verbal Behavior* 7:501–509.

Kavanaugh, Robert D. 1979. Observations on the role of logically constrained sentences in the comprehension of *before* and *after, Journal of Child Language* 6:353–357.

Kay, Paul and Charles J. Fillmore. 1999. Grammatical constructions and linguistic generalizations: the *What's X doing Y?* construction, *Language* 75:1–33.

Keenan, Edward and Sarah Hawkins. 1987. The psychological validity of the accessibility hierarchy, in Edward Keenan, *Universal Grammar: 15 Essays*, 60–85, London: Croom Helm.

Kidd, Evan and Edith L. Bavin. 2002. English-speaking children's comprehension of relative clauses: evidence for general-cognitive and language-specific constraints on development, *Journal of Psycholinguistic Research* 31:599–617.

Kim, Young-Joo. 1989. Theoretical implications of complement structure acquisition in Korean, *Journal of Child Language* 16:573–598.

Köpcke, Klaus-Michael. 1988. Schemas in German plural formation, *Lingua* 74:303–335.

1993. *Schemata und Pluralbildung im Deutschen. Versuch einer kognitiven Morphologie*, Tübingen: Narr.

1998. The acquisition of plural marking in English and German revisited: schemata versus rules, *Journal of Child Language* 25:293–319.

Kroch, Anthony S. 1989. Reflexes of grammar in patterns of language change, *Language Variation and Change* 1:199–244.

Kuhn, Deanna and Henry Phelps. 1976. The development of children's comprehension of causal direction, *Child Development 1976*: 248–251.

Kuno, Susumo. 1973. Constraints on internal clauses and sentential subjects, *Linguistic Inquiry* 4:363–385.

  1974. The position of relative clauses and conjunctions, *Linguistic Inquiry* 5:117–136.

Kyratzis, Amy and Susan Ervin-Tripp. 1999. The development of discourse markers in peer interaction, *Journal of Pragmatics* 31:1321–1338.

Labelle, Marie. 1990. Prediction, WH-movement and the development of relative clauses, *Language Acquisition* 1:95–120.

  1996. The acquisition of relative clauses: movement or no movement? *Language Acquisition* 5:65–82.

Lakoff, George. 1974. Syntactic amalgams, *Chicago Linguistic Society* 10:321–344.

  1987. *Women, Fire, and Dangerous Things*, Chicago: Chicago University Press.

Lambrecht, Knud. 1988. There was a farmer had a dog: syntactic amalgams revisited, *Berkeley Linguistics Society* 14:319–339.

  1994. *Information Structure and Sentence Form. Topic, Focus and the Mental Representation of Discourse Referents*, Cambridge: Cambridge University Press.

Langacker, Ronald W. 1987a. *Foundations of Cognitive Grammar*, Vol. I, *Theoretical Prerequisites*, Stanford: Stanford University Press.

  1987b. Nouns and verbs, *Language* 63:53–94.

  1988. A usage-based model, in Brygida Rudzka-Ostyn (ed.), *Topics in Cognitive Linguistics*, 127–161, Amsterdam: John Benjamins.

  1991. *Foundations of Cognitive Grammar*, Vol. II, *Descriptive Application*, Stanford: Stanford University Press.

  2000. A dynamic usage-based model, in Barlow and Kemmer (eds.), 24–63.

Lebeaux, David. 1990. The grammatical nature of the acquisition sequence: adjoin-A and the formation of relative clauses, in Frazier and de Villiers (eds.), 12–82.

Lederberg, Amy R. and Michael P. Maratsos. 1981. Children's use of semantic analysis in the interpretation of missing subjects: further evidence against MPD, *Journal of Psycholinguistic Research* 10:89–110.

Leech, Geoffrey, Brain Francis, and Xunfang Xu. 1994. The use of computer corpora in the textual demonstrability of gradience in linguistic categories, in C. Fuchs and B. Victorri (eds.), *Continuity in Linguistic Semantics*, 57–76, Amsterdam: John Benjamins.

Lehmann, Christian. 1988. Towards a typology of clause linkage, in Haiman and Thompson (eds.), 181–225.

  1995. *Thoughts on Grammaticalization*. Munich: Lincom Europa.

Lieven, Elena V. M., Julian M. Pine, and Gillian Baldwin. 1997. Lexically-based learning and early grammatical development, *Journal of Child Language* 24:187–219.

Lillard, Angeline S. 1993. Pretend play skills and the child's theory of mind, *Child Development* 64:348–371.

Limber, John. 1973. The genesis of complex sentences, in Timothy E. Moore (ed.), *Cognitive Development and the Acquisition of Language*, 169–185, New York: Academic Press.

1976. Unraveling competence, performance and pragmatics in the speech of young children, *Journal of Child Language* 3:309–318.

Lohmann, Heidemarie and Michael Tomasello. 2003. The role of language in the development of false belief understanding: a training study, *Child Development* 74:1130–1144.

Lust, Barbara (ed.) 1986. *Studies in the Acquisition of Anaphora*, Vol. I, Boston: Reidel.
(ed.) 1987. *Studies in the Acquisition of Anaphora*, Vol. II, Boston: Reidel.

Lust Barbara and Cynthia A. Mervis. 1980. Development of coordination in the natural speech of young children, *Journal of Child Language* 7:279–304.

MacWhinney, Brian. 1975. Pragmatic patterns in child syntax, *Stanford Papers and Reports on Child Language Development* 10:153–165.
1978. The acquisition of Morphology, *Monographs of the Society for Research in Child Development* 43.
1987. The competition model, in Brian MacWhinney (eds.), *Mechanism of Language Acquisition*, 249–308, Hillsdale, NJ: Lawrence Erlbaum.
1995. *The CHILDES Project. Tools for Analyzing Talk*, 2nd edn. Hillsdale, NJ: Lawrence Erlbaum.
2000. *The CHILDES Project. Tools for Analyzing Talk*, Vol. II, *The Database*, 3rd edn. Hillsdale, NJ: Lawrence Erlbaum.

MacWhinney, Brian and Csaba Pléh. 1988. The processing of restrictive relative clauses in Hungarian, *Cognition* 29:95–141.

Maratsos, Michael P. 1974. How preschool children understand missing complement subjects, *Child Development* 45:700–706.

Marcus, G. F. 2001. *The Algebraic Mind. Integrating Connectionism and Cognitive Science*, Cambridge: Bradford.

Marcus, G. F., M. Ullman, S. Pinker, M. Hollander, T. J. Rosen, and F. Xu. 1992. Overgeneralization in language acquisition, *Monographs of the Society for research in Child Development* 57.

Marcus, G. F., S. Vijayan, S. Bandi Rao, and P. M. Vishton. 1999. Rule learning in seven month-old infants, *Science* 283:77–80.

Matthiessen, Christian and Sandra A. Thompson. 1988. The structure of discourse and 'subordination', in Haiman and Thompson (eds.), 275–329.

McCabe, Allyssa, Susan Evely, Rona Abramovitch, Carl M. Corter, and Debra J. Pepler. 1983. Conditional statements in young children's spontaneous speech, *Journal of Child Language* 10:253–258.

McCabe, Allyssa and Carole Peterson. 1985. A naturalistic study of the production of causal connectives by children, *Journal of Child Language* 12:145–159.

McCarthy, John and Alan Prince. 1990. Foot and word in prosodic morphology: the Arabic broken plural, *Natural Language and Linguistic Theory* 8:209–283.

McClelland, James L. and Jeffrey L. Elman. 1986. The TRACE model of speech perception, *Cognitive Psychology* 18:1–86.

McDaniel, Dana and Helen Smith Cairns. 1990. The processing and acquisition of control structures by young children, in Frazier and de Villiers (eds.), 313–325.

McDaniel, Dana, Helen Smith Cairns, and Jennifer Ryan Hsu. 1991. Control principles in the grammars of young children, *Language Acquisition* 1:297–335.

McKee, Cecile and Dana McDaniel. 2001. Resumptive pronouns in English relative clauses, *Language Acquisition* 9:113–156.

McKee, Cecile, Dana McDaniel, and Jesse Snedeker. 1998. Relatives children say, *Journal of Psycholinguistic Research* 27:573–596.

Meisel, Jürgen M. 1994. Parameters in acquisition, in Plaul Fletcher and Brain MacWhinney (eds.), *Handbook of Child Language*, 9–35, Oxford: Blackwell.

Menyuk, Paula. 1969. *Sentences Children Use*, Cambridge, Mass.: MIT Press.

Michaelis, Laura and Knud Lambrecht. 1996. Towards a construction-based theory of language function: the case of nominal extraposition, *Language* 72:215–247.

Mintz, Toben H., Elissa L. Newport, and Thomas G. Bever. 2002. The distributional structure of grammatical categories in the speech to young children, *Cognitive Science* 26:393–424.

Morris William C., Garrison W. Cottrell, and Jeffrey Elman. 2000. A connectionist simulation of the empirical acquisition of grammatical relations, in Stefan Wermter and Run Sun (eds.) *Hybrid Neural Symbolic Integration*, 175–193, New York: Springer-Verlag.

Nedjalkov, Vladimir (ed.). 1983. *Typology of Resultative Constructions*, Amsterdam: John Benjamins.

Newmeyer, Frederick J. 1998. *Language Form and Language Function*, Cambridge, Mass.: MIT Press.

Newport, Elissa L. 1990. Maturation constraints on language learning, *Cognitive Science* 14:11–28.

Nishigauchi, Taisuke and Thomas Roeper. 1987. Deductive parameters and the growth of empty categories, in Thomas Roeper and Edwin Williams (eds.), *Parameter Setting*, 91–121, Boston: Reidel.

Noonan, Michael. 1985. Complementation, in Shopen (ed.), Vol. III, 42–140.

Nosofsky, R. M. 1988. Similarity, frequency and category representation, *Journal of Experimental Psychology: Learning, Memory and Cognition* 14:54–65.

Nunberg, Geoffry, Ivan A. Sag, and Thomas Wasow. 1994. Idioms, *Language* 70:491–538.

O'Grady, William. 1997. *Syntactic Development*, Chicago: The University of Chicago Press.

Ono, Tsuyoshi and Sandra A. Thompson. 1995. What can conversations tell us about syntax, in Philip W. Davies (ed.), *Alternative Linguistics. Descriptive and Theoretical Models*, 213–271, Amsterdam: John Benjamins.

Pawley, Andrew and Hodgetts Syder. 1983. Two puzzles for linguistic theory: native like selection and native like fluency, in Jack C. Richards and Richard W. Schmidt (eds.), *Language and Communication*, 193–226, London: Longman.

Pérez-Leroux, Ana. 1995. Resumptives in the acquisition of relative clauses, *Language Acquisition* 4:105–138.

Perner, Josef. 1991. *Understanding the Representational Mind*, Cambridge, Mass.: Bradford Books/MIT Press.

Peterson, Carole. 1986. Semantic and pragmatic uses of *but*, *Journal of Child Language* 13:583–590.

Peterson, Carole and Allyssa McCabe. 1985. Understanding *because*: how important is the task?, *Journal of Psycholinguistic Research* 14:199–218.

1987. The connective *and*: do older children use it less as they learn other connectives?, *Journal of Child Language* 14:375–381.

1988. The connective *and* as discourse glue, *First language* 8:19–28.

Phinney, Marianne. 1981. *Syntactic Constraints and the Acquisition of Embedded Sentential Complements*, dissertation, Amherst, Mass.: University of Massachusetts.

Piaget, Jean. 1948. *Language and Thought in the Child*, London: Routledge & Kegan Paul.

Pine, Julian M. and Elena V. M. Lieven. 1993. Reanalyzing rote-learned phrases: individual differences in the transition to multi-word speech, *Journal of Child Language* 20:551–571.

Pine, Julian M, Elena V. M. Lieven, and Caroline Rowland. 1998. Comparing different models of the development of the English verb category, *Linguistics* 36:4–40.

Pinker, Steven. 1984. *Language Learnability and Language Development*, Cambridge, Mass.: Harvard University Press.

1994. *The Language Instinct*, New York: Harper Collins.

1999. *Words and Rules. The ingredients of Language*, New York: Basic Books.

Pinker, Steven and Alan Prince. 1988. On language and connectionism: analysis of a Parallel Distributed Processing model of language acquisition, *Cognition* 28:73–193.

Plunkett, Kim and Virginia Marchman. 1991. U-shaped learning and frequency effects in a multi-layered perceptron: implications for child language acquisition, *Cognition* 48:43–102.

Plunkett, Kim and Virginia Marchman. 1993. From rote learning to system building: acquiring verb morphology in children and connectionist nets, *Cognition* 48:21–69.

Plunkett, Kim and Ramin Charles Nakisa. 1997. A connectionist model of the Arabic plural system, *Language and Cognitive Processes* 12:807–836.

Pollard, Carl and Ivan A. Sag. 1994. *Head-Driven Phase Structure Grammar*, Chicago: Chicago University Press.

Pullum, Geoffrey K. 1996. Learnability, hyperlearning, and the poverty of the stimulus, *Berkeley Linguistic Society (parasession on the role of learnability of grammatical theory)* 22:498–513.

Pullum, Geoffrey K. and Barbara C. Scholz. 2002. Empirical assessment of stimulus poverty arguments, *The Linguistic Review* 19:9–50.

Pullum, Geoffrey K. and Arnold Zwicky. 1991. Condition duplication, paradigm homonymy, and transconstructional constraints, *Berkeley Linguistics Society* 17:252–266.

Prasada, Sandeep and Steven Pinker. 1993. Generalizations of regular and irregular morphological patterns, *Language and Cognitive Processes* 8:1–56.

Prince, Ellen F. 1978. A comparison of WH-clefts and *it*-clefts in discourse, *Language* 54:883–906.

Quirk, Randolph, Sidney Greenbaum, Geoffrey Leech, and Jan Svartvik. 1985. *A Grammar of Contemporary English*, London: Longman.

Ramscar, Michael. 2002. The role of meaing in inflection: why the past tense does not require a rule, *Cognitive Psychology* 45:45–94.

Rattermann, Mary Jo and Dedre Gentner. 1998. More evidence for a relational shift in the development of analogy: children's performance on a causal-mapping task, *Cognitive Development* 13:453–478.

Redington, Martin and Nick Chater. 1998. Connectionist and statistical approaches to language acquisition: a distributional analysis, *Language and Cognitive Processes* 13:129–191.

Redington, Martin, Nick Chater, and Steven Finch. 1998. Distributional information: a powerful cue for acquiring syntactic categories, *Cognitive Science* 22:435–469.

Reilly, Judy Snitzer. 1986. The acquisition of temporals and conditionals, in Traugott et al. (eds.), 309–331.

Reinhart, Tanya. 1983. *Anaphora and Semantic Interpretation*, Chicago: University of Chicago Press.

1984. Principles of gestalt perception in the temporal organization of narrative texts, *Linguistics* 22:779–809.

Roeper, Thomas and Jürgen Weissenborn. 1990. How to make parameters work, in Frazier and de Villiers (eds.), 147–162.

Roeper, Thomas and Jill G. de Villiers. 1994. Lexical links in the WH-chain, in Barbara Lust, Gabriella Hermon, and Jaklin Kornfilt (eds.), *Syntactic Theory and First Language Acquisition: Cross-linguistic Perspectives*, Vol. II, *Binding, Dependencies, and Learnability*, 357–390, Hillsdale, NJ: Lawrence Erlbaum.

Rosenbaum, Peter S. 1967. *The Grammar of English Predicate Constructions*, Cambridge, Mass.: MIT Press.

Ross, John Robert. 1970. Gapping and the order of constituents, in Manfred Bierwisch and Karl-Erich Heidolph (eds.), *Progress in Linguistics*, 249–259, The Hague: Mouton.

1986. *Infinite Syntax*, Norwood, NJ: Ablex.

Roth, Froma P. 1984. Accelerating language learning in young children, *Journal of Child Language* 11:89–107.

Rothweiler, Monika. 1993. *Der Erwerb von Nebensätzen im Deutschen. Eine Pilotstudie.* Tübingen: Max Niemeyer.

Rumelhart, David E. and James L. McClelland (eds.). 1986a. *Parallel Distributed Processing. Explanation in Microstructures of Cognition*, Vols I–II, Cambridge, Mass.: MIT Press.

1986b. On learning the past tense of English verbs, in Rumelhart and McClelland (eds.), Vol. II, 216–271.

Rumelhart, David E., Geoffrey Hinton, and James L. McClelland. 1986. A general framework for parallel distributed processing, in Rumelhart and McClelland (eds.), Vol. I, 45–76.

Rumelhart, David E., Paul Smolensky, James L. McClelland, and Geoffrey Hinton. 1986. Schemata and sequential thought processes in PDP models, in Rumelhart and McClelland (eds.), Vol. II, 7–57.

Sachs, Jacqueline. 1983. Talking about there and then: the emergence of displaced reference in parent–child discourse, in K. E. Nelson (ed.), *Children's Language*, Vol. IV, 359–438, Hillsdale, NJ: Lawrence Erlbaum.

Saffran, Jenny R. 2001. Words in a sea of sounds: the output of infant statistical learning, *Cognition* 81:149–169.

Saffran, Jenney R., Richard N. Aslin, and Elissa L. Newport. 1996. Statistical learning by 8-months-old infants, *Science* 274:1926–1928.

Sag, Ivan A. 1997. English relative clauses, *Journal of Linguistics* 33:431–483.

Santelmann, Lynn M. and Peter W. Jusczyk. 1998. Sensitivity to discontinuous dependencies in language learners: evidence for limitations in processing space, *Cognition* 69:105–134.

Sasse, Hans Jürgen. 1993. Syntactic categories and subcategories, in Joachim Jacobs, Arnim von Stechow, Wolfgang Sternefeld, and Theo Vennemann (eds.), *Syntax*, 646–686, Berlin: Mouton de Gruyter.

Saussure, Ferdinand de. 1916. *Cours de linguistique générale*, Paris: Payot.

Schuele, C. Melanie and Lisa M. Nicholls. 2000. Relative clauses: evidence of continued linguistic vulnerability in children with specific language impairment, *Clinical Linguistics and Phonetics* 14:563–585.

Schultz, Petra. 2000. Children's interpretation of factive and non-factive verbs in English, in Mieke Beers, Beppie van den Bogaerde, Gerard Bol, Jan de Jong, and Carola Rooijmans (eds.), *From Sound to Sentence. Studies in First Language Acquisition*, 141–153, Groningen: Center for Language and Cognition.

Searle, John R. 1979. The classification of illocutionary acts, in John R. Searle, *Expression and Meaning*, 1–29, Cambridge: Cambridge University Press [reprinted from *Language in Society* 5:1–24].

Shatz, Marilyn, Henry M. Wellman, and Sharon Silber. 1983. The acquisition of mental verbs: a systematic investigation of the first reference to mental state, *Cognition* 14:301–321.

Sheldon, Amy. 1974. The role of parallel function in the acquisition of relative clauses in English, *Journal of Verbal Learning and Verbal Behavior* 13:272–281.

1977. On strategies for processing relative clauses: a comparison of children and adults, *Journal of Psycholinguistic Research* 6:305–318.

Sherman, Janet Cohen. 1987. Evidence against the Minimal Distance Principle in first language acquisition of anaphora, in Lust (ed.), Vol. II, 89–101.

Sherman, Janet Cohen and Barbara Lust. 1986. Syntactic and lexical constraints on the acquisition of control in complement sentences, in Lust (ed.), Vol. I, 279–308.

1993. Children are in control, *Cognition* 46:1–51.

Shopen, Timothy (ed.). 1985. *Language Typology and Syntactic Description*, Vols. I–III, Cambridge: Cambridge University Press.

Silva, Marilyn. 1991. Simultaneity in children's narratives: the case of *when*, *while* and *as*, *Journal of Child Language* 18:641–662.

Slobin, Dan I. 1973. Cognitive prerequisites for the development of grammar, in Ferguson and Slobin (eds.), 175–208.

1986, The acquisition and use of relative clauses in Turkic and Indo-European languages, in Dan I. Slobin and Karl Zimmer (eds.), *Studies in Turkish Linguistics*, 273–294, Amsterdam: John Benjamins.

1997, The origins of grammaticizable notions: beyond the individual mind, in Dan I. Slobin (ed.), *The Crosslinguistic Study of Language Acquisition*, Vol. V, *Expanding the Context*, 265–323, London: Lawrence Erlbaum.

Slobin, Dan I. and Charles A. Welsh. 1973. Elicited imitation as a research tool in developmental psycholinguistics, in Ferguson and Slobin (eds.), 485–497.

Slobin, Dan I. and Thomas Bever. 1982. Children use canonical sentence schemas: a cross-linguistic study of word order and inflection, *Cognition* 12:229–265.

Smith, Michael D. 1974. Relative clause formation between 29–36 months: a preliminary report, *Stanford Papers and Reports on Child Language Development* 8:104–110.

Suppes, Patrick. 1973. The semantics of children's language, *American Psychologist* 88:103–114.

Tager-Flusberg, Helen B. 1982. The development of relative clauses in child speech, *Papers and Reports on Child Language Development* 21:104–111.

Tallal, P., R. Ross, and S. Curtis. 1989. Familial aggregation in specific language impairment, *Journal of Speech and Hearing Disorders* 54:157–173.

Talmy, Leonard. 1978. Figure and ground in complex sentences, in Joseph H. Greenberg (ed.), *Universals of Human Language*, Vol. IV, 625–649, Stanford: Stanford University Press.

1988. The relation between grammar and cognition, in B. Rudzka-Ostyn (ed.), *Topics in Cognitive Linguistics*, 165–205, Amsterdam: John Benjamins.

2000. *Toward a Cognitive Semantics*, Vol. I, *Concept Structuring Systems*, Cambridge: Cambridge University Press.

Tavakolian, Susan L. 1977. *Structural Principles in the Acquisition of Complex Sentences*, dissertation Amherst: University of Massachusetts.

1981a. The conjoined clause analysis of relative clauses, in Tavakolian (ed.), 167–187.

(ed.). 1981b. *Language Acquisition and Linguistic Theory*, Cambridge, Mass.: MIT Press.

Theakston, Anna L. 2003. The acquisition of auxiliary syntax: *be* and *have*, Ms.

Theakston, Anna L., Elena V. M. Lieven, Julian M. Pine, and Caroline F. Rowland. 2001. The role of performance limitations in the acquisition of verb-argument structure, *Journal of Child Language* 28:157–172.

Thompson, Sandra A. 1985. Grammar and written discourse: initial vs. final purpose clauses in English, *Text* 4:55–84.

1987. 'Subordination' and narrative event structure, in Russell Tomlin (ed.), *Coherence and Grounding in Discourse*, 435–454, Amsterdam: John Benjamins.

2002. 'Object complements' and conversation: towards a realistic account, *Studies in Language* 26:125–164.

Thompson, Sandra A. and Robert E. Longacre. 1985. Adverbial clauses, in Shopen (ed.), Vol. II, 171–234.

Thompson, Sandra A. and Anthony Mulac. 1991. A quantitative perspective on the grammaticalization of epistemic parentheticals in English, in Bernd Heine and Elizabeth Closs Traugott (eds.), *Approaches to Grammaticalization*, Vol. II, 313–329, Amsterdam: John Benjmains.

Thompson, Sandra A. and Paul Hopper. 2001. Transitivity, clause structure, and argument structure: evidence from conversation, in Bybee and Hopper (eds.), 27–60.

Tibbits, Donald F. 1980. Oral production of linguistically complex sentences with meaning relationships of time, *Journal of Psycholinguistic Research* 9:545–564.

Tomasello, Michael. 1992. *First Verbs. A Case Study of Early Grammatical Development*, Cambridge: Cambridge University Press.

1999. *The Cultural Origins of Human Cognition*, Cambridge, Mass.: Harvard University Press.

2000a. Do young children have adult syntactic competence?, *Cognition* 74:209–253.

2000b, The item-based nature of children's early syntactic development, *Trends in Cognitive Science* 4:156–163.

2003. *Constructing a Language. A Usage-based Theory of Language Acquisition*, Cambridge, Mass.: Harvard University Press.

Tomlin, Russell S. 1985. Foreground–background information and the syntax of subordination, in Talmy Givón (ed.), *Quantified Studies in Discourse*, special issue of *Text* 5:85–122.

Tottie, Gunnel. 1995. Lexical diffusion in syntactic change: frequency as a determinant of linguistic conservatism in the development of negation in English, in Dieter Kastovsky (ed.), *Historical English Syntax*, 439–467, Berlin: Mouton de Gruyter.

Townsend, David J., David Ottaviano, and Thomas Bever. 1979. Immediate memory for words from main and subordinate clauses at different age levels, *Journal of Psycholinguistic Research* 8:83–101.

Townsend, David J. and Norma Ravelo. 1980. The development of complex sentence processing strategies, *Journal of Experimental Psychology* 29:60–73.

Townsend, David J. and Thomas G. Bever. 2001. *Sentence Comprehension. The Integration of Habits and Rules*, Cambridge, Mass.: MIT Press.

Trask, R. L. 1993. *A Dictionary of Grammatical Terms in Linguistics*, London: Routledge.

Traugott, Elizabeth Closs, Alice ter Meulen, Judy Snitzer Reilly, and Charles A. Ferguson (eds.), 1986. *On Conditionals*, Cambridge: Cambridge University Press.

Vainikka, Anne and Thomas Roeper. 1995. Abstract operators in early acquisition, *The Linguistic Review* 12:275–310.

Van Dijk, T. A. 1979. Pragmatic connectives, *Journal of Pragmatics* 3:447–456.

1981. *Studies in the Pragmatics of Discourse*, New York: Mouton.

Van Valin, Robert and Randy LaPolla. 1997. *Syntax*, Cambridge: Cambridge University Press.

Vendler, Zeno. 1967. *Linguistics in Philosophy*, Ithaca: Cornell University Press.

Verhagen, Arie. 2001. Subordination and discourse segmentation revisited, or: Why matrix clauses may be more dependent than complements, in Ted Sanders, Joost Schilperoord, and Wilbert Spooren (eds.), *Text Representation. Linguistic and Psychological Aspects*, 337–357, Amsterdam: John Benjamins.

Wanner, Eric and Michael Maratsos. 1978. An ATN approach to comprehension, in Morris Halle, Joan Bresnan, and George A. Miller (eds.), *Linguistic Theory and Psychological Reality*, 119–161, Cambridge, Mass.: MIT Press.

Wasow, Thomas. 2002. *Postverbal Behavior*, Stanford: CSLI Publications.

Weissenborn, Jürgen. 1992. Null subjects in early grammars: implications for parameter-setting theory, in Jürgen Weissenborn, Helen Goodluck, and Thomas Roeper (eds.), *Theoretical Issues in Language Acquisition: Continuity and Change in Development*, 269–299, Hillsdale, NJ: Lawrence Erlbaum.

Wellman, Henry M. 1990. *The Child's Theory of Mind*, Cambridge: Bradford.

Wexler, Kenneth. 1999. Maturation and growth of grammar, in William C. Ritchie and Tej K. Bhatia (eds.), 1999, *Handbook of Child Language Acquisition*, 55–109, Oxford: Blackwell.

Wierzbicka, Anna. 1988. *The Semantics of Grammar*, Amsterdam: John Benjamins.

Wilson, Stephen. 2003. Lexically specific constructions in the acquisition of inflection in English, *Journal of Child Language* 30:75–115.

Wing, Clara S. and Ellin Kofsky Scholnick. 1981. Children's comprehension of pragmatic concepts expressed in *because*, *although*, *if* and *unless*, *Journal of Child Language* 8:347–365.

Wray, Alison and Michael R. Perkins. 2000. The functions of formulaic language: an integral model, *Language and Communication* 20:1–28.

Zwicky, Arnold. 1987. Constructions in monostratal syntax, *Chicago Linguistic Society* 23:389–401.

1994. Dealing out meaning: fundamentals of syntactic constructions, *Berkeley Linguistics Society* 20:611–625.

Author index

Abott-Smith, K., 5
Abramovitch, C. M., 151
Aissen, J., 26
Amidon, A., 149
Ammon, P., 51
Ardery, G., 157
Aslin, R. N., 36
Astington, J. W., 114
Austin, L. J., 82–83

Baldwin, G., 5, 144
Barlow, M., 2, 13, 26
Bartsch, K., 79, 110, 114
Bates, E., 13, 26, 31, 33, 149
Bavin, E. L., 117, 119
Bebout, L. J., 150, 151
Behne, D., 53
Behrens, H., 32
Bell, A., 21
Bencini, G. M. L., 15
Berman, R. A., 143
Bever, T. G., 36, 118, 121, 122, 144, 146–147, 149
Bloom, L. P., 8, 50, 54, 55, 65, 77, 78, 80, 149, 150, 151, 158–160
Boas, H., 17
Bock, J. K., 31
Borer, H., 39
Bowerman, M., 2, 5, 173
Braine, M. D. S., 144, 150, 183
Braunwald, S. R., 149, 150, 151
Brent, M. R., 36
Brent, S. B., 149
Bresnan, J., 26
Brooks, P. J., 5
Brown, H. D., 116, 119
Brown, R., 8, 9
Brown, A. L., 149, 150

Bruner, J., 83
Bybee, J., 2, 13, 18, 19, 21, 23, 24, 26, 29, 30, 31, 32, 33

Cairns, H. S., 50, 52, 54
Cambon, J., 51
Capatides, J. B., 160
Carey, P., 149
Carni, E., 150
Cartwright, T. A., 36
Chafe, W. L., 168
Chapman, R. S., 150, 151, 163
Chater, N., 36
Chipman, H. H., 50, 52
Chomsky, C., 50–51, 53, 174
Chomsky, N., 13, 15, 34, 35, 37, 38, 56
Clahsen, H., 32, 33
Clancy, P., 116, 119, 123, 149, 150, 151
Clark, E. V., 38, 149, 150, 151, 152, 163, 168, 173, 174
Clark, H. H., 149
Claudi, U., 23
Clifton, C., 119, 120
Cohen, D., 116, 122, 146
Coker, P. L., 149, 152
Corrêa, L. M. S., 116, 119
Corrigan, R., 149, 151
Corter, C. M., 151
Cottrell, G. W., 13, 28
Crain, S., 35, 36, 39, 116, 147
Cristofaro, S., 154
Croft, W., 13, 14, 15, 18, 28, 29, 37, 45
Cromer, R., 51
Cruse, A., 18
Culicover, P. W., 14
Curtis, S., 35
Custer, W. L., 101

Dabrowska, E., 5
Dasinger, L., 117
Daugherty, K. G., 31, 32, 33
Davidse, K., 135
de Villiers, J. G., 39, 79, 114, 116, 119, 120, 122, 146
de Villiers, P. A., 79, 114, 122
Diessel, H., 5, 17, 24, 25, 33, 34, 37, 103, 117, 120, 121, 122, 143, 146, 154, 155, 172
Dixon, R. M. W., 24
Donaldson, M. L., 163
Dryer, M., 25, 36, 37, 118
DuBois, J. A., 37

Eisenberg, A. R., 149, 150, 151, 158, 160, 164
Eisenberg, S. L., 50, 52, 54, 116
Elman, J. L., 13, 18, 23, 26, 28, 31, 32, 33, 35, 147, 178
Emerson, H. F., 149, 151, 152
Erman, B., 21
Ervin-Tripp, S., 149
Evely, S., 151

Fabian-Kraus, V., 51
Feagans, L., 150, 151, 152
Ferreiro, E., 149, 151, 152
Fiengo, R., 50, 52, 54
Fillmore, C. J., 2, 5, 13, 14, 15, 16, 17, 18, 20, 131
Finch, S., 36
Flickinger, D., 182
Fliess, K., 149, 150, 151
Flynn, S., 116
Foley, W. A., 43
Ford, C. E., 168
Fosler-Lussier, E., 21
Fox, B. A., 129, 133, 147
Francis, B., 34
Frazier, L., 25, 119, 120
French, L. A., 149, 150

Gartner, B., 77, 78
Gawlitzek-Maiwald, I., 50, 54
Gentner, D., 183, 184
Gerard, J., 50, 52
Gerhardt, J., 50
Gibson, E., 120
Givón, T., 19, 37, 43, 58, 59, 64, 66, 168
Glenberg, A. M., 15

Goldberg, A. E., 2, 13, 14, 15, 16, 17, 19, 20, 28, 30, 182
Goodluck, H., 50, 52–54, 116, 121, 143, 147, 157
Gravitt, C. B., 149, 151
Greenbaum, S., 55, 81, 128, 152
Gregory, M., 21, 24
Gries, S. T., 17, 34

Hafitz, J., 77, 78
Haiman, J., 25, 26, 37, 48, 154
Hakes, D. T., 119
Hakuta, K., 116, 119, 122, 123, 146
Halliday, M. A. K., 43
Hamburger, H., 116, 147
Hare, M., 15, 31, 32, 33
Haspelmath, M., 154
Hawkins, J. A., 25, 26, 34, 120
Hawkins, S., 116
Heine, B., 23
Hildebrand, J., 116, 119, 120
Hinton, G., 28
Höhle, B., 36
Hollander, M., 33
Homzie, M. J., 149, 151
Hood, L., 149, 150, 151, 160
Hooper, J. B., 87
Hopper, P. J., 2, 19, 20, 21, 23, 24, 26, 29, 37, 45
Hsu, J. R., 50, 52, 54
Hudson, R. A., 16
Hünnemeyer, F., 23
Hyams, N., 34

Irwin, J. W., 150
Israel, M., 5

Jackendoff, R., 14, 15
Jacobsen, T., 149, 150, 151
Jenkins, J. M., 114
Jisa, H., 117, 143
Johnson, C., 5, 100
Johnson, E., 13, 26, 33
Johnson, H. L., 149, 151, 152, 163
Johansson, B. S., 149
Jurafsky, D., 21, 24
Jusczyk, P. W., 36

Kail, M., 150
Karmiloff-Smith, A., 13, 26, 33

Kaschak, M. P., 15
Katz, E. W., 149
Kavanaugh, R. D., 149, 150
Kay, P., 2, 5, 13, 14, 16, 20, 131
Keenan, E., 116
Kemmer, S., 2, 13, 26
Kern, S., 117, 143
Kidd, E., 116, 119
Kim, Y. J., 50, 54
Köpcke, K. M., 32
Kroch, A. S., 31
Kuhn, D., 149, 151, 163
Kuno, S., 118
Kyratzis, A., 149

Labelle, M., 116, 121
Lahey, M., 50, 54, 55, 65, 149, 150, 151
Lakoff, G., 2, 13, 14, 15, 17, 28, 135, 182
Lambrecht, K., 4, 17, 42, 128, 132, 133, 134, 135, 168
Langacker, R. W., 2, 13, 14, 15, 16, 18, 20, 21, 22, 23, 26, 28, 29, 31, 36, 40, 41, 42, 46, 128, 182
LaPolla, R., 14, 16, 41, 50, 58
Lebeaux, D., 126
Lederberg, A. R., 50, 52
Lee, K. D., 116
Leech, G., 34, 55, 81, 128, 152
Lehmann, C., 23, 42, 48, 154, 155
Lieven, E. V. M., 5, 144
Lifter, K., 149, 150, 151
Lillard, A. S., 102
Limber, J., 50, 54–55, 68, 78, 80, 117, 142
Lohmann, H., 7
Longacre, R. E., 168
Lust, B., 50, 52, 116, 149, 151

MacWhinney, B., 5, 7, 8, 19, 26, 29, 31, 116, 158
Maratsos, M. P., 50, 52, 53, 119, 120
Marchman, V., 29, 31, 32, 33
Marcus, G. F. S., 18, 19, 32, 33, 36
Matthiessen, C., 43, 45, 154
McCabe, A., 150, 151, 160
McCarthy, J., 32
McClelland, J. L., 18, 26, 28, 31, 33
McDaniel, D., 50, 52, 54, 116, 121
McKee, C., 116, 121
Median, J., 183
Meisel, J. M., 39
Mervis, C. A., 149, 151, 157

Menyuk, P., 50, 117
Michaelis, L., 17
Mintz, T. H., 36
Morris, W. C., 13, 28
Mulac, A., 77, 87, 92

Nakisa, R. C., 33
Nedjalkov, V., 17
Nelson, K., 150
Newmeyer, F. J., 13, 15
Newport, E. L., 36, 178
Nicholls, L. M., 116
Nishigauchi, T., 39
Noonan, M., 56, 80, 81
Nosofsky, R. M., 20
Nunberg, G., 16

O'Connor, C., 2, 5, 13, 14, 16
O'Grady, W., 2, 118, 121, 126
Ono, T., 18
Ottaviano, D., 149

Pagliuca, W., 23
Parisi, D., 13, 26
Pawley, A., 21
Pepler, D. J., 151
Pérez-Leroux, A., 121
Perkins, M. R., 21
Perkins, R., 23
Perner, J., 101, 114
Peterson, C., 150, 151, 160
Phelps, H., 149, 151, 163
Phinney, M., 79
Piaget, J., 149, 151, 174
Pietroski, P., 35, 39
Pine, J. M., 5, 144
Pinker, S., 13, 18, 19, 33, 35, 36, 40, 55, 77
Pléh, C., 116
Pollard, C., 16, 182
Plunkett, K., 13, 26, 29, 31, 32, 33
Prasada, G. K., 33
Prince, A., 18, 19, 32
Prince, E. F., 14
Pullum, G. K., 14, 35
Pulver, C. J., 150

Quirk, R., 55, 56, 81, 128, 135, 152, 153, 155

Ramscar, M., 18
Rao, S. B., 36
Rapp, M., 50

Rattermann, M. J., 183
Ravelo, N., 150
Raymond, W. D., 21
Rayner, K., 25
Redington, M., 36
Reilly, J. S., 149
Reinhart, T., 45, 154
Rispoli, M., 77, 78
Roeper, T., 39, 79
Rosen, T. J., 33
Rosenbaum, P. S., 51
Ross, J. R., 154, 155
Ross, R., 35
Roth, F. P., 119
Rothweiler, M., 2, 32, 33, 78, 149
Rowland, C., 5
Rumain, B., 150
Rumelhart, D. E., 18, 26, 28, 31, 33

Sachs, J., 8
Saffran, J. R., 36
Sag, I. A., 14, 16
Santelmann, L. M., 36
Sasse, H. J., 36
Saussure, F., 15
Scheibman, J., 21, 29, 30
Schlisselberg, G., 50, 54
Scholnick, E. K., 150
Scholz, B. C., 35
Schuele, C. M., 116
Schulz, P., 79
Searle, J. R., 83
Segalowitz, S. J., 150, 151
Shatz, M., 7, 78–79
Sheldon, A., 116, 117, 118, 123, 124, 125, 126, 174
Sherman, J. C., 50, 52
Silber, S., 7, 78
Silva, M., 149, 150
Sinclair, H., 51, 149, 151, 152
Sjöln, B., 149
Slobin, D. I., 16, 32, 116, 117, 118, 122, 143, 146
Smith, M. D., 116, 117, 119
Snedeker, J., 121
Stojanovic, D., 121
Suppes, P., 8
Svartvik, J., 55, 81, 128, 153
Syder, H., 21

Tackeff, J., 50, 54, 55, 65
Tager-Flusberg, H. B., 116, 146
Tallal, P., 35
Talmy, L., 24, 45
Tavakolian, S. L., 50, 116, 118, 124, 125, 126, 143, 147, 174
Theakston, A. L., 5
Thompson, S. A., 18, 19, 20, 21, 30, 31, 34, 37, 43, 44, 45, 46, 48, 77, 80, 87, 92, 129, 133, 147, 154, 168
Tibbits, D. F., 150
Tomasello, M., 5, 7, 38, 40, 83, 103, 117, 120, 121, 122, 143, 146, 183
Tomlin, R. S., 44, 45, 154
Tottie, G., 31
Toupin, C., 117
Townsend, D. J., 122, 146, 149
Trask, R. L., 53
Traugott, E. C., 23, 24

Ullman, M., 33

Vainikka, A., 79
Van Dijk, T. A., 160
Van Valin, R., 14, 16, 41, 43, 50, 58
Vendler, Z., 41
Verhagen, A., 46, 86
Vijayan, S., 36
Vishton, P. M., 36

Wanner, E., 119, 120
Warren, B., 21
Wasow, T., 16, 26, 34, 182
Weissenborn, J., 36, 39, 150
Welsh, C. A., 116
Wellman, H. M., 7, 78, 79, 110, 114
Wexler, K., 39
White, G. J., 150, 151
Wierzbicka, A., 14
Wilson, S., 5
Wing, C. S., 150
Woest, A., 32, 33
Wray, A., 21

Xu, F., 33
Xu, X., 34

Zoh, M. H., 116
Zwicky, A., 14

Subject index

acquisition of the English past tense, 28, 31–32
activation value, 27, 28, (*see also* entrenchment)
adverbial clause, 1–2, 4, 12, 33–34, 43–44, 46, 47, 48, 149–173, 177, 181
  cognitive and linguistic development, 150–151
  discrepancy between observational and experimental studies, 150
  final adverbial clause, 157
  initial adverbial clause, 157, 168–169, 172–173, 177, 180
  nonfinite adverbial clause, 11, 12, 156
  order of acquisition, 150–151
  relationship between adverbial and coordinate clauses, 152–156
  after, 151–152, 153, 157, 165, 169
  although, 151, 153, 157
  because, 151, 153, 155, 157, 160–163, 164–165, 170
  before, 151, 152, 153, 157, 165
  if, 151, 153, 157, 165, 168–169, 172
  since, 151, 153, 157, 169
  unless, 153
  until, 157, 165
  when, 151, 153, 155, 157, 165, 166, 168–169
  whereas, 153, 157
  while, 151, 157, 165, 169
adverbial conjunction
  morphological form, 153
  semantic classification, 153
  semantic feature analysis, 152
ambient language, 39, 73, 74–76, 113, 115, 126, 144–147, 171–172, 177
analogy, 37, 40

causal clause, 151, 152, (*see also* adverbial clause)
CHILDES, 7–10, 158
clause (definition), 41–42
clause expansion, 4, 49, 73, 116, 142, 175
clause integration, 4, 149, 171, 175
Cognitive Grammar, 14
competing motivations (competing forces), 33
complement clause, 1–2, 12, 43, 47, 48, 59, 72, 73, 77–115, 134, 176, 180–181, 182–183
  IF-complement, 80–81, 90, 91, 105–107, 112, 176
  S-complement, 80–81, 90–105, 112, 113, 176
  WH-complement, 80, 81, 90, 91, 105–106, 107–111, 112, 176
  assertive matrix clause, 81–82, 85–86, 87, 88–89, 90, 94, 98, 100, 104, 107, 110, 111, 112–113, 114
  formulaic matrix clause, 86–89, 90, 94, 95, 96, 98, 99, 104, 107, 108, 111–112, 113, 114
  performative matrix clause, 81, 82–86, 87–89, 90, 94, 100, 101, 104, 107, 110, 111, 112–113, 114
  lexically-specific utterance frame, 106, 108, 112, 176
  long-distance dependency, 79
  nonfinite complement clause (*see* infinitival and participial complement construction)
  parenthetical use of matrix clause (*see* formulaic matrix clause)
complementizer, 80, 81, 87, 90, 92, 95, 103, 105, 125
comprehension vs. production studies, 174–175

concessive clause, 157, (*see also* adverbial clause)
conditional clause, 152, 165, 166, 173, (*see also* adverbial clause)
conjoined clause, 12, 115, 149–173, 177, 181, (*see also* adverbial and coordinate clauses)
  definition of conjoined clause, 12, 149–173
conjoined clause hypothesis, 118, 124–126, 142, 174
conjunction (*see* adverbial conjunction, complementizer)
conjunctive adverb, 153, 156
connectionism, 26–28, 29, 31, 33, 147
Construction Grammar, 2, 14–23, 28
construction, 14–23, 25, 41
  lexically-specific construction, 4–6, 30, 72, 141, 144, 180–184
  morphological construction, 18, 32–33
  relationship between constructions, 19–20
  schematic construction (*see* schema)
constructional schema (*see* schema)
continuity hypothesis, 40
control construction, 56–57
coordinate clause, 1–2, 4, 12, 42, 43, 47, 48, 149–173, 177, 181
  and, 151, 153, 157, 158–160, 164–165
  but, 151, 153, 157, 163–165
  for, 153
  or, 153, 157
  so, 151, 153, 157, 160, 163, 164–165
coordination (*see* coordinate clause)

entrenchment, 23, 29–31, 37, (*see also* activation value)
exemplar-based model, 20
explicit performantive utterance, 82

filler-gap hypothesis, 118, 119–121
frequency, 6–7, 23, 24, 29–31, 39, 177
  token frequency, 29–31
  type frequency, 19, 29, 30, 31, 32, 33

generative grammar, 13, 15–16, 21, 23, 25, 26, 34, 36, 38, 39
gradual development, 39–40, 143, 147, 177
grammar-lexicon continuum, 16–18, 22
grammaticalization, 23–26, 37, 86, 87, 96, 111
growth, 37–40

habituation, 25–26, 37
Head Driven Phrase Structure Grammar, 14

incremental development (*see* gradual development)
idiomatic expression, 16–18, 20
infinitival and participial complement construction, 3, 12, 49–76, 115, 175–176
  aspectual verb, 49, 56, 64, 175, 176
  bare infinitive, 56, 57, 59, 60, 61, 63, 65–66, 69, 72, 73, 75
  equi (*see* control construction)
  for-infinitive, 57
  modal verb, 49, 57, 59, 63, 64, 175, 176
  NP-V-VP construction, 56, 57, 59, 60, 61, 62–67, 68, 72, 73–74
  NP-V-NP-VP construction, 56, 57, 59, 60, 61, 62, 66, 68, 70, 72, 73, 74–76
  participial complement, 56, 57, 59, 60, 61, 63, 65, 66, 72, 73
  to-infinitive, 55, 56, 57, 59, 60, 61, 63, 65–66, 72, 73
  wh-infinitive, 56, 57, 59, 61, 63, 65–66, 72, 73, 74, 178
infinitive marker (*see to*-infinitive)
innateness hypothesis, 34–37, 40
input (*see* ambient language)

learning, 37–40
localization of brain functions, 34
low-frequency default pattern, 32–33

maturation hypothesis, 39
mean proportions, 60
minimal distance principle, 51–52
Minimalism, 13, 15

network model, 26–29, 40, 147, 181–183
noninterruption hypothesis, 118–119, 142
NVN-schema hypothesis, 118, 121–123, 142, 146–147

Optimality Theory, 26
order-of-mention principle, 151–152, 163, 174

parallel-function hypothesis, 118, 123–124
pied-piping, 137

poverty of the stimulus, 35–36
Principles and Parameters Theory, 13, 25, 126
productivity, 19, 22, 31–34
profile, 46, 48, 81
prototype, 19–20

raising, 56–57
relative clause, 1–2, 4, 12, 43, 47, 48, 115, 116, 148, 176–177, 181
    amalgam construction, 116, 134–135, 137, 141, 142, 145
    center-embedded relative clause, 118–119, 142
    communicative function of children's early relative clauses, 144
    comprehension vs. production, 142–143
    external syntax, 131–136
    infinitival and participial relative clauses, 11, 12, 129, 139–141
    information structure of children's early relative clauses, 133, 144
    internal syntax, 136–139, 145–147
    intransitive/transitive relative clause, 138–139, 147
    locational relative clause, 130
    nonfinite relative clause (*see* infinitival and participial relative clauses)
    pragmatic functions of relative clauses, 128–129, 147
    restrictive/non-restrictive, 127–128
    resumptive pronoun, 120–121

similarity between children's early relative constructions and simple sentences, 146–147
relative pronoun, 128, 136
Role and Reference Grammar, 14
rule, 18–20

schema, 18–20, 21, 22, 28, 29, 30–34, 40, 104–105, 112, 121–123, 180–184
schematization, 40
semantic role principle, 52, 53
situation (definition), 41–42
SLI children, 35
social-cognitive basis of language acquisition, 38
subordinate clause, 1–2, 42–48
    figure-ground organization, 45–46
    morphological features, 44
    nonfinite subordinate clause, 42, 178–179
    processing, 46–48
    semantic features, 44–46
    syntactic features, 43–44
subordination (*see* subordinate clause)

temporal clause, 151–152, 165, 166, (*see also* adverbial clause)
theory of mind, 7, 114, 180
Transformational Grammar, 56
triggering problem, 39

underspecification, 20
universals, 36–37
usage-based model, 2, 23–34, 37, 38, 40